THE NEW ETHNICITY:

Perspectives from Ethnology

THE NEW ETHNICITY:
Perspectives from Ethnology

1973 Proceedings of
THE AMERICAN ETHNOLOGICAL SOCIETY
Robert F. Spencer, *General Editor*

Edited by
JOHN W. BENNETT
Washington University, St. Louis

WEST PUBLISHING CO.
St. Paul · New York · Boston
Los Angeles · San Francisco

GN
320
N48
cop. 2

COPYRIGHT © 1975 by WEST PUBLISHING CO.

All rights reserved

Printed in the United States of America

Library of Congress Catalog No.: 75–7510

ISBN 0–8299–0032–2

Foreword

With this, the 1973 issue of the *Proceedings of the American Eth-nological Society*, a new publishing venture begins. The Society is pleased to report its association with West Publishing Company, St. Paul, Minnesota; beginning in 1974, all future publications of both Monographs and Proceedings will be issued by West. The Society is gratified to have made this new arrangement and foresees the appearance of its publications on a regularized basis. A reflection of this change in publisher is seen in the new format of this issue. We look forward to a pleasant and continuing association with West Publishing Company.

The meeting in which the papers appearing here were generated was held March 7–10 at the Blockade Runner Hotel in Wrightsville Beach, North Carolina. The American Ethnological Society met jointly with the Southern Anthropological Association. The program and local arrangements were handled by Professors Thomas K. Fitzgerald and Harriet J. Kupferer, University of North Carolina, Greensboro, while the outgoing president of the American Ethnological Society, Professor John W. Bennett, Washington University, St. Louis, assumed responsibility for arranging the symposium on the general subject of ethnicity. Dr. Bennett has served as editor of the present volume.

Robert F. Spencer, Editor, AES

University of Minnesota

*

Preface

The American Ethnological Society (founded 1842) plans an annual symposium on a particular topic presented at a meeting with another anthropological scholarly group. The papers in this symposium on ethnicity were presented in joint meeting with the Southern Anthropological Society at Wrightsville Beach, North Carolina, March 7–10, 1973. Two papers, those by Ethel Nurge on German national identity and Edward Robbins on a Canadian industrial community, were not presented at the meeting. Aware of their papers, I invited Drs. Nurge and Robbins to contribute them to this issue of the *Proceedings of the American Ethnological Society*. With Robbins's paper, I hoped to fill a gap in the roster: the relationship between ethnicity and class in modern complex society. Similarly, the Nurge paper shed some new light on the difference between ethnic character and national character. Both papers seemed ready-made for the purpose.

J. W. B.

St. Louis
January 1, 1975

*

Contents

*

THE NEW ETHNICITY:

Perspectives from Ethnology

INTRODUCTION

*

1

A Guide to the Collection

JOHN W. BENNETT
Washington University, St. Louis

The title of these 1973 *Proceedings of the American Ethnological Society,* "The New Ethnicity," has a double meaning. First, the "newness" implies something new in the world—or at least something newly noticed by anthropologists: the proclivity of people to seize on traditional cultural symbols as a definition of their own identity—either to assert the Self over and above the impersonal State, or to obtain the resources one needs to survive and to consume.

Nancie Gonzalez, in her paper on the Dominican Republic, uses the term "ethnogenesis," borrowed from John Murra. It is really another term for the "new ethnicity," since it refers to the conscious, that is, the cognitive construction of an identity for the individual and the group out of traditional cultural symbols: "a self-conscious ideological framework which glorifies and crystallizes the new collectivity." It, is a phenomenon of new-statehood, of what Gonzalez calls "neoteric" societies; a part of our modern history; and an ethnological version of "nationalism."

The second meaning of the new ethnicity is intradisciplinary: it refers to the shift from a culture-population-group frame of reference in anthropology to a cognitive and behavioral-strategy frame, which views ethnicity as a component of social participation. This, I would assume, represents a substantial shift in basic theoretical outlook. There are two major sources of this shift: the first is the work of Frederik Barth on ethnic boundaries and identity; the second is the general field of social transactionism and strategy analysis.

In arranging these papers I had two alternatives. One was simply to put them in geographical order: North American Indian, South American and Caribbean, and so on. The other alternative was to put them in an order which reflected the major themes of the new (and old) ethnicity. After listening to the papers at the meeting, and then reading them over, it occurred to me that there were four major themes: (1) ethnicity as an identity phenomenon, which has two meanings: the search for the self and the definition of group boundaries; (2) ethnicity as a set of strategies for acquiring the resources one needs to survive and to consume at the desired level; (3) ethnicity as a part of the distinctive characteristics of nations, and of some of the groups composing nations (an older concept of ethnicity—the "old ethnicity," perhaps, in contrast to the "new"); (4) Edward Robbins' paper, which was not presented at the meetings, stands alone. It is concerned with ethnicity in relationship to class, and because it is, it contains a view of ethnicity which collapses the distinction between ethnicity as a cultural or group phenomenon, and as an identity phenomenon. Robbins holds that in either case, ethnicity is a cultural construct—as behavior pattern, value, or ideology, and because this is so, it cannot explain itself. He believes that the concept of class, since it defines "structural" relations between people, can provide much of the explanation of social relations in complex societies.

We begin with a special invited address by Everett Hughes, who elected to set the stage for the conference historically with an examination of the cognitive categories of "colonies, colonization, and colonialism" as these emerged out of a notion of empty lands—"empty" from the Western point of view, and ready for filling up with "civilization." Colonization continues today, Hughes asserts, in the form of economic expansion and hegemony; it is a new type of exploitation, and while its past wrongs are being redressed, its new versions create a fresh round of problems.

Thus, the original meaning of "ethnic" pertained to the inhabitants of "empty" lands: the notion of exotic, less than civilized, and probably less than human creatures out there for the taking; and for the ethnologist, there for studying and preserving, like wild species. The ethnologist, despite his understanding, his sympathy, and his empathy, was after all part of the system, and his concepts inevitably came to reflect this mixed role, as William Willis so cogently shows in his paper on Franz Boas. Ethnicity for years meant, as Sydelle Levy points out in her Elsie Clews Parsons prize student paper on the Hassidim (the first in the "identity" series), "a group of people who share fundamental cultural values expressed by unified cultural forms"; that is, a native species, a natural population living and dying in a known geographical range. She goes on to note that the concept "You are what you are by virtue of your birth" was the root of the idea, and ethnic culture was therefore tied firmly to socialization in a particular group. It was what distinguished you and yours from them and theirs. Some groups expressed contempt of them and theirs; others, such as the Guatemalans described years ago by Sol Tax, had a native doctrine of cultural relativity; the different ways of farming or praying were simply *es costumbre*, "it's just a custom." The old notion of ethnicity as the thing that distinguished one tribe from another made a certain amount of sense when such populations were relatively isolated, and the notion was even not entirely wrong when it was applied to older nations as a form of "cultural character." Nations, until recently, also experienced relative isolation, and thus their distinctive cultural styles had an opportunity to flower. (Ethel Nurge provides us with a contemporary review of a particular series of attempts to define national cultural ethnicity—in this case, the Germans.)

Times change, however, and the history of ethnicity changes with it. Robert Dirks criticizes the "mistaken tendency to create homologies between population aggregates and ethnic categories" in his paper on ethnic concepts in a typical modern, pluralistic crossroads, the Virgin Islands. He is implying, I would assume, that the old concepts, founded on isolation, no longer work in a world of intercommunication and movement, of nations and classes, of assertive life style and political rights. In such a world, ethnicity becomes a cognitive category, a definition of the *self*, as Robert Breunig flatly asserts in his paper on the Hopi. Whether the cognitive idea of ethnic identity coincides with actual population aggregates and cultural styles becomes for the new ethnologist an empirical question. Dirks shows that such an ethnic self need not "be founded on a genuine native tradition at all"; it is a "collective representation," imagined out of needs for assertion and defense, for maintaining one's boundaries in a world of competition and usurpation of resources. Tom Fitzgerald, in his paper on the Maori, even speaks of "a cultural identity without a culture."

One dominant theme in these papers on identity would appear to be *boundary maintenance*—or, at any rate, the need to define the ethnic self always in the context of some "outside" group. Thomas Collins shows us that changing economic opportunities imposed on the Ute reservation create social heterogeneity among the "traditional full bloods", the "laborers," and the "underemployed" (see his paper for definitions)—a situation which automatically creates an urge among all of these people to "keep things Indian." This has resulted in increasing outward symbolization of Indian culture, as evidenced by dress, speech, adornment, and so forth. These symbolic displays do not seem to vary importantly by occupational and economic status. Hence, as the "outside" forces create inside heterogeneity, the beleaguered (or aspiring) group responds, in this latter day, by emphasizing homogeneity. I would suggest that Collins has not sufficiently weighed the possibility that this growing homogeneity of cultural style is symbolic and superficial only, and that it might be a prelude to a cultural breakdown along class lines when the enthusiasm wears off. I am not predicting—I really don't know—but the new ethnologist must be sensitive to constant historical change in these cognitive-behavioral-display categories.

George Hicks compares two Amerind groups, the Catawba and the Monhegans, and in both cases he finds the choice of identity label (and symbols) is channeled by the nature of the outside reference group: the Mormons in the case of the Catawba and the blacks in the case of the Monhegans. Catawba may remain Catawba, but they have chosen Mormonism as a symbol and route of upward mobility in a white society. Monhegans, who have intermarried with blacks, must assert their Indianness in opposition to blackness in an effort to escape from racist stereotypes. Catawba are thus Catawba (Indian) on the inside; Monhegan are Monhegan (Indian) *to* the outside.

These are all "badge" phenomena: cognitive definitions of the self and the group-self, the collective representation. One other major theme represented in these papers is ethnicity as a device, a *strategy* for achieving what one wants and needs. Leo Despres is concerned with a complex new nation—Guyana—where a series of ethnic groups compete for scarce resources in a national framework. Ethnicity, as it is becoming everywhere, is a device for political assertion, a means for obtaining votes and favors, a basis for claims on resources and advantages. But since the competition for scarce resources always means that someone wins (relatively) and someone loses (relatively), the ethnic groups become ranked by access to resources, and ethnicity then begins to be indistinguishable from stratification—and *then*, as Despres observes, it also becomes part of the problem of exploitation and power. Or, ethnology becomes political science.

Hoy Steele, in his paper on urban Indians, sees the boundary-maintaining process as a matter of "badges" which the Indian adopts because they are imposed on the Indian group or somehow required by outside majority groups. Here ethnicity becomes a device to create a community of solidarity which can act as a unit against exploitation. Steele speaks of "successful adaptation" to the city. I am not sure what he means here, but it would seem not to be the old assimilation, but the new ethnicity: the organizing of a group for bargaining purposes that proclaims its right to resources by its badges; that is, its outward display of cultural symbols and its (hopefully) inner sense of cognitive and emotional unity.

Bobby Thompson and John Peterson observe similar processes among the Choctaw, but they take the analysis one step further. They see the formation of a Choctaw symbolic identity as desirable for forging unity among the Choctaw, but as a poor strategy for gaining what the Choctaw really need in the way of resources. This can be accomplished only when Indian groups such as the Choctaw are willing to surrender some of their group identity to a larger identity: that of the American Indian.

S. J. Makielski, like Despres, is concerned with a large sociopolitical entity, the American South, and the change in ethnic politics taking place since the civil rights struggles of the 1950s and 1960s. He proposes that

> Southern politics has been undergoing a significant change in its stylistic base. With this change—a shift from a politics of white ethnic identification to one of coalition politics—have emerged new opportunities for the black Southerner. It has also been argued, however, that the change is less than complete. Identifica-

tion politics are rooted in cultural rather than purely political or economic variables, and cultural norms change slowly.

But if the writers of the other papers are right about the new ethnicity, it is not really a matter of "cultural norms," but rather of identity, or definition of the self. It is coalition for advantage, and white ethnic identification, however "cultural" or "normative" it might be, can change very rapidly to identity-ethnicity, and bargaining with black ethnic groups can take place on a basis of full equal rational shares, once the step from cultural norm to cognitive identity is taken.

However, Robbins's paper raises an additional point in regard to this question. In his view, I suspect, Makielski is saying that ethnicity is becoming weaker; or that Southern black politicians are leaving behind the cultural ideology of ethnicity, for the underlying structural reality of power—the power that goes with true class relations, in the classic Marxist sense of shares in the system of production. In Robbins's own paper, on a small industrial community in Newfoundland, he shows that while ethnicity does provide a focus for certain associations, class is more important in forging key social relations in the work force.

Muriel Crespi takes us to Ecuador, where a traditional culturally and natally based system of ethnic categories is changing toward the new identity-ethnicity and its concomitant use as a bargaining strategy. In the preindustrial hacienda economy, ancestry was the major criterion for access to survival needs. And so it remains. Outside the hacienda, however, in the new economy based more on achievement and ability, the Indians can play a different role: one not dependent on their inherited Indianness and all the symbols this implies to the non-Indian majority group, but rather one of the free individual bargaining for resources with his abilities. Crespi shows how these two systems actually interlock and overlap in the transitional society of Ecuador, creating a variety of ethnic identities for the Indians.

As already noted, the concept of ethnicity still figures in the idea of national cultural character, or the distinctive characteristics attributed to the members of a nation by outsiders. This has always been a difficult problem, moving between purely stereotypic attributions and empirical or statistical tendencies in behavior and attitude. The growing heterogeneity of the world, and the interpenetration of national entities by the commonalities of industrial mass culture have obscured many such peculiarities, and one scarcely knows how and where to look for the evidence. Yet the concepts persist, and Ethel Nurge pulls them together in her long, scholarly study of analyses of German character, in the first of the papers in the next section.

Along with Nurge's paper I have placed two others. Stanley Walens presents the symbolic meaning of old Virginia City for Americans: a tourist place where one can find the collective identity of American history and its meaning for the individual. Cultural character is defined for us all by the Old West: we are all Westerners; this was our finest hour. That this meaning contains attitudes and behaviors outmoded and even dangerous for this age of hypercompetition for resources is another question, which Walens mentions, but perhaps does not do full justice to. It is there, just as the disastrous consequences of the new ethnicity generally can be observed in Northern Ireland. While the new ethnicity may be a desirable strategy to combat the exploitation of colonialism, as it is for Hughes, it can also lead to madness and mayhem, as has so often occurred in the new nations of Africa.

With Gwen Neville's paper we come almost full circle back to the old notion of ethnicity as a group-cultural phenomenon—but with a subtle difference. Neville reminds us that ethnicity, however cognitive it might be, can nevertheless lead to community—to shared solidarity. She proposes that "ethnic" be applied not only to groups in the population who define themselves as ethnic groups, or who are "forced into cultural separation," but also to all groups that are "interacting networks which retain a sense of shared cultural past. . . ." This is of course correct. What Neville may forget, however, is that many of these latter "networks" are self-constituted groups: they emerge out of those who define themselves as ethnic, and then *become* networks, and *acquire* the shared meanings. She is talking here about Presbyterians; I could talk about Hutterites, Amish, and other sectarian "intentional communities" who most certainly have ethnicity, but it is a cognitive ethnicity, a self-chosen ethnicity.

One meaning of Presbyterianness for Americans is simply this: these Protestant groups have for generations equated their ways with the ways of the nation; their cultural sharedness was self-defined as the national character. This may have forged solidarity among them, but it has also created intolerable friction in the larger society. It has contributed to the stratification of American society and to the subordination-superordination patterns of religious prejudice and racial stereotype.

Perhaps as ethnologists we have no business celebrating ethnicity in any form; we might have in the age of cultural isolation, but that age is past, gone forever, and cultural ethnicity is now one of its lag phenomena. The new ethnicity, as I have already implied, is an answer, though no cure. It, too, leads to disorder and early sorrow; it, too, is a symptom of what is out of joint in the human mentality as the human population becomes worldwide.

William Willis's historical paper closes our book. He takes one of our own disciplinary heroes—the great Franz Boas—and demonstrates the complex mixture of tolerance and stereotypy which the sympathetic academic in the age of cultural ethnicity and stereotypic prejudice could not escape. Patronizing the Negroes by collecting their folklore was for Boas an ethnological act which solved a problem: the explanation for the cultural difference of American Negroes. But this had a social cost: the implication of cultural inferiority or incapability. As Willis shows, Boas accepted too narrow a definition of culture, the "intimate" or immediate domestic existence, and ignored the segregated community—that community which forced blacks back into their own traditions both as a defense against exploitation and discrimination and as an escape from reality. That such mechanisms were operative in that age was known to many social scientists; anthropologists like Boas, Parsons, and others were in sympathy with the aims of racial reform, but their conceptual apparatus was unconsciously feeding the status quo, or at least blinding them to larger cultural-political realities. Willis does not accuse Boas and his contemporaries of fostering racism, but he does show how the theoretical approach of anthropology has had to overcome the influence of the age of cultural ethnicity. Thus our theories emerge out of history; and history is influenced by our theories; we are all, in some final sense, creatures of our time, and ethnology cannot escape culture.

INVITED ESSAY

*

2

Colonies, Colonization and Colonialism*

EVERETT C. HUGHES

Boston University

These words, and their relatives, have been current and important in European languages for a long time. They pervade history, literature, economics, politics, and ethics; more recently they have become important concepts in biology. Since Fanon's *Les Damnés de la Terre* and Memmi's answer, *Les Colonisés et les Colonisateurs,* "colony" words have become the key pejorative terms in discussion of poverty and oppression, with or without explicit reference to racial and ethnic contacts. I have no quarrel with people who use these words in such a way, although I do think this usage tends to obscure other more important aspects of the historic phenomena to which the terms earlier referred. In the new pejorative sense, *colonizing* has come to include the tendency of middle-class people to spread their ideas and institutions

* Cambridge, Mass. March 1973.

to all people within their own country or countries. Perhaps what I have to say leads to the same destination, but by another road.

The mother of all the "colony" words is the Latin irregular verb, *colo*, whose past participle is *cultum*. The first meaning of the verb was "to till the ground"; it expanded to include every kind of cultivation—of the arts, of philosophy, or even of a person. It also had reference to place, in the sense of inhabiting. The simplest derived noun is *colonia*, a farm or estate; the words referring to people are *colonus*, a farmer, and *colona*, a countrywoman. In these words, the citizen (the city man, the Roman), is referring to the rural (to people and things not of the city).

The meaning took on imperial dimension to include "the settlements of Roman citizens in a hostile or newly conquered country." A less political meaning in eighteenth century English (and no doubt earlier) was "a number of people of one nationality residing in a foreign city or country." [1]

In ecology, the colony words are key concepts; they refer to symbiotic and competitive aggregations of organisms, the manner in which these aggregations develop, and how they destroy and succeed one another.

Recently a counter-colonial vocabulary has appeared: colonia*lism*, *neo*colonialism, *de*colonization. All these terms carry the pejorative sense mentioned earlier. There is a hint of this change in the titles of pertinent articles from the *Encyclopaedia of the Social Sciences*, 1930, to the *International Encyclopedia of the Social Sciences*, 1968. In the newer encyclopedia, the two articles on the subject are put under the general heading, "Colonialism." I do not find the term colonia*lism* in the titles or texts of the older work. The articles in the newer encyclopedia reflect the events of the nearly forty years between the old and the new, with their emphasis on *de*colonization, of which alleged *neo*colonia*lism* is a function.

The longest of the articles in the older volumes is entitled simply "Colonies." It is a history of colonies from Greece and Rome on down to the period after the First World War. It ends thus:

> In brief, modern colonization has been mainly an expansion of European ideas and methods. Since the inception of the age of power machinery no alternative has appeared able to impose more

than temporary checks to the movement. At the present advanced stage the main problem seems to be that of salvaging those intrinsically valuable elements in older systems of society, which might be destroyed in a too sudden transition.[2]

I take it that the movement Knight, the author of this article, refers to is the continuing spread of European ideas and methods, not the establishment of new colonies by conquest of new territories. We must leave open the question whether there will be a reverse movement of ideas and methods from some other center into the territories now dominated by the European methods we have known (including our "own" territory). Knight, by the way, talks of colonies, colonization; and colonial systems, not of colonialism. A *colonialism,* in the *Shorter Oxford* of 1936, is simply "a colonial practice, idiom, or manner"—presumably as seen from the center of the empire. (A pretty cockney waitress once asked me what colony I had come from.)

In the newer encyclopedia, Rupert Emerson defines colonialism as "the establishment and maintenance, for an extended time, of rule over an alien people that is separated from and subordinate to the ruling power." He later adds "separation by salt water from the imperial power" as a characteristic. He is, of course, documenting a change of emphasis in the meaning of the colony words by leaving out any reference to settlement abroad of citizens of a country. He makes a beginning at defining colonialism from the point of view of the people colonized. This occurs in most social movements; the defining of terms is taken over by the underdogs and those who sympathize with them. In the case of the colony words, this process has been accompanied by a great extension of meaning of the terms.

Our own country shows an interesting history of the use of colony words. Even more select in membership than the staid Daughters of the American Revolution are the Colonial Dames; an aspiring Dame must prove that at least one of her ancestors amounted to something under British rule of the colonies. The key words, *colony* and *revolution,* in the names of these organizations, have undergone a change of meaning in the course of our history. We are now against all revolutions, and we do not admit to having established any colonies after independence from Britain. We moved west into what we considered open country, using the term *frontier* in a new sense of "the edge of settlement." When we came to another kind of frontier, that of Spanish America, we invaded the territory and more or less settled it; we never allow it said that our people who took over from the Mexicans in all of the states that now bear Spanish names were colonists. Nor did we call Hawaii a colony, although it was a real throwback to the classical colonies in which Europeans made themselves owners of semitropical islands and imported labor of other races from across salt water to cultivate sugar cane for the world market. The accident of having first established ourselves in colonial settlements on the coast of an "empty" continent allowed us to spread our population and our European ideas and methods without crossing salt water again, except for a slight expansion into Hawaii and Alaska later on.

Our country was in the unique ecological position of being partly in temperate regions where ethnically homogeneous settlement was possible and partly in subtropical regions, in which developed the usual "colonial" formula of large-scale agriculture using involuntary labor from what is now called the Third World. As early as 1827, Thomas Macaulay had stated and refuted all the racist arguments in favor of slavery.[3] He saw the problem of the West Indies not in the laziness of people with black skins nor in that of their white masters, but in the nature of the sugar industry. Sugar could be sold on the world market only by paying labor little or nothing. He praised Massachusetts as the ideal colony; Englishmen tilled their own soil there and developed a decent society. We in this country (I am not quoting Macaulay now) have been caught in the dilemma of having both Massachusetts and Alabama in the same so-called nation-state.

Yet all parts of our country are as surely products of the expansion of European ideas and methods—of colonization—as were the Portuguese, Spanish, Dutch, French, and British empires. We were created by the same forces. The whole modern world is a product of colonizing—of people, ideas, military power, machines, and methods going out from cities—and of generating great currents, cross-currents, and migrations of people, plants, animals, diseases—and even of science and religions. We appear to have reached the end, or at least the slowing-down point, of the most stupendous expansion any one race and civilization has ever carried out. Already we have competitors with increasing power of expansion; they, too, are products of European colonization of ideas and methods. Edward Shils speaks of the lingering intellectual dominance of the West, indicating that even with complete political independence the other continents, no matter how proud their intellectual tradition, are dependent upon the West for their modern intellectual activities and styles.[4] This may be the most lingering phase of colonizing. There is reason to believe, however, that even while the old lingers, new waves of colonization may spread from other centers than those with a dominant population of European descent.

Leaving that question for the futurologists, let us look at some earlier analyses and judgments of the nature and ethics of colonization, and also at the language of ecology.

In 1748, Montesquieu wrote what he would say if asked to justify the enslavement of black Africans.[5] He was evidently repeating, with full irony, what others did say. Sugar cane was a new crop not suitable to cultivation in Europe; new land had to be found. The suitable land had no suitable labor; it was, in that sense, empty. Who could question the right of good Christian men with pale skins to have their sugar and to get human or not-quite-human labor to produce the sugar by whatever means. The means might include destroying the manhood of those black people, who probably had no souls in any case. (It didn't take a Freud to think of castration as a demeaning device.) The whole ideology of race had been worked out in detail before 1748.

Thus, the basic biracial or multiracial institution of subtropical colonies had been established and justified: the *plantation.* European ownership, large tracts of land in a favorable climate, and labor brought from non-European regions by whatever means to produce goods for the European and world market—that was the basic colonizing formula. Perhaps it was also the favoring wind for machine industry in the emerging capitalism of Europe. One might propose that the colony created the métropole.

Not long after Montesquieu, Diderot took up the theme of colonizing. Under what circumstances, he asked, is it permissible to colonize a region (*contrée*)? One must, he went on, distinguish three cases: "where the region is without inhabitants (*déserte*); where it is partly uninhabited and partly inhabited; and where it is completely populated. . . . An uninhabited land is the only one that one can appropriate." In populated country, "I can only legitimately claim the hospitality and succor which man owes to man. . . . When one shall have given me asylum, fire, water, bread and salt, he will have fulfilled his duty to me. If I demand more, I become a thief and an assassin." [6]

Diderot and the other angry iconoclasts of the Enlightenment were condemning the great historic drive of their time. Even some republicans, said Diderot with regret, had fallen into the temptation of colonial trade, as did Holland after having heroically thrown off the yoke of Spain and Rome. Once colonization, particularly in subtropical regions, had taken hold, much of the world outside Europe seemed *déserte,* empty, less than fully populated and used. Diderot himself said that "the fanaticism of religion and the spirit of conquest, those great disturbers of the world, are no longer what they once were." In another place, he suggested that there are other forces which drive men on to conquering the world.

> In these mercantile societies, the discovery of an island, the importation of a new article of consumption (*denrée*), the invention of a machine, the establishment of a firm, innovation of a branch of commerce, the construction of a harbor become events of greatest importance.[7]

One might indeed say that any one of these discoveries or inventions makes new regions empty, or *déserte,* in some specific sense. Diderot himself (not that it is important that it was he who said these things) stated that only unpopulated territory can be justly colonized or appropriated. But what is meant by empty, or unoccupied, regions or sites? Here we come to ecology, for *empty site,* is an ecological concept.

Scott A. Boorman, in his review of a book on geographical ecology in *Science,* suggests analogues that might be useful in the social sciences.

> Another major set of themes in *Geographic Ecology* is the importance of the dual processes of extinction of local populations and colonization of vacant sites. Several sections of the book are devoted to the circumstances surrounding these phenomena. A number of the most intriguing results are connected with the effects of species packing upon likelihood of extinction. For example, it is shown in quantitative terms (pp. 44ff) how difficult will typically be the position of a species sandwiched between two other species along a resource continuum, a model situation which should be suggestive to theorists of oligopoly. The focus on extinction and colonization is especially strong in the discussion of the island view of competition, which views a species as consisting of a network of largely isolated subpopulations having a comparatively high frequency of local extinction. . . . The emphasis on colonization and extinction events is in sharp contrast to the tendency of most social science to evade the analogous problems in its mathematical models. Sociological model-building sel-

dom progresses beyond dealing with processes involving fixed sets of categories such as attitudes or social classes; the ontogeny or dissolution of such a categorical system, even in a highly local environment, is almost never tackled from a formal standpoint.[8]

Colonization appears here as a major concept. Let me point to the phrase, "dual processes of extinction of local population and colonization of vacant sites." These are the complementary aspects of a common process. It might be well to look at human colonizing in the same way.

But what is an empty country, region, or even a vacant lot? The Romans made country empty by conquering the natives and setting up their own kind of agriculture. The European colonizers of the fifteenth, sixteenth, and seventeenth centuries were generally met by natives when they landed in what was to them a new country; to these Europeans much of the New World was empty. A vacant lot may be populated with boys playing ball, until someone with a land title, a building permit, some capital, and a bulldozer turns up. To the builder the site has been vacant. There is quite a turmoil in Canada now about the James Bay region. There is talk of developing it, which means building a huge power dam deep in the northern forest. Anthropologists fear lest this destroy the habitat of the Indians of the region. One can fly over that country for hours and see no sign of human life; human life is so human that there are no skyscrapers to be seen from a plane. From the standpoint of the Indians and of the Quebecois writer, Yves Theriault, it is not empty; [9] it is rich in the material of which so-called savage minds develop their science of the concrete. The dam will empty it of Indians and their environment. It will be fully used and occupied, for a time, in the terms of the society we live in. I will turn on a light in Cambridge and use the water of an almost equally remote dam on the Manicuoagan River far beyond the Saguenay on the north shore of the St Lawrence.[10]

Whether a region is empty or not is an ecological statement, whose terms include every aspect of cultures and social systems. Any culture is a set of ways of occupying and using an environment. One of the concepts of ecology is "the carrying capacity" of an environment; carrying capacity is obviously relative to technology, social organization, and other characteristics of social systems. Perhaps one should think of an internal logic or dynamics of any culture and social system. Our system seems to require new products, new inventions, and the whole list Diderot mentioned. We even reach for the moon. It is as if the system itself were fanatical, even when its individual members have lost their fervor. The city is still the problem; and every man in our part of the world is the city man.

We are all party to colonization in the basic sense of encouraging, even in our simplest actions of consuming goods and services, the expansion of our system beyond present boundaries and into new dimensions. To understand it we will have to invent the terms of a human ecology. Since all humans are of the same species, we will need terms for the categories within the species which approximate for long periods of time, in their struggles for survival and expansion, something very like species. In the past, we have all too quickly solved the problem and our consciences by defining in terms of individual biology the differences in the ways in which humans of various backgrounds and culture occupy environments, colonize, destroy, and displace one another, or live in various kinds of symbiosis and competition. That is because humans live in moral worlds and in ecological communities at the same time.

We will not solve the problem by making *colonizing* a bad word, a catchall for all the evil that men do to each other, and especially that which has been done in the growth of the modern world. We will all, I trust, join fiercely and intelligently in righting the wrongs done to *les damnés de la terre*.

NOTES

[1] The references are to the Latin dictionary which I used in college, and to *The Shorter Oxford English Dictionary*, 2nd edition, 1936. The Greeks were colonizers, having established cities in many places far from Greece, but they lost out to the Romans. We use the Latin terms, the terms of the surviving power.

[2] Melvin M. Knight, "Colonies," *Encyclopædia of the Social Sciences*, 3 (1930), pp. 653–663.

[3] Robert Macaulay, "The Social and Industrial Capacities of Negroes," *Race: A Journal of Race and Group Relations*, 13 (October 1971), pp. 133–164.

[4] Edward Shils, "Traditions of Intellectuals," *Daedalus*, Spring, 1972, pp. 21–34.

[5] Montesquieu, "Of the Enslaving of the Negroes," *The Spirit of the Laws*, Bk. 15, ch. 5.

6 Quoted in Yves Benot, *Diderot, de L'Athéisme a L'Anticolonialisme* (Paris, François Vaspero, 1970), pp. 195, 196, 197. Translation by ECH.

7 *Ibid.*, p. 195.

8 Scott A. Boorman, "Analogues in the Social Sciences," *Science*, 178 (October 27, 1972), pp. 391–393. This is a review of Robert H. MacArthur, *Geographical Ecology, Patterns in the Distribution of Species* (New York: Harper and Row, 1972).

9 Yves Theriault, *N'Tsuk* (Montreal: Harvest House, 1972), and *Ashini* (Montreal: Harvest House, 1973). See also "The James Bay Project," *Bulletin of the Canadian Sociology and Anthropology Association*, No. 29, January 1973.

10 Claude Lévi-Strauss, "The Science of the Concrete," *The Savage Mind* (Chicago: University of Chicago Press, 1966), ch. 1.

*

ETHNICITY AS IDENTITY

*

3

Shifting Patterns of Ethnic Identification among the Hassidim*

SYDELLE BROOKS LEVY

Graduate Center, City University of New York

This paper discusses shifting patterns of ethnic identification among members of a particular Jewish group, the Lubovitcher Hassidim. Hassidism is one of many forms of Judaic beliefs and practices. To the larger Jewish community, Hassidim are characterized by their ultra-orthodox practices and mystical ideology. Every Hassidic group has a leader, known as the Rebbe. The Rebbe's followers believe that he is the personification of all core values that they hold dear.

Hassidism flourished in Eastern Europe from the time of its inception in the late eighteenth century until the early twentieth century. Members of many Hassidic groups were killed or forced to disperse during World War II. A large number of Hassidim chose to leave the confines of their "shtetl" communities [1] and seek a different life, away from their Rebbe and away from traditional Judaism. The Lubovitcher Rebbe, leader of the Lubovitcher Hassidim, came to the

* This was the American Ethnological Society's Elsie Clews Parsons Prize Paper for 1973. This prize is awarded annually to the winner of a special graduate student competition. The study was assisted by grants from CUNY —Dissertation Year Fellowship and NDEA.

25

United States in 1941 and established his headquarters in Brooklyn, New York. Although Lubovitch is not the largest Hassidic group in Brooklyn, it claims the largest worldwide membership.

Many cultural forms differentiate Hassidim from a larger, more assimilated Jewish population. Allegiance to the Lubovitcher Rebbe distinguishes this particular Hassidic group from all others. In this paper I plan to demonstrate that an individual's strong ethnic ties to Lubovitch are not manifested in cultural forms alone, but rather in manipulation of symbols and approved social behavior that provide opportunities for a moving or floating identity. The decision to employ Lubovitch symbols is made by individual members in particular situations, in their attempt to meet the problems of life and reach their intended goals.

Among anthropologists it is common to identify an ethnic enclave as a group of people who share fundamental cultural values expressed by unified cultural forms (Narroll 1964). This "cultural" approach to the study of ethnic groups incorporates two central ideas. The first, shared cultural values, applies, in general, to a macroculture and denotes an ascribed status vis-à-vis other such groups. The single term—ancestry—is the key idea that reflects this ascribed status. You are what you are by virtue of your birth. The second idea, cultural forms, concerns the particular behavioral traits, customs, and patterns that embody the values and frequently create a social boundary around the group. Although the boundary markers are distinctive cultural forms, the very existence of clear markers which differentiate those who are encapsulated from those who surround them leads us to consider the sociological significance of the boundary and raises the possibility of a social definition of ethnicity.

In nonurban settings, ethnic groups, with sharply defined social boundaries, present distinctive cultural forms articulated in a social organization which impinges little on the surrounding society. These kinds of groups voluntarily separate themselves from the larger encapsulating culture (see Zborowski and Herzog 1952; Orans 1965; Mayer 1961). Alternatively, ethnic groups may persist because policies and attitudes of the encapsulating society deliberately exclude them from participation in the mainstream culture (see Siverts 1969; Smith 1965; Ablon 1965). In both situations the boundary is not only social but may be spatial as well. Neither the anthropologist nor the ethnic group members have any difficulty specifying those who are the insiders from those who are the outsiders.

Now let us consider ethnicity in urban centers. The growing literature on urbanization and urbanism reveals many technological, political,
economic, and demographic factors which mitigate against the development of spatial boundaries to demarcate one urban ethnic group from
another and from the surrounding society (see Whitten 1969; Hodge
1969; Little 1966). More significant is the fact that, given a cultural
definition of ethnic identity—where status as ethnic group members is
ascribed—any distinctive cultural forms shared by the members must
be seen by the anthropologist as markers for ethnic identification.
Empirically, this position is not verifiable. Each successive generation
of ethnic group members carry an ethnic designation by virtue of ancestry alone. They may however, continually discard some of the cultural forms that have traditionally characterized their group (see
Cronin 1970; Glazer and Moynihan 1963). Ultimately, the ascribed
status persists, even though the associated cultural forms may be totally
absent. The meaning of a culturally defined category of ethnicity is
thus obscured by the historical record.

The paradox of this situation derives from the fact that, although
many studies have documented the loss of cultural forms among culturally defined ethnic groups, we are currently experiencing a resur-
gence of ethnic identification throughout the world. Selected cultural forms, both old and new, are displays of positive ethnic identification.
It is likely that, today, many ethnic groups in urban areas use cultural
forms not only for purposes of self-identification, but also to articulate
a social organization (Cohen 1969). Barth has expressed this social
definition of ethnicity as self-ascription and ascription by others
(1969:13).

I approached the field situation with hypotheses based on Barth's
model of ethnic identity. I expected that my research would reveal a
group that used many distinctive cultural forms to develop and maintain
strong self-identification and which articulated a corporate type of organization. But the longer I stayed in the field, the more difficulty I
had determining who was a Lubovitcher Hassid and who was not. The
cultural forms not only displayed a broad range of variation within the
group, but were differentially used by individual members in pursuit of
particular goals. Moreover, it became quite clear that the criteria for
ethnic group membership defined by the Lubovitchers themselves was
significantly different from the way in which members of the larger
society defined the Lubovitchers.

The problem of deciding who is, and who is not, a member of a particular ethnic group is critical for the urban anthropologist. It is not unique to my own field study. Cultural forms among self-ascribed ethnic group members are frequently diffuse, extremely variable, or even nonexistent. They do not adequately define boundary markers for urban ethnic groups. Cultural forms are even less useful to explain the intensity of ethnic identity of those who count themselves as group members on the basis of ancestry alone (see Leibow 1967; Hodge 1969).

This paper proposes that ethnicity is a symbolic system which may be activated by members of a group or its leaders as one of many strategic alternatives in the pursuit of individual or group goals. By using selected cultural forms as charters and banners, group members may be extraordinarily flexible in their choice of behavioral alternatives. Particular cultural forms which express a group's boundaries are invoked as meaningful and appropriate behavior by individual members only at certain times. At other times, in different situations, members use a range of symbols which are so different that they deny ethnicity. Such members, in these situations, deem the use of nonethnic symbols as strategically relevant.

When Lubovitch is viewed as a group by outsiders, an image of homogeneity in shared values is projected. This suggests cultural uniformity among all of the members as well as a strongly bounded group. But, if we observe an individual Lubovitcher, a vast array of acceptable behavioral alternatives are available within a cultural framework that suggests great heterogeneity.

An individual member's decision about when to employ particular ethnic symbols, or when to wave the ethnic banner, is situationally determined and based upon that person's assessment of his goals and his options to attain those goals. When deemed appropriate, an individual can neatly tuck the flag of ethnicity in an inconspicuous drawer. At the same time, he will creatively employ a whole new set of symbols, which may or may not be related to his ethnicity, to use for particular desired ends. The decision to employ ethnic identification, like all other role behaviors, is situationally defined, strategically determined, and goal oriented.

Sociologically, the roots of strategic decision making may be traced to Thomas's work on the Polish peasant, in which he spoke of the "definition of the situation" as a primary behavioral determinant (1918: Vol. 1). Individuals identify and classify not only those with whom they are dealing, but also the goals and consequences of the intended social action. The selected use of relevant ethnic symbols is one of many alternative models available to an individual in his choice of situationally appropriate role behavior.

While the Lubovitchers are viewed by the world at large as a single ethnic group, the Lubovitchers themselves can be divided into four distinct subgroups or categories. Each category uses the ethnic charter differently. Together, these four categories reveal the enormous range of flexibility within that charter for alternative behavioral choices. For any given social interaction there are special markers to determine who is, and who is not, a member of each category.

In part, the four ethnic categories reflect status groups within the community. They are easily understood in terms of concentric circles. At the center is the leader, the Lubovitcher Rebbe, who personifies those symbols which uniquely set Lubovitchers apart from the rest of the Jewish population and from society in general. As one moves from the center outward, the identification with Lubovitch changes, both in terms of its intensity and the cultural forms associated with each category. Within each category individuals manipulate the ethnic charter in a two-directional way. On the one hand, symbols and cultural forms are employed to preserve the markers between categories. At the same time, with reference to non-Lubovitchers, the barriers between categories are totally obliviated and efforts are made to display a unified Lubovitch image. Only Lubovitchers themselves, or those outsiders who are intimately familiar with Lubovitch, recognize the different ethnic categories. To the outsider, all Lubovitchers appear very much the same.

Let us consider the four categories as they tend to be defined by Lubovitchers:

Category I (core group). These are people who are defined as Lubovitch if their ancestral ties, especially in the parental generation, are Lubovitch. They live a full ritual Jewish life and have the closest personal and organizational ties to the Rebbe.

Category II. The second group, working outward from the center, consists of those who have been raised in orthodox Jewish homes.[2] Their immediate ancestors were not Lubovitch. They accept and have always accepted Jewish law as divine and practice the proper Jewish ritual, but only as adults have they come to accept the Rebbe as spiritual leader of all the Jews.

Category III. In the third concentric ring are people who are regarded as recent converts (Baal Tshuvah).[3] They have no long-term ties to orthodox Judaism; most came to Lubovitch to learn basic Jewish law and ritual. They profess acceptance of the divine nature of Jewish law and agree to try to practice the appropriate ritual. In so doing, they also claim strong allegiance to the Rebbe as spiritual leader of all Jews.

Category IV. On the outer perimeter is a group of both observant and nonobservant Jews who have not accepted many of the cultural forms, or even the ritual that is normally associated with orthodox Judaic belief. They acknowledge, however, an emotional tie to Judaism. These people, in what they deem appropriate situations, will accept the sanctity of the Rebbe and will follow his advice and identify with Lubovitch. They may also frequently participate in Lubovitch ritual.

There is much interaction between members of all categories. Many live within the spatial limits of a Lubovitch community, but each category manipulates the Lubovitch charter in a different way. During the course of a Lubovitcher's daily routine, his activity and movement is sometimes limited by the markers between groups, and it is not always possible or even necessary to bridge the gap between categories. A Lubovitcher's identity—and this may be true of all ethnic identity—is constantly affected by his general need and desire to elevate himself within the matrix of his ethnic group as well as his need and desire to accomplish certain ends within the larger society. An individual's use of an ethnic charter must be viewed from this double purpose, namely, the need to succeed within, and the need to succeed without. Because ethnic identity depends on the existence of a larger encapsulating cultural group, it must be analyzed in terms of this double-edged sword. This paper demonstrates precisely how such a two-pronged approach is strategically viable and successful for the Lubovitch ethnic group.

The largest and most important Lubovitch community is located in Brooklyn, New York, in what is called the Crown Heights area. Crown Heights is one of many Lubovitch communities around the world. It is the home of the present Lubovitcher Rebbe, and is the geographical nerve center of a vast worldwide communications network of Lubovitcher Hassidim. Crown Heights, like other sections of Brooklyn, has no hard and fast boundaries. Although it is well-known in Brooklyn as a Hassidic section, it houses a multitude of other people, most notably blacks and non-Hassidic Jews. The total Lubovitch population of Crown Heights is smaller than that of other Hassidic communities in the Williamsburg and Boro Park sections of Brooklyn.

The residential pattern of the community is determined by each person's desire to live as close to the Lubovitch headquarters as possible. This not only represents a status symbol, of closeness to the Rebbe, but is also dictated by a prohibition against traveling in any fashion except on foot during the Sabbath and all holidays. In order for a Hassid to pray with his Rebbe on these days, he must walk to his "shul", which is located at 770 Eastern Parkway.[4] Interestingly enough, many people would be much closer to "770" if they chose housing in the northern area of Crown Heights. There are few, if any, Hassidim who live there, because the section is heavily populated by blacks, is in a slum condition, and is therefore rejected.

"770" is the heart of all Lubovitch operations as well as the locus of the expression of distinctiveness of all people who wave the Lubovitch banner. Because these people espouse the divine nature of Jewish law and constantly strive to achieve the divinely given Mitzvot (good deeds), we must recognize that in many respects they are more similar to, than different from, other observant or orthodox Jews. Lubovitchers are set apart from other Hassidic groups, not in terms of a range of distinctive cultural forms, but rather in terms of one central value, which is recognition of the Rebbe, their leader, as the leader of all Jewish people. Lubovitch distinctiveness is manifested by the assertion of this single symbol that implies sociological goals as well as institutionalized behavior. This symbol is the charismatic leadership of and response to the Rebbe.

Devotion to the Rebbe and associated cultural forms are glorified through "770." "770" is a rather large and old building on Eastern Parkway and Kingston Avenue that houses the Lubovitcher synagogue, the Rebbe's offices, and administrative machinery designed to coordinate worldwide Lubovitch communications, education, and mission work. "770" is a meeting place, a house of worship, a place to congregate to exchange gossip, an employment agency, and the place where a Jew shows himself to be a Lubovitcher. It is the physical manifes-

Ethnicity as Identity

tation of an emotional and ideological decision to carry forward the banner of Lubovitch.

On most Jewish religious occasions, "770" is open to anyone wishing to participate in Jewish ritual. All people are welcomed as brother and sister Jews, and no distinctions are made among any of the categories of Lubovitchers. In addition to Lubovitchers, one will find, on any ritual occasion, visitors—almost always Jewish—who have had no prior affiliation with Lubovitch, but who have been encouraged to participate. They are not only welcomed, but accorded the grandest treatment possible. Members of Categories I, II, and III always urge nonadherents to join them in a ritual that is "Jewish." Frequently, members of Category IV attend these functions and bring others in their networks along. In this fashion, many people who have only a token identification with Judaism are incorporated into Lubovitch circles.

Members of the encapsulating society often identify Hassidim on the basis of dress. The popular image of Hassidim in the minds of other Jews is one of extreme conservatism in dress. More specifically, they are regarded as carrying over traditional Eastern European dress to contemporary United States fashions. Perhaps this is an adequate description for those Hassidic groups where men not only have long beards and sidelocks, but are frequently seen in black coats, white shirts without ties, black knickers, white knee socks and black ballet-type slippers (Poll 1962; Levine 1972). The Lubovitcher Hassidim do not reflect this image.

The Lubovitch style of dress is dictated by Jewish precepts of ethical and moral behavior (modesty).[5] While preserving the rules of modesty, however, the dress code illustrates how well a group can integrate into the larger society. For a Lubovitcher, dress is not one of the distinctive cultural characteristics that set him apart from the larger society. Moreover, it is never possible to differentiate members of Categories I, II, III, or IV on the basis of dress.

A Lubovitch man is far more distinctive than a Lubovitch woman. He is usually seen with a narrow-brimmed hat, a dark suit, and a beard. His sidelocks, if he has grown them at all, will be tucked behind his ears. Most Lubovitch men do not grow sidelocks. In recent years, men have frequently worn colored shirts and patterned ties. There are two basic deviations from this style. The first occurs on the Sabbath and festival days when many Lubovitchers, though not all, don black silk suits. The jacket is longer than is customary for everyday wear. This type of suit serves to identify each man to the other and is a method of marking the many non-Lubovitch guests at "770." This is a rather insignificant pattern, however, because even on special days, there are many Lubovitch men who maintain ordinary dress patterns. The second deviation occurs among young unmarried males in Categories I–III. These men also dress in dark suits, white shirts, and narrow-brimmed hats, but they are distinguished by the absence of a tie. Although this is not an enforced rule, it is commonly observed. It immediately differentiates Hassidic and non-Hassidic young men.

The more important function of this custom is to identify a male who is "learning." [6] This status cuts across the boundaries of Categories I–IV and marks one who is involved in learning, the highest pursuit of all. In practice, not wearing a tie denotes two particular male categories. The first is comprised of unmarried males, who are observed as potential spouses. The second includes those men who are married, but spend most of their time learning in "kolel" class.[7] During the early years of marriage, Lubovitchers encourage a woman to work and her husband to "learn." In most cases, by the time the first child is born, the father has received his rabbinical degree and stops full-time study. Usually, he takes a job, and this is his signal to put on a tie. I have also observed some older men, returning from work, who remove their ties when they go to "770" to learn.

There is an array of other cultural forms which Lubovitchers practice but which do not specifically mark them as Lubovitchers. Every male wears a "Tallis Katan" underneath his shirt. This white garment covers his chest and ends with long strings exposed outside of the trousers. The strings hang between the waist and the thigh. The Tallis Katan has a religious significance and may be worn by any Jewish male. It identifies an observant Jew, not necessarily a Hassid. Like many other observant Jews, a Lubovitcher male always has his head covered. If he is not wearing a narrow-brimmed black hat, he is wearing a skullcap. Many men wear skullcaps underneath larger hats. If the outer hat falls off, their heads will not be left uncovered. Many observant Jews put on hats only for prayer and ritual functions, but a Hassid wears a head covering at all times.

The customary dress of a Lubovitch male places him directly in the center of a diversity of dress styles, ranging from those of the larger society on one extreme, to those of other Hassidic groups on the opposite. Nonobservant Jews and non-Jewish members of the larger society interpret the conservative Lubovitch dress, the beard, and the hat as markers of a distinctive cultural group—Hassidim. My field observations reveal, however, that a large number of Lubovitch men do not fit this pattern and are thus undistinguishable by members of the larger society.

Women are even less identifiable. The female code of dress varies with current styles of the larger society but stays within the limits of what Lubovitchers regard as appropriately modest. The general guideline is that arms should be covered at least up to the elbow, and legs should be covered at least up to the knee. This rule is not a Lubovitch, or even Hassidic rule, because it derives from Jewish law and is applicable to all observant Jewish women. When miniskirts were fashionable, a Hassidic woman was most conspicuous, but the years of midiskirt popularity provided a more adequate disguise for them.

All married women are required by Jewish law to keep their heads covered. Unmarried women are permitted to display their natural hair. This, of course, reflects a status marker, but does not make it possible to differentiate a Lubovitch woman from any other orthodox Jewish woman. A married woman usually wears a wig (called a shavtl) in public. Because wigs are so popular among urban women, the presence of one is no longer an identifiable marker of an orthodox Jewish woman, and certainly not a Lubovitch woman.

Because of the rules of modesty, an observant Jewish woman is more easily discernible in the summer than in the winter. Even in the hottest weather, she will wear clothing that covers her arms and has a high neckline. Frequently, Hassidic women are not able to wear fashionable clothing and are commonly regarded as old-fashioned. No Hassidic woman or girl past the age of twelve wears trousers. Women are regarded as immodest if they do, and in my year in the field, I never saw a Lubovitch woman in pants.

Lubovitch distinctiveness, within the ethnic group and with respect to the larger urban population, is created and maintained through their marriage system. The genealogical data reveals a major trend of preferred endogamous marriage. Marriage patterns are used by Lubovitchers to differentiate members of Categories I–IV. Although most Lubovitchers marry other Lubovitchers, the preferred pattern is to seek a mate from within one's particular category. In order to accomplish this, family name assumes an important role in mate selection. Status markers within the community are most evident in this area.

A concerted effort is made by members of Categories I, II, and III to create an image of egalitarianism between the categories. Lubovitchers speak of total acceptance of each other, rich or poor, educated or uneducated. They argue that every Jew has equal consideration from, and access to, the Rebbe. To some extent this is true. But some are more equal than others. Much covert conflict is generated within the Lubovitch community by its members' overt insistence of equality between categories and by the strong desire of members of Category I to marry spouses from that same category. By and large, members of Categories I–III marry others in their category. No Lubovitch male, however, is ever publicly regarded as ineligible for any Lubovitch female. On one occasion I heard a woman speak about a group of Baal Tshuvah (Category III) young men. She said, "Oh, they will find nice Baal Tshuvah girls." The community repercussions of this public comment were severe. There was much negative gossip about this woman, who, in effect, voiced what everyone practices; that is, she indicated that members do not usually seek spouses outside of their own category. Over 90 percent of all marriages recorded in my genealogies were either marriages to members of the same category or of the one deviant form that is acceptable, hypergamy. Hypergamy is a frequent occurrence, but hypogamy is rare. Hypogamous marriages are usually to men who have no Lubovitch connections at all.

A newly married couple always sets up an independent nuclear household, separate and distinct from either set of families. Yet, marriage is regarded as a bond between two families. This is especially true for Lubovitchers of Russian descent, who trace their roots to the original Lubovitcher Rebbe. Russian Lubovitchers are the dominant members in Category I and occupy the highest status positions. The men of Russian descent are usually those closest to the Rebbe and provide the core of Lubovitch organizational and administrative strength.

Although marriage of two Russian Lubovitchers is the preferred pattern in Category I, such marriages do not always occur. A marriage between any two people of Category I Lubovitch families is regarded as an approved union. It is also acceptable to choose a spouse from Category II, since both categories have a known background of strict ritual observance. Nonetheless, the status accrued to a marriage in these categories depends upon the status of the particular families involved in the union.

One major deviation from this pattern is that a Lubovitch male can gain approval to marry a non-Lubovitch female, provided that she is an observant Jewish woman. Hypergamy is effective because Lubovitchers believe that a woman usually follows her husband's customs and beliefs. If she can maintain a ritually correct Jewish home, Lubovitchers expect that the husband will keep his Lubovitch ties and raise his children accordingly.[8] Many women who marry into Lubovitch come to accept the sanctity and authority of the Rebbe. If they participate in the Lubovitch ideals of service to the Jewish people and good deeds, they are generally accepted by the community as members of their husbands' category. The old nature-culture dichotomy looms large here, since Lubovitch status is carried through males only, but the biologically ascribed "Jewishness" is traced through the female (a Jew is a child born of a Jewish mother).

One interesting case concerns a young man from a wealthy and prominent Lubovitch family. He married a girl who had no prior observant Jewish background. Her parents lived in a town that had a small Jewish population and were convinced that their daughter had to be placed in a "more Jewish environment" so that she would marry a Jewish man. They sent her to the Lubovitch school in New York. During her years at the school she made many friends and began to practice Jewish ritual. Within five years of her marriage to a prominent Lubovitch man, she became a respected member of Category I. She no longer regards herself as an outsider, nor is she so considered by others. In cases where the woman does not embrace Lubovitch, but only maintains a Jewish home in the appropriate way, her husband and children do not suffer a significant loss of status.

The reverse situation, hypogamy, occurs infrequently and is generally regarded with disapproval. Because of the belief that a woman follows her husband's life style, Lubovitchers discourage hypogamous marriages. My genealogical records bear this out. In cases where a Lubovitch woman marries a non-Lubovitch man, she either moves to another Hassidic group or out of Hassidism altogether. One of my female informants wanted permission to marry a non-Lubovitch orthodox Jewish man. Her family did not overtly oppose the proposed union. They sought to convince her that he was not sufficiently orthodox, and that, over time, he would lose his ties to Judaism. In particular, they pointed to his custom of wearing a hat only for ritual occasions instead of at all times. Her family felt that he was not very proud of his Jewishness. The marriage did take place and the girl has since given up many of her associations with Lubovitch.

Aside from selected cases of exogamous marriages, as discussed above, the most frequently occurring unions are endogamous within categories. These marriage patterns are strengthened by the fact that most Lubovitch marriages are arranged by families. From the time of puberty, boys and girls are separated and have little contact with each other. When parents feel their child is ready for marriage (ages eighteen to twenty for girls and twenty to twenty-four for boys), a meeting is arranged between the two potential mates. Very often, a girl's brothers know the boy who has been recommended and will answer any questions she may have. A similar scene occurs for a boy who speaks to his sisters about a proposed "match." The boy and girl have their first meeting in the presence of a married couple who knows them both. The four people spend several hours together. If the boy wishes to see the girl again, he will call her directly. She agrees to see him alone only if she considers him a prospective bridegroom. Dating patterns among Lubovitchers differ significantly from the larger society in that a boy and girl never touch each other. They take walks, visit friends, and within a few weeks decide whether to marry. They need not seek parental approval because the initial arranged meeting had carried with it implied parental consent. The young couple needs only to gain the Rebbe's approval. If both individuals are members of the same category, this is assured. The Rebbe also generally approves most hypergamous marriages. But he has been known to withhold his letter of blessing in hypogamous unions.

The primary cultural mechanisms that encourage Lubovitch endogamous marriages are sexual separation and self-maintained schools. Sexual separation, which I shall consider first, is one of the most significant influences in a person's life during the formative years. Because there is so little contact between the sexes, young adults are ill-equipped to handle sociosexual interaction with members of the larger society. Lubovitchers, as young adults, turn inward to other Lubovitchers for social contacts. An informal separation begins during early childhood, when sons accompany fathers to the synagogue while daughters remain at home with sisters and mothers. This pattern is reinforced at school as early as kindergarten, where girls, attending sexually segregated classes, hold Sabbath parties.[9] Girls play the roles of father, mother and children and recreate the scene that occurs each Sabbath at home. Boys tend to concentrate on their studies and have little involvement in domestic life during their early years. Sexual separation is an enforced rule on all age levels in the Lubovitch schools in Crown Heights. Most Jewish orthodox day schools have sexually segregated classes. Lubovitchers simply carry the separation to a greater degree by sanctioning more behavior patterns which demand sexual separation.

Outside of the school environment, prepubescent children are permitted to interact and join in games of mutual interest. A child, however, perceives adult patterns of strict separation and tends to mimic the behavior of adults. Beginning at age twelve, boys and girls have separate social functions, activities, and clubs and rarely interact with members of the opposite sex outside of their home environment.

The theory underlying sexual separation of adults stems from the code of Jewish law which defines a menstruating woman as ritually unclean (polluted) and forbids a male from coming into contact with her until she has been ritually purified. Since a woman's pollution-purity status is indeterminable by appearance, men insure their own purity by sustaining customs that prohibit any physical contact between men and women, except for the marital relationship. Therefore, males and females of marriageable age have had no physical contact whatsoever with members of the opposite sex. During the period of courtship, a young couple will have discussed feelings, attitudes, life goals, and aspirations but avoided all physical contact. Such avoidance creates great anxiety among both males and females, but they claim to have a far deeper understanding of each other than would be possible if physical contact were permitted.

Anxiety is particularly obvious among Lubovitch women. When a girl is engaged, she is expected to attend Kallah (bridal) classes. They are a series of lectures about Jewish rituals of family purity. Essentially, the bridal classes teach girls how to obey laws of ritual purity and pollution. There is no need to discuss other aspects of a Jewish home since all Lubovitch girls are familiar with these laws. Young girls in Category III who have had no prior study of family purity laws usually learn them well during their first year of living with Lubovitchers. In this fashion, all women know how to keep a kosher home and are familiar with the general expectations of the husband-wife relationship. Subjects that are sexual in nature are never openly discussed. The Kallah classes provide a forum where some of the girls' questions may be answered.

There is no doubt that cultural forms expressed under the rubric of sexual separation mitigate against any outmarriage. Little opportunity exists for a Category I or II Lubovitcher to meet anyone outside of the Lubovitch group. In addition, lack of knowledge of appropriate behavior between the sexes acts as a deterrent to social contacts. Category III Lubovitchers have generally spent their early years among members of the larger society. But in choosing to identify with Lubovitch, they adopt the appropriate cultural rules of behavior. Even so, they do not have the status necessary to acquire marriage partners outside of their category. It is most significant that, for purposes of marriage, members of Category IV are considered non-Lubovitch and are not deemed appropriate mates for members of any of the other categories.

Education for Lubovitch children in the Lubovitch Yeshivah [10] day school system is the second cultural mechanism that maintains boundedness and distinctiveness. The establishment of separate schools for Lubovitch children minimizes any real or potential contacts with non-Lubovitchers. Close-knit and bounded peer group relationships that are formed at school are maintained in other areas of life. These friendships cut across categorical groupings of the parental generation. Frequently, Category I children form close friendships with Category III children. Such relationships provide a vehicle of upward mobility for the children of Categories II and III when they mature and marry.

In all Jewish orthodox day schools, the primary emphasis is on Jewish studies. In this respect, Lubovitch schools compare favorably with non-Lubovitch Yeshivah schools. For the male student, a rabbinical degree is offered, and Lubovitch students are not encouraged to pursue higher secular learning. The Lubovitch schools are distinctive in that they provide an addition to traditional Jewish studies, namely, Hassidus, the philosophy and beliefs of Hassidism. Both boys and girls learn Hassidus, but the emphasis on this subject is greater in the boys' schools. Unfortunately, I did not have access to classes in the boys' schools, and the information presented here depends on the accuracy of my informants.

In Brooklyn, there are three Lubovitch Yeshivas for boys. One of them is new and is located outside of the Crown Heights area. Many Lubovitch boys are bused to school there. This Yeshivah maintains an English and Hebrew curriculum. The second Lubovitch Yeshivah is located in Crown Heights and differs significantly from the first in that it does not have an English studies program. All instruction is given in Yiddish, which is the preferred language of Hassidim. Each Lubovitch family is free to decide which Yeshivah they prefer for their children.

Within the Lubovitch community, the Yiddish school is the most prestigious one. It is the preferred school for children of Category I parents because the curriculum is completely Jewish in orientation. Earlier, I asserted that peer relationships formed at school provided a vehicle of upward mobility for the students. Although this is true, we may now introduce a constraining mechanism on such mobility. Parental selection of a school is partially determined by the family's desire to reinforce the boundaries between categories. A Yeshivah is a manifestation of a status position. Parents pick and choose a school according to status criteria, thereby limiting the range of peer group associations for a child. The potential for upward mobility through school relationships is thus somewhat constrained.

It is common to find members of Category III, recent converts, more rigid in their interpretation of Jewish law and more overtly demonstrative of their devotion to the Rebbe. In an effort to establish themselves as "real Lubovitchers," many Category III families elect to send their children to the Yiddish speaking school. In so doing, they increase the possibility of upward mobility for their children within the ethnic group and decrease the probability that these children will gain the secular and technical skills necessary for employment in the economy of the larger society. All Lubovitchers are aware of the potential usefulness of secular skills and an English curriculum, but few Category I families elect the bilingual school for their children.

There is another important strategic factor that a Lubovitcher considers when choosing a Yeshivah. The bilingual Lubovitch Yeshivah is located in a section of Brooklyn that offers better housing and lower crime rates than Crown Heights. Each Lubovitcher must weigh a desire to be close to the Rebbe against a desire for improved environmental conditions. The choice of school can create a reasonable excuse to seek better housing, albeit farther away from the Rebbe. A family choosing this alternative will not lose its Lubovitch status, but moving out of Crown Heights will impair its potential for upward mobility. The factors to be considered in the decision-making process are very great and it is possible to implement personal goals within the framework of the Lubovitch banner.

The purpose of the third Yeshivah is quite different. It was established as a Jewish school for college-age boys who have had little or no prior Jewish learning. Lubovitchers provide housing and jobs and encourage boys to spend at least one year "learning". During this time, the boys are introduced to Hassidism and participate in Lubovitch life. Those who choose to remain as Lubovitchers enter the community as members of Category III.

There is only one Yeshivah for Lubovitch girls, and it teaches both Jewish studies and an English program. Girls enter school at three and one-half years of age in a full day nursery program. Classes continue until graduation from high school. For girls who complete the high school curriculum, Lubovitch features an optional two-year Seminary program that trains students to be teachers. The afternoon English program does not have New York State accreditation. My many hours of classroom observation demonstrated why. The library facilities are inadequate. The curriculum highlights reading and math, and other subjects are included only tangentially. Because the school administration does not regard the English program as an important feature of Yeshivah training, most of the money, energy, and initiative is channeled into the Hebrew program. The salary scale for teachers is very low and it is difficult to attract New York State licensed teachers. The school administration is attempting to upgrade the English program and, toward that end, offers higher salaries to accredited teachers than to teachers who are graduates of the Lubovitch seminary. I interviewed one New York State licensed teacher at the Yeshivah. Her college major was in the field of speech. In the Lubovitch school, she taught speech, history, and hygiene. In these last two fields she had had one college course.

When a girl completes the high school curriculum, she is not encouraged to pursue a secular college education. This is true for all categories of Lubovitch females. Instead, she is directed to the seminary program, which will train her to be a teacher in any Hebrew day school. When a girl completes the two year course of study at the seminary, she either marries or seeks a job in the educational field.

Since she is not qualified in a New York State certified school, her employment opportunities are limited to the Lubovitch school system, a non-Lubovitch Yeshivah, or an after-school Talmud Torah (school of Jewish studies).

Because the Lubovitch status system encourages Jewish, rather than secular learning, most of the graduates of the top half of the seminary class accept employment as Hebrew teachers in the Hebrew or Yiddish part of a bilingual Yeshivah program. Graduates who rank in the lower half of the class accept positions as English teachers in similar bilingual Yeshivah schools. Since these positions do not carry much respect, many young women choose to take nonteaching jobs. Many are secretaries, switchboard operators, clerks, or assume other positions which permit them to take days off on Jewish holidays and to depart early at the start of the Sabbath. There is currently a shortage of teachers in the English program at the girls' Lubovitch Yeshivah. In an effort to fill teaching vacancies, many girls who are seminary students accept part-time jobs as English teachers in the school. As a result, the level of instruction is exceedingly poor.

Rarely does one find a teacher in the Lubovitch girls' school with more than a few years of teaching experience. A Lubovitch girl reaches marriageable age after approximately one year of teaching experience. The most frequent pattern is for a girl to maintain her teaching position for only one year after marriage. During that first year of marriage, her husband is "learning," and she is the major source of financial support. After one year, she is usually pregnant, and leaves to have her baby and raise her family. The coordinator of English studies for the lower grades of the girls' Yeshivah complained to me about the lack of "commitment" of teachers to students. The teachers argued that they had demonstrated their good will and dedication to the Rebbe by accepting a position in the Yeshivah at a lower salary than New York State certified teachers who were employed there.

Secular college education and professional training are good examples of conflicting Lubovitch values. Lubovitchers, following Jewish tradition, place great stress on education of any kind. The Rebbe is not only a Torah scholar but has attended classes at two universities. Children are encouraged to study and learn, but are discouraged from entering a secular college immediately after high school graduation. This is generally not a problem for boys, since they are committed to study full time for a rabbinical degree. This degree is usually conferred between the ages of twenty and twenty-five. At the time of ordination most men are married, frequently with families of their own to support. Only a few will decide to pursue a secular college education. Girls have greater opportunities to attend a secular college because rabbinical degrees are prohibited to women. But they meet greater resistance when they attempt it. Instead, they are encouraged to attend the Lubovitch seminary for two years, marry, bear children, and then, if they wish, return to school for a secular education. The pervasive attitude among Lubovitchers is that if a Jewish woman is married to a Lubovitch man and is raising children there is little possibility of her losing a Jewish life style.[11] But if a Lubovitch woman attends a secular college prior to her marriage, they feel she will be exposed to a dangerous secularizing influence in terms of intellectual pursuits and social interaction.

Lubovitchers are very proud of their college graduates and boast of their achievements. Moreover, individual skills, talents, and abilities are used whenever and wherever possible to promote Lubovitch activities throughout the world. Simultaneously, Lubovitchers are not encouraged to develop their secular abilities. By and large, members of Category III have achieved the greatest amount of secular schooling. Many were highly skilled before they joined Lubovitch and continue in their fields of endeavor. These fields include medicine, dentistry, engineering, mathematics, chemistry, and many more. Fewer members of Categories I and II have secular degrees of any kind. A large number of Category I Lubovitchers, probably a majority, came to the United States after World War II, and their children, who are now of college age, show little evidence of seeking higher secular education.

The strategies discussed above are visible only to members of the Lubovitch group. How do people beyond the boundary see the Lubovitchers? There are a multitude of cultural forms, expressed through ritual behavior, that appear to distinguish Hassidim from other social groups. Are these cultural forms sufficient to provide markers for a Lubovitch ethnic group? Most of the previously published accounts of Hassidim dwell either on their mystical beliefs (Buber 1947–48; Mintz 1968; Scholem 1955), or on descriptions of orthodox Jewish ritual that Hassidim are known to practice (Rubin 1972; Gersh and Miller 1959; Weiner 1969). Virtually all of the ritual practiced by Lubovitchers stems from the Bible and its commentaries and, hence, is an integral part of traditional Jewish life. Empirically, there is no way to differentiate between any Jew who observes prescribed ritual and a Lubovitcher, except by the latter's allegiance to the Rebbe. Currently, in the larger Jewish community, there has been much movement away from adherence to ritual. Today, only a small percentage of the Jewish population attempts to follow the full, traditional Jewish ritual. Intense ritual observance, as a cultural form, has come to characterize Hassidim by default. Hassidic groups, defined by the larger society as keepers of traditional Judaism, are often confused with observant non-Hassidic Jews. It would be a most difficult, if not impossible task, to separate these groups on the basis of cultural forms. Most differ only insofar as minor interpretations of ritual is concerned. For example, when a Jewish woman attends a ritual bath for purification after her menstrual period, the number of times she immerses herself in the water will vary from group to group. But the fact that all observant Jewish women must attend a ritual bath and must immerse themselves in the water is constant among all the groups.

In general, rituals are associated with religious occasions and festival days. They also mark a transfer from one status in the life cycle to another. Ritual serves as a method of communication between all Jews and especially between observant Jews. Among all Jews, observance or nonobservance of ritual marks the extent an individual wishes to be identified with other Jews. But traditional Jewish ritual rarely differentiates between Lubovitchers and other observant Jews.

One of the most pervasive forces in the lives of Lubovitchers and other orthodox Jews is observance of laws relating to family purity. One aspect of these laws is a mandated period of sexual separation during the time a woman is "impure". A woman is considered impure or polluted a minimum of five days during her menstrual period and at least seven days thereafter, to insure that all signs of bleeding are gone. For at least twelve days a woman is untouchable to any man. Her period of pollution ends when, having counted seven "clean" days, she immerses herself in a ritual bath. Lubovitchers explain that pollution occurs when any potential life-creating force is destroyed. Menstrual blood is polluting because it is associated with an unfertilized ovum. Semen is polluting for the same reason and many Lubovitch men purify themselves in a ritual bath the morning following sexual intercourse.[12] The Bible does not mandate a ritual bath for men but does specifically indicate the necessity for female purification. Many observant Jewish men never attend a ritual bath because it is not specifically required.

The explanations may differ, but the ritual behavior is similar among all observant Jews.

The behavioral consequences of these cultural forms are exceedingly varied among different Jewish groups. Many orthodox men refrain from any physical contact with their wives during her polluted state. Most Hassidic men avoid contact with all women since they never know which ones are impure. This is a simple procedure for husbands and wives. A wife, during her period of pollution, does not touch her husband, sleeps in a separate bed, and avoids all physical contact with him. A Hassid's relationship with other women, however, may cause him problems. How does he know whether he may touch a woman? Is she polluted at that given moment? A Hassid's answer to this problem is never to touch a woman. This rule is extended to unmarried men as well, such that after puberty, but before marriage, male-female physical contact is prohibited.

Except for those rituals specifically mandated in Jewish law, the Lubovitch community exhibits much variation in the range of accepted behavioral patterns. The amount and type of interaction with the larger society varies from individual to individual. For example, the Rebbe has made public his negative feelings about television, but many Lubovitchers have TV sets, which they watch with moderation. In a Lubovitch home, with its total dedication to Judaism, it is not uncommon to find copies of Yiddish publications as well as the *New York Times*, *Life Magazine*, and *New York Magazine*.

Lubovitch participation in many areas of mass culture is tacitly discouraged by the Lubovitch elite of Category I, but is ultimately an individual decision. Many Lubovitchers attend movies, but only those rated G or GP. When they see a film, sexual separation is the rule, and women will attend with other female friends. More women than men attend films. Concerts and the theater are occasionally part of a Lubovitcher's social activity. Whenever possible, people carefully choose seats near members of the same sex. Some Lubovitchers choose not to attend these activities because proper seating arrangements cannot be assured. From time to time, Lubovitch organizations sponsor concerts of Jewish music or other cultural items. They are very well attended.

There is no particular behavioral pattern that can be discerned within each category of the Lubovitch community. Rather, a random assortment of individuals select activities of the larger culture that they deem desirable and appropriate. For many Lubovitchers, guidelines of participation are determined by rules of modesty and educational value. For example, Lubovitch participation in sports is minimal, but apparent. Many men and women swim, but only at separate times. Lubovitch men often report that athletic activities are a waste of precious time that should be spent in learning.

Although many Lubovitchers view the social mores of the larger society with disdain, they understand that they are intrinsically tied to the larger society for political, economic, and material benefits. Many aspects of Lubovitch life-styles differ from those of the encapsulating group, but Lubovitchers glean every possible advantage from the larger society. Lubovitchers are assimilated in that they are capable of merging with the surrounding group in many different fields. Virtually all Lubovitchers speak English, as well as many other languages. They participate in the economy of the larger society through various occupations. The range includes shopkeepers in all branches of retailing, owners and employees of wholesale and manufacturing businesses in the soft and hard goods industries, computer programmers, engineers, teachers, secretaries and many more. Many Lubovitch men and women are teachers in the Jewish day school system or the after-school Jewish educational programs.

Lubovitchers accept many different kinds of technological innovations. They use electrical systems that automatically turn lights and TV sets on and off on those days when Jewish law prohibits an individual from so doing. Most men, and many women, drive late model automobiles. In terms of cars, patterns of conspicuous consumption abound. Lubovitchers are an integral part of the urban system of charge accounts and credit cards. They are known for their political acumen in that they form a strong voting bloc. They have been able to maximize benefits to the Lubovitch community from community-based, city-funded projects. In addition, Lubovitchers take advantage of food stamp programs, social security benefits, and other government programs. Whenever possible, Lubovitch political activity concentrates on projects that offer benefits either directly to the Lubovitch community or to the Jewish community in general.

The emergent idea about ethnic boundedness for this particular group is that distinctive cultural forms that enhance ethnic identity are few. If an ethnic group is viewed as a cultural type in a complex society, then Lubovitchers cannot be differentiated from other Hassidic or non-Hassidic orthodox Jewish groups. Indeed, a cultural definition of Lubovitch will grow to include many other Jewish groups because ritual observance creates behavioral similarities among all of them. If our theoretical emphasis can be shifted to the area of social relations, to self-identification in particular, then a strong ethnic tie to a specific group emerges.

The degree of identification and expression of ethnicity within Lubovitch is situationally determined. When it is expressed, however, ethnicity is distinctively Lubovitch. More significant than the clothing one wears, the way the ritual is practiced, or where one lives, is the successful manipulation of kinship, marriage, educational institutions, and other types of social relations to promote individual goals while simultaneously preserving the image of Lubovitch to the larger society.

NOTES

[1] A *shtetl* is a small town or hamlet, and characterizes the culture of the Eastern European Jews during the nineteenth and early twentieth centuries.

[2] The term *orthodox* describes a constellation of ritual and beliefs which dictate a life style for those Jews who choose to observe most aspects of traditional Judaism. It is applied to any Jew regardless of his affiliation to a particular subgroup.

[3] *Baal Tshuvah* is a Hebrew term which means Master of Repentence. It is used by Lubovitchers to specifically mark those individuals who were not observant Jews when they came to Lubovitch and have since "repented" and are now living a good Jewish life. In many ways, Lubovitchers believe that a Baal Tshuvah can attain a higher state of goodness, because he has spent many years as a sinner.

[4] *Shul* is a Yiddish word for synagogue. Lubovitchers never use the word synagogue but always refer to their house of worship as "shul."

[5] The rules governing modest behavior are called "Tznias." This term is used to denote improper behavior by saying that something is not Tzniasdik.

[6] In some respects "learning" is similar to studying. But its meaning goes beyond the term study, and reflects a total immersion in certain scholarly pursuits. It is not used for secular study. One "learns" when one studies Torah.

[7] Kolel classes are special classes for men who are newly married. During the first year, and sometimes for two years, Lubovitch men "learn" while their wives work and support them. Lubovitchers believe it to be very important for all men to spend at least one year full time at Kolel class.

8 Jews believe that the home is the core of Jewish life. Without a "Jewish home," no individual can be a good and proper Jew. Therefore it is exceedingly important to marry a woman who can observe the appropriate ritual and provide an environment in which the husband can observe Judaism in its entirety.

9 Not all orthodox Yeshivah schools are sexually segregated in all the grades. Many have coed classes in the lower grades, or separate classes of boys or girls in the same building. All high school classes are single sexed. However, where there are enough students to fill a school with one sex or the other, this pattern will generally be found.

10 A Yeshivah is a Rabbinical Academy. However, in modern usage it refers to a Jewish parochial school (for boys or girls) which practices and teaches orthodoxy.

11 One of my informants is a convert to Judaism, and a new member of Lubovitch. She is a professor at a secular university and argued strongly for not permitting Jewish children, especially girls to attend a university before they are married and have families. By that time, she felt it would be "safe."

12 Since a ritual bath for men is not mandated by Jewish law, there are no ritual baths that operate for men only. Rather, among certain groups, designated periods of time are set aside for the men to use the baths, and at all other times the bath house is reserved for women.

LITERATURE CITED

Ablon, Joan
  1965   American Indian Relocation: Problems in Dependence and Management in the City. Phylon 26:362–371.

Barth, Fredrik, Ed.
  1969   Ethnic Groups and Boundaries. Boston: Little, Brown and Co.

Buber, Martin
  1947–48   Tales of the Hasidim. New York: Schocken Books.

Cohen, Abner
  1969   Custom and Politics in Urban Africa: A Study of Hausa Migrants in Yoruba Towns. Berkeley: University of California Press.

Cronin, Constance
  1970   The Sting of Change: Sicilians in Sicily and Australia. Chicago: University of Chicago Press.

Gersh, H., and S. Miller
  1959   Satmar in Brooklyn. Commentary 28:389–399.

Glazer, Nathan, and Daniel P. Moynihan
  1963   Beyond the Melting Pot. Cambridge: MIT Press.

Hodge, Wm.
   1969   The Albuquerque Navahos. Anthropological Papers of the
          University of Arizona. Tucson: University of Arizona Press.

Leibow, Elliot
   1967   Tally's Corner: A Study of Negro Streetcorner Men. Boston:
          Little, Brown and Co.

Little, Kenneth
   1966   West African Urbanization: A Study of Voluntary Associations
          in Social Change. Cambridge: Cambridge University Press.

Mayer, Philip
   1961   Townsmen and Tribesmen: Conservatism and the Process of
          Urbanization in a South African City. Capetown: Oxford
          University Press.

Mintz, Jerome
   1968   Legends of the Hasidim. Chicago: University of Chicago Press.

Narroll, R.
   1964   Ethnic Unit Classification. Current Anthropology, 5; 4; 283–
          312.

Orans, Martin
   1965   The Santal: A Tribe in Search of a Great Tradition. Detroit:
          Wayne University Press.

Poll, Solomon
   1962   The Hasidic Community of Williamsburg. New York: Schocken
          Books.

Rubin, Israel
   1972   Satmar: An Island in the City. Chicago: Quadrangle Books.

Scholem, Gershon
   1955   Major Trends in Jewish Mysticism. London: Thames and Hud-
          son.

Siverts, Henning
   1969   Ethnic Stability and Boundary Dynamics in Southern Mexico.
          In Ethnic Groups and Boundaries. Fredrik Barth, Ed. Boston:
          Little, Brown and Co. pp. 101–116.

Smith, M. G.
   1965   Stratification in Granada. Berkeley: University of California
          Press.

Thomas, W. I., and F. Znaniecki
   1918   The Polish Peasant in Europe and America, Vol 1. Methodo-
          logical Note. Chicago: University of Chicago Press.

Weiner, Herbert
 1969 Nine and a Half Mystics: The Kabbala Today. New York:
   Holt, Rinehart and Winston.

Whitten, N.
 1969 Strategies of Adaptive Mobility in the Columbian–Equadorian
   Littoral. American Anthropologist 71:228–242.

Zborowski, M., and E. Herzog
 1952 Life is with People. New York: Schocken Books.

4

Schools and the Hopi Self*

ROBERT G. BREUNIG
Northern Arizona University

INTRODUCTION

For nearly 100 years there have been schools on the Hopi Indian Reservation in Arizona. The organization and curriculum—in fact, the very nature of formal education—has been defined for the Hopis by representatives of the "dominant" Anglo-American society. This definition of the institution of the school and the kind of interrelationship between Anglos and Hopis in the educational context not only has placed the Hopi in a subordinate relationship with regard to Anglos, but has affected their own definitions of themselves. Exclusion from the decision-making processes of the school has resulted in feelings of inadequacy or incompetence in school matters.

* The preparation of this paper has been supported in part by grants from the U. S. Office of Education (OEG–0–8–522422–4433 and O.E. Project No. 2–0647). Points of view or opinions stated do not necessarily represent official government position or policy.

In this paper, I wish to examine this effect on the self as it is manifest in comments Hopis make about how they feel about themselves when they meet Anglos. These comments were made in response to questions asked during fieldwork on community-school relations on the Hopi Reservation from January to July 1972.

HISTORICAL REVIEW

In order to explain the general educational context today, I will briefly review the origin and development of the schools on the Hopi Reservation. We must consider how the schools were established, how they came to be defined through time by the school authorities and the Hopi, and what the consequences were of those definitions.

The following statement, written by the Hopi agent in 1882, reflects the prevailing Anglo sentiment of the time, a sentiment that pervades the *Annual Reports of the Commissioner of Indian Affairs*:

> There is much to be said to the credit of these Indians. They are affectionate and not at all quarrelsome. As far as they understand the right they seem inclined to follow it. Still they are children in understanding; sometimes they act like spoiled children, and the policy that has yielded to gratuitous giving has, in a measure, confirmed them in that course. They must be taught self-reliance, and that beggary is a disgrace, if they are to be made men and women in the true sense of the terms. I have never yet attended any of their dances, and cannot speak from personal knowledge; but, judging from reliable authority, the great evils in the way of their ultimate civilization lie in these dances. The dark superstitions and unhallowed rites of a heathenism as gross as that of India or Central Africa still infects them with its insidious poison, which, unless replaced by Christian civilization, must sap their very life blood (*A.R.C.I.A.* 1882:5).

Given this definition of the Hopi by those responsible for the schools, the schools became instruments by which Hopis were to be assimilated into the dominant (Anglo) society.

The first Hopi school, established in 1874, was a boarding school run by the Protestant Mission Board located at Keams Canyon, Arizona. According to the Indian Service agent, the school was well-attended and the children had, to his apparent surprise, "an aptness and capacity to acquire a knowledge of letters" equal to that of white children. (*A.R.C.I.A.*1876) The agent favored the boarding school concept, believing that Hopi children would progress faster away from parental influence. The agent noted, however, that the Hopis insisted that the schools be located near the mesas so that children could spend the evening hours at home. In 1876, the school closed—apparently due to lack of funds. (*A.R.C.I.A.*1876)

Ten years later, in 1886, a group of Hopi leaders from Second Mesa sent a letter to Washington requesting the establishment of a school near their homes so that the children could "learn the Americans' tongue and their ways of work." They quickly added, "We pray that they [the children] may follow in their father's footsteps and grow up good of heart and pure of breath." (*A.R.C.I.A.*1886) The letter was signed by twenty religious leaders and indicates that at least some Hopis were willing to accept new innovations from Americans but within the context of their own cultural traditions.

In 1887, a new government school, consisting of buildings rented from Tom Keams, was established at Keams Canyon. The girls worked in the dining room and were taught to launder, cook, and sew. The boys cut wood, hauled water, worked a garden patch, and maintained the buildings. For academics, they were taught the basic skills of arithmetic, reading, and writing. A heavy dose of Christianity was also taught.

After several years, school attendance dropped dramatically, and some villages refused to send their children at all. In 1890, a government team was sent to the villages to get the children back into school. In several villages, children were forcibly removed from hiding places and carted away in wagons. At the Second Mesa village of Shipaulovi, the government party barged into a kiva and removed boys while their initiation into an adult secret society was taking place. (Donaldson 1893:59)

An agent, Steward, who was charged with the responsibility of determining why so much opposition existed to the schools discovered that

> one of the principal objections is the religious education, which they say is a large part of the instruction. They feel that their own religion, to which they, like all other races cling with fanatical tenacity, is thus undermined and taken from them by this process of education; also that their families are separated by drawing their children away from the beliefs which have been taught by their fathers for thousands of years. . . . They are willing that their children should be taught how to read and how

to make figures and learn all the practical business ways of the white race, so that they will be able to deal with white people and not be cheated, but want schools in their villages, and also think they should be left the right of religious liberty . . . and should only be given a secular education. I am of the opinion that whatever in our religion is superior to theirs will inevitably be accepted, absorbed by them in time, both consciously and unconsciously, through their increasing intelligence and association with the white race. (Donaldson 1893:60).

The above quotation perhaps contains the key to many of the difficulties between American educators and the Hopi. The Americans viewed the schools as institutions for transforming Indian children into individuals more culturally acceptable to them, while the Hopi saw the schools as practical adjuncts to their traditional educational practices.

Given such a view by Anglos, the boarding school, removed from the influences of village life, was an effective instrument for implementing the policy. The Hopi, willing to learn new things in order to meet a new set of circumstances, wanted the schools too. They perceived advantages to incorporating the language and material items of the Americans into their own basic cultural framework. But they did not bargain for an all-out war on the Hopi Way.

These differences in goals led to difficult conflicts over the role of the Anglo school in Hopi society. Nevertheless, the schools remained and continued their assimilation policy. Over the next few decades the government had to make repeated attempts to force the children of villages into the schools. As the school as an institution gradually became entrenched, something fundamental happened; the nature of what formal education was to be was defined by the Anglos for the Hopis— the Anglo concept of schooling prevailed.

From that time on, the schools on the reservation were viewed as white institutions, not Hopi ones. This, of course, was the definition whites gave to the schools, and was the one the Hopi were forced to accept. Parents were excluded from the formal decision-making processes related to the school. Formal education had become the exclusive province of white men; and the only legitimate educators, according to this definition, were white people trained as teachers.

CONTEMPORARY DEFINITIONS

Because most Hopis who are today parents and grandparents went to school where this definition prevailed, they have accepted that definition. This has resulted in the creation of a superordinate-subordinate relationship between Anglos and Hopis with rgard to the schools. It has also profoundly affected the Hopis'[1] perceptions of themselves vis-à-vis Anglos within the context of the new institutions.

To analyze the situation more closely, it might be useful to look at the concept of the *self* as it applies here. In part, our feelings about ourselves in certain situations are a result of our joint interactions with other people and how we and they define the particular situations we are in. When peoples meet, the parties on both sides bring a set of assumptions about the other to the interaction. These assumptions may be stated explicitly or be implicitly imbedded in the very structure of the relationship. As we talk and act among other peoples, as we begin to observe their actions and they ours, we begin to modify our behavior both in accordance with our own definition of the situation and according to how we think the other party defines it. As the interaction proceeds, and as we see how others respond to us, we begin to form an image of ourselves as we are performing and shaping our behavior in that situation.

Having been placed in a subordinate position to Anglos within the school context, Hopis, over several generations, have come to feel that they are inferior and thus incompetent to make educational decisions. Hence, the schools should be what Anglos say they should be because they as educational experts "must know what they are talking about if they are in there."[2]

This feeling of subordination is most clearly expressed with regard to the use of English. From the founding of the schools to very recent years, Anglo educational administrators have insisted that only English be taught in the schools. Fluency in English has become the criteria for success and a measure of intelligence. Many Hopis have accepted this interpretation of English. One older Hopi woman expressed it to me this way: "When I went down here to school at Oraibi, we weren't allowed to talk Hopi; if we did we were hit with a strap. So I learned never to talk it on campus. That's why I think they should talk English down there. They can always talk Hopi at home" (Fieldnotes 5/11/72).

A few nights later, the same woman, an aide at the school, told of an incident there: "I heard some Second Mesa boys talking Hopi in the hall of the school so I went up to them and said, 'Boys, would you mind speaking in English here at school. You can talk Hopi at home but you came here to learn English so I wish you would.' And so they said 'all right' and walked off talking English" (Fieldnotes 5/15/72).

Anxiety over this matter of English is commonly expressed by Hopi parents who insist that above all their children should learn to speak English well. Although many want children to learn "good English" for pragmatic reasons (such as getting a new job), others express a more profound reason directly related to the child's image of himself. Here are some examples of this when Hopi parents were asked, "What do Hopi children need to learn the most?":

> *Father*: English! Definitely English!
>
> *Interviewer*: Why English?
>
> *Father*: Our people are going off the reservation more often. A lot go over to Flagstaff and the white people are coming here. A lot of these people feel stupid when they meet up with white people. They get tongue-tied and can't talk English good so they *feel* dumb. They have to get over that. That's why they need to learn good English in school. (Fieldnotes, 3/10/72) [emphasis mine]
>
> *Mother*: I feel it's English and math. What we are going through now, they will need those things the most. Of course, I teach them Hopi culture at home, but they should learn English at school.
>
> *Interviewer*: I don't understand what you mean by 'what we are going through now.'
>
> *Mother*: They might have a real need for this in the higher levels and when they go off the reservation. When white people come around here and I don't know how to talk to them, it's hard and I can't translate to English well. It's hard to put Hopi words into English so I want them to learn good English. (Fieldnotes, 5/72).
>
> *Mother*: The sports and music, and English too.
>
> *Father*: That's what we've been heading for; we never made it. Now days you have to compare with whites to get a job. We aren't educated and it's hard to communicate. You go to get a job and you talk to the man there. Well, sometimes he thinks you are a dumb Indian. *Because you can't speak English he thinks you are dumb.* But when you get to know them, you find that you are smarter than they are. Sometimes I get real mad and say, 'Ok, you ——— you want to find out how dumb I am? Well, here's my fist!' (Fieldnotes, 4/72) [emphasis mine]
>
> *Mother*: I'm happy they are going to school and learning all they can, not like us dumb ones who can't get anything into

our heads. They should learn more English so they can speak for themselves when speaking to white people and so they can speak for us. I'm thankful they [her children] all went to school. I've got two in college. I'm glad they didn't grow up to be like their mother, not dumb like me. (Fieldnotes 5/72).

A parent aide at a school explained why English is so important for education of Hopis because they "need to learn English so they can speak up for themselves and *present themselves* right to white people." (Fieldnotes, 4/72) [emphasis mine]

When speaking of English usage, a common theme runs through these and other responses of informants. These individuals are referring to how they feel in relation to whites, how they think they present themselves or appear to whites, and how they think whites look at them.

When a Hopi who cannot speak "good English" enters into interaction with an Anglo (especially one who appears articulate in English, well-educated, and professional) he may feel a loss of dignity or equality and the kind of assurance which he might exhibit in his interactions with other Hopis.

It should be noted here that Hopis actually feel very ambivalent toward Anglos. In many respects Hopis think Anglos are "dumb," or materialistic, aggressive, and lacking in the rich ceremonialism of the Hopi. These opinions are most vividly expressed by Hopi clowns who mimic white behavior at Hopi dances. In fact, within purely Hopi contexts, the situation is quite different from that described above. In terms of internal village matters, as in the organization and coordination of ceremonial dances, Hopis feel quite good about their roles and institutional abilities.

Feelings of subordination are, then, situational—depending upon the context of the interaction. Hopi feelings of subordination with respect to the school as an institution are a product of joint Hopi-Anglo interactions over the last century. The nature of Hopi-Anglo interactions with regard to schooling has not only affected the power relationship between the two groups, but has also affected Hopi definitions of themselves vis-à-vis their interactions with those who run the schools.

NOTES

[1] See the concept of the self as used by Mead (1962) and Goffman (1959).

[2] Many statements such as this were made to me during my fieldwork. This specific quote was made on April 17, 1972.

LITERATURE CITED

Breunig, Robert
January–July 1972   Fieldnotes, Hopi Reservation, Arizona.

Dept. of the Interior
1871–96   Annual Report of the Commissioner of Indian Affairs. Washington, DC: Government Printing Office.

Donaldson, Thomas
1893   Moqui Pueblo Indians of Arizona and Pueblo Indians of New Mexico. Washington, DC: United States Census Printing Office.

Goffman, Erving
1959   The Presentation of Self in Everyday Life. New York: Anchor Doubleday Books.

Mead, George Herbert
1962   Mind, Self, and Society. Chicago: University of Chicago Press.

5

Behavioral Change and Ethnic Maintenance among the Northern Ute: Some Political Considerations

THOMAS W. COLLINS

Memphis State University

The northern Ute Indian reservation of northeastern Utah has undergone dramatic socioeconomic change in the past two decades in response to a successful development program. The new reservation situation has brought expected behavioral adjustments in nearly every segment of the Ute population. However, certain norms have not been altered, particularly those that tend to be most exclusively Indian. The Ute response does not appear to be different from that of 65 million other ethnic Americans who have manipulated certain aspects of their traditional culture to maintain their exclusiveness for political reasons. As Gans (1967:211) suggest, "some norms are maintained simply because they have become political symbols, and people are unwilling to give

59

them up because this would be interpreted as a loss of power." Although Gans does not refer to this political phenomenon as ethnicity, other scholars (cf. Cohen 1969; Glazer and Moynihan 1970; Levy and Kramer 1972; Suttles 1972) have pointed out the importance of ethnic status in political struggles in both this country and Africa. The proposition is an interesting one and offers an alternative to the thesis that norms are maintained by the conservative nature of cultural groups.

This situational analysis is by no means innovative in anthropology. The acculturation models in reservation studies, exemplified in the earlier work of Bruner (1956), Spindler (1955), Voget (1952), and others, have nearly been discarded by the current generation of anthropologists. At present, reservation segments once considered "traditionalist" or "native oriented," and therefore the major vehicle of surviving aboriginal elements, are now considered highly adaptive. These behavior patterns are viewed as necessary responses to economic deprivation (cf. James 1961; Kupferer 1962; Stern 1966; Wax 1971). Such traits as sharing or residence patterns in extended families and social networks are normal given the condition of poverty. Excessive use of alcohol is considered a response to the frustration, despair, and disorganization. In short, the literature of the past decade projects the Indian-American on reservations as just rural poor folk, thoroughly dissatisfied with their lot and powerless to change their situation. One gains the perspective that if the economic situation were to change, all identifiable traces of Indianness would evaporate into the proverbial melting pot. Thus far, the political dimension of ethnicity is nearly ignored in the situation analysis of reservations. In spite of many behavioral adjustments, the Utes continue to emphasize their exclusiveness, as I propose to demonstrate.

SOCIAL AND ECONOMIC CONDITIONS

Located in an economically depressed region of Utah called the Uintah Basin, the 1,700 tribal members and the 8,000 white residents have not enjoyed long periods of prosperity. The major source of employment, until quite recently, has been agriculture and federal service agencies, such as the Departments of Interior and Agriculture. Unfavorable soil, climate, and uneven terrain have combined with high transportation costs to make agriculture a precarious industry.

Accelerated economic change began on the reservation in the early 1950s, when the tribe began receiving large sums of investment capital through land claim settlements and mineral royalties. Additional capital was made available through several federal agencies engaged in regional development and the amelioration of poverty. This money, amounting to over $35 million, has been spent in direct payments to individual families, improving social conditions, and developing several tribal enterprises. Also, during this period, 499 . mixed-blood tribal members (those designated by the government as having less than five-eighths Indian ancestry) voluntarily terminated their status in the tribe. This event was economically significant, since this segment formerly held most of the stable employment in the reservation bureaucracy. Full bloods who possessed fewer job skills and less formal education now had the opportunity to assume nonagricultural employment for the first time.

During this period, the tribe was forced to shift its focus from individual and family development to larger corporate economic enterprises. As in most rural areas, mechanization made it impossible for small ranchers and farmers to compete in agricultural industry. Tribal leaders realized it was futile to encourage individuals to pursue agriculture. While a significant number of whites have emigrated to industrial areas outside the region, tribal members have pressed for employment and improved living conditions on the reservation. In the early 1960s, only 30 percent of the Ute labor force had achieved stable employment, while the remaining 70 percent attempted to pick up what casual labor remained in the dwindling job market. Thus, the tribe had no alternative; it had to develop large corporate enterprises in manufacturing, tourism, agriculture, and craft industry. This change had achieved enough success by 1972 to make the Ute reservation a showplace among United States Indian reservations.

Today, the Utes operate a ranch, utilizing most of the available land and water for their 7,500 head of cattle. A cabinet and furniture plant, begun in 1968 with a modest building and ten employees, has been expanded to a large plant employing 120 members. The tribe opened a multi-million-dollar motel-resort in 1970, in which it hires 100 members in various capacities from manager to maid. Several other smaller operations have been established, such as an environmental research laboratory, a domestic water system, a casting shop, a custom hunting and fishing enterprise, and coin-operated laundries. In short, the reservation economy has moved from a labor surplus to a labor shortage in less than ten years. Individuals who had migrated to seek employment in urban areas in the past have returned to the reservation.

Furthermore, the tribe has not neglected problems of housing, recreation, and youth. A Mutual Self-help Project has constructed 250 new suburban-type homes, complete with modern facilities. Existing homes have been refurbished through the Housing Improvement Program. Manpower programs have been liberally funded to train and educate those members with low skills. The Neighborhood Youth Corp employs most of the young people unable to obtain employment in the tribal enterprises. The Bureau of Indian Affairs has assured the Utes that these programs will continue, by designating them for the Rapid Acceleration Program, which makes the tribe eligible for unlimited funding.

BEHAVIORAL CHANGE

The new economic situation has affected reservation behavior. For example, there is greater social heterogeneity today than when Lang (1954) carried out his fieldwork in the early 1950s.[1] Differences in occupational opportunities, with corresponding levels of income and prestige, have formed distinguishable social categories or classes. Each of these classes are crosscut with smaller social networks of family and peer ties. The social categories are distinguished by differences in set modes of action, social relationships and aspirations. Behavior of women in each of these categories varies substantially from their male counterparts. Generally, their desire for improved housing, education and job opportunities has led them to support tribal development efforts. Politically, they are more assertive in both reservation and off-reservation activities and institutions.

For analytic purposes, in this study the members have been divided into three general categories: elite, laborer and underemployed. These categories, roughly 35, 50, and 15 percent respectively, are based primarily on occupational characteristics on the assumption that the type of job one holds is an index of behavior and attitudes. The elite, who determine who will be employed, have used their power to unofficially sanction certain behavior. In other words, there is a selection process for hiring based not only on skill and work experience, but also on personal activities of job applicants. Administrative or managerial positions, for example, are occupied by those who demonstrate a commitment to tribal economic development. Usually, this means individuals who have been educated or have worked off the reservation for some length of time. This experience, in itself, is an indication of aspiration for job mobility. It is understood that elite members will not consume alcohol publicly or engage in activity that will reflect on the tribe negatively. Some tribal managers have been fired for such minor offenses as drunken driving. Usually, the elite maintain steady work habits, are involved in community activities, and support the tribal council on most issues. They tend to form stable marriages, with both partners taking an active interest in the management of family affairs and rearing of children. Consumer habits do not vary from non-Indian families in the region. The elite acknowledge that economic change has had certain disadvantages, particularly in the loosening of ties among extended kin. One individual commented that "my brothers and cousins rarely get together for anything, except at funerals or Christmas. We just can't relate to each other anymore." He continued, "I feel like we [the elite] have lost a great deal not having a close family."

Those in the laborer category occupy the nonsalaried, semiskilled, or unskilled jobs, in the tribal enterprise or BIA. This work is stable and relatively easy to obtain. There is a high rate of job turnover but only among individuals who are shifting to higher-paying positions. Absenteeism is not any greater than that in similar industry in the wider society. Generally, these individuals do not identify with their work in the same manner as the elite. A number have expressed the view that they would just as soon be home or away in the mountains. But since the work provides a steady income, they prefer employment to the deprivation they once had to endure.

Life-styles in this category vary quite widely from network to network. Members of the Peyote Cult, for example, adhere to their religious ethic regarding the use of alcohol. Their weekends are occupied with religious activities. Other laborers spend their leisure time with their single-sex peer groups or relatives hunting, fishing or partying. Interaction in these networks frequently involves the use of alcohol. These people, however, tend to demonstrate considerable skill in avoiding trouble or public intoxication that may result in arrest. As one put it, "I may show up for work drunk or I may not show up at all but I know just how much I can get away with before I get into trouble." Kinship ties have remained relatively close with strong emphasis placed on maximizing leisure activity within the household groups.

Those in the final category, the underemployed, have derived the least material benefits from corporate economic development. This category includes old people and families with female heads or physically handicapped men. Most of these individuals receive at least part of their subsistence from tribal and county relief payments. The size of this group has been reduced (35 percent of 1965 to 15 percent today) to where it now compares to the non-Indian welfare population of the region. Housing is provided by the tribe, in addition to services such as Head Start and community recreational activities. Indian craft work produced by women is marketed through the tribe for higher prices. Nevertheless, incomes remain substantially lower in this category. Hence, the change in life-style has not kept pace with that of other Utes. Since most of the public assistance is channeled through women, they tend to hold more power in these households. For example, they are more dominant in their own households and ultimately make the decision as to who may reside in their home.

Another tribal segment included in this underemployed category is that of the adult males (about thirty in number) who have developed a reputation for excessive use of alcohol. They are marginally attached to the households of the women mentioned above, but they spend most of their time with close male companions. These network relationships are personally so satisfying that men are unwilling to give them up for long-term stable employment. Furthermore, the tribe will not provide them with employment until they demonstrate a more "responsible" life style. Since these individuals are not threatened by economic deprivation, tribal sanctions regarding public drunkenness are not effective. Drinking is regarded as a social criterion for assigning status. They refuse to exercise the same skill other groups do as to when and where they choose to drink. Arrest for public intoxication is frequent, both on and off the reservation. Thus, this limited minority of members tends to reinforce the stereotype the local white population holds of Utes—as lazy and excessive drinkers.

Generally, the individuals in the underemployed category are not involved in reservation organization, nor do they identify with tribal development efforts. In fact, most of the overt reservation hostility directed toward the tribal council is generated within this group. They consider the council as a "white man's thing" and the members as "just a bunch of kids spending our money." To them, the only rational solution to personal economic problems is to divide all tribal assets equally, including land, water resources, cattle, and tribal money. It is impossible for underemployed members to understand why they have to seek welfare assistance from the state or county, when the tribe has several million dollars in the bank. As one individual described it, "We own the bank in Roosevelt (where the tribe has $15 million on deposit) but we can't get credit. The BIA won't let us have our kids' money [trust accounts] that belongs to us. I just don't understand those people down there." In short, this group wants money, not programs or the jobs that programs provide. They maintain that their economic difficulties are caused by the federal government's failure to fulfil its treaty obligations.

In summary, the new opportunity structure created by the recent economic change on the Ute reservation has led to extensive social heterogeneity among the formerly traditional full bloods. Predictably, full bloods with greater occupational skills have been able to assume the positions vacated by the termination of the mixed bloods in 1955. Full bloods with aspirations for a middle-class life-style have been able to move into the white-collar and managerial positions created by economic development.

The elite group is economically well off by reservation standards and by the standards of the neighboring white community. Since both the men and women tend to have greater occupational skills than other Utes, in many families both married adults hold down high-paying positions. Moreover, these families have the advantages of free medical care, college scholarships for their children, and an equal share in the profits that the tribal enterprises pay to all Ute members. In some cases, these families have received government housing at a minimal cost and surplus food supplements. It is not surprising that few of these individuals ever seek employment off the reservation. It is also understandable that those Utes who have left the reservation for employment in larger urban areas tend to return to the reservation as new opportunities are created.

The laborers have profited from economic development, but their life-style has not changed as drastically as that of the elite. The men are not achievement oriented. They hold little aspiration for political office, and they view their jobs only as means of avoiding welfare. Social relationships are oriented toward the extended family and peer group. Their world view does not extend beyond the local community or the reservation. Perhaps the most visible change within this group is the growing involvement of women in reservation politics. Their increased skills, particularly in English, have increased their influence in the formal political process.

The remaining category, the underemployed, has been influenced the least by the economic changes of the past decade. Since most of their income is derived from public assistance, they are unaffected by the social sanctions created by tribal leaders. Generally, they view tribal projects with disdain, as just one more attempt by the government to avoid its treaty obligations.

ETHNIC MAINTENANCE

There exists a considerable consensus among all segments of the reservation on the desire "to keep things Indian." This attitude was true in the 1950s, as it is today. Therefore, economic change has not appreciably affected those norms or elements considered most exclusively Ute, such as dress, ceremonials, religion, and native language. The following analysis reviews those aspects of reservation life with which the Ute tend to identify as Indian.

Dress for normal, everyday wear by men is predominantly that which characterizes western ranchers: boots, western hats, and jeans. Lang (1953) also found a preference for such clothing. At that time beadwork jewelry, as well are large black hats and braids, were only worn by the older full blood men with some status as leaders. Adult women wore the traditional shawl when out in public. Lang noted that elaborate beadwork was produced for special occasions such as the Sun Dance and other ceremonies. Today, Indian jewelry is used frequently by both adult men and women. Tribal leaders rarely leave the reservation on business trips without displaying at least a bolo tie or pendant. Only the very old women still wear shawls, but other Indian items are used by younger women, such as moccasins or beaded barrettes. Headbands and moccasins are now popular among highschool-age Utes.

Perhaps the most conspicuous aspect of native attire on the reservation is the popularity of long braids. Only two years ago the preferred style was short hair; just two men wore braids. When a non-Ute Indian was hired by the tribe at that time, he was chastised by the males in the laborer category. As one put it: "A long time ago Indians all wore braids but now we have short hair. Why is he trying to be different from us?" This attitude has been reversed—long hair and braids are nearly as common among men as they are among women. In fact, the tribal council is now involved in a legal suit with the conservative local school board, which does not permit children with this new hairstyle to attend public schools. The tribal leaders claim their civil rights have been violated by not allowing children to follow Indian customs in long hair. The same individual who had criticized the non-Ute for wearing braids now wears his own hair in that style. He stated, "When tourists visit our resort, they want to see Indians, not someone dressed like a white man. I'm selling a product, my Indianness."

On special occasions such as war-dance contests, powwows, or local fairs, a number of Utes turn out in elaborate ceremonial dress of buck-skin and fine beadwork. Most of these costumes are not new, but informants agree that these are more common today since people have more money to buy the necessary materials to make them. The elite appear to own more costumes and wear them more frequently than other tribal segments.

Reservation activities involving Indian dances and pageantry are now held more frequently and with greater enthusiasm. The Bear Dance, one of the oldest aboriginal ceremonies, is still held each spring in two communities, with a feast provided by the tribe. A number of new events are sponsored by the tribal council, in part to promote tourism in the Basin. But these events are also provided by the tribe in response to a greater demand by the members for more Indian-type activities. For example, a large powwow is held near the motel each July. Smaller powwows are conducted each summer by the individual Ute communities, with the tribe providing cash prizes for dance competition. Some teenagers have formed their own singing and drumming groups to participate in these contests. This growth in participation is due somewhat to the increase in tribal financial encouragement, but it is also an indication of the level of enthusiasm for Indian activity. Only four years ago young people tended to reject participation in such activities because it was considered too conservative. Today, they not only take their turn along with the older men in singing, but they also assist in the organization of these events.

Indian religion, manifest in the two annual Sun Dances and somewhat less in the Peyote Cult, continues as a meaningful element in Ute identity. Most Utes attend each Sun Dance, although only about twenty-five to fifty men actually participate in the rigors of dancing. Many of the adult males take part in the other activities of the ceremony. On occasion, some of the most active members in Christian churches will solicit curing or have their infants blessed by the Sun Dance Chief. All Utes identify in some degree with the extensive mythology supporting the ceremony. A surprisingly high number of people have openly acknowledged that Indians have an afterlife separate from that of whites.

As is the case for religion nationally, the commitment to the Sun Dance has declined in recent years (cf. Jones 1955). Nonetheless, it is a significant reservation social activity. It is a time for visiting with relatives and friends from other reservations. Individuals who do not have the opportunity to gamble or engage in hand games through the rest of the year do so at this time. A common complaint by the Sun Dance leaders is that people seem more interested in gambling than in the performance of the dancers. Indeed, many more Indians are found observing the gambling than are found in the Sun Dance enclosure at any time during the four days of the ceremony. One of the leaders said he was disgusted with the way the people acted while in the enclosure. He said, "They would not carry on like that in the white man's church." Another informant added, "It has become something like the white man's Christmas. People don't take it seriously." In spite of this lack of religious devotion, participation in the ceremony or mere attendance at the Dance grounds offers evidence to other Indians and non-Indians of a continuing commitment to a Ute way of life.

The Peyote Cult has remained viable but limited in membership over the past two decades. There are those who only attend peyote meetings when they are held to cure or aid a relative. The more active peyotists, about forty-five in number, will attend between twenty and forty meetings a year for purposes of curing or to commemorate holidays and special events, such as high school graduations. This latter segment forms a close-knit social network and appears to be thoroughly committed to the ethics of the religion. That the peyote ceremony is quite a demanding activity in terms of time and physical discomfort could explain the lack of wider reservation involvement in the religion (cf. Stewart 1948).

Perhaps the major symbol of Indian exclusiveness is the native language. Reservation members judge the degree of "Uteness" by the ability to speak and understand the language. It is not uncommon for tribal members who have spent long periods of time away from the reservation to declare their identity on the basis of their language. As one youth put it, "I may have lived six years in a white home, but I can still speak good Ute. I still got a right to claim what is coming to me as an Indian." Ute is often used in the home, at social gatherings, and in public meetings. Frequently, opening prayers are given in Ute at biracial events, such as dedications. Tribal members are often critical of elected leaders who cannot converse with them in Ute. Young adults aspiring to tribal offices maintain that being able to converse with the older people in their native language is a political advantage. By the same token, parents consider it a great accomplishment when their children use Ute at home.

In spite of this present viability among adults, reservation children are not showing an interest in the language. To counteract this trend, high-status members have actively promoted the teaching of Ute. Some, for example, have attempted to have language classes incorporated in the public school curriculum. Perhaps the apprehension about language loss is best demonstrated in a statement by a former leader, quoted by his daughter (Willie 1971:195):

> Be sure to teach the kids to speak Ute. . . . Some day it's going to be asked who is the Indian, who's an Indian now? Who's got their right heritage to claim this land? And you know what he is going to say? "Okay prove to me that you're an Indian." And what are we going to say? "Well, I'm so and so's daughter, my grandparents are this." And he's gonna say, "No, that's not what I'm looking for." And some day somebody that'll say it's (Ute); and that's the one that that man's gonna say to. "Right you're an Indian, the only Indian that's left." The only Indian that's gonna get all this reward or whatever is going to be at the end of that time.

In brief, the Ute life-style of the early 1950s was altered to accommodate the new reservation economic situation while those elements which emphasize Ute exclusiveness have become more prominent in all segments of the reservation. Thus far, there is no indication that a stable income and a standard of living comparable to that of the wider society will make these elements any less relevant to the Ute. For an explanation of this phenomenon, it is necessary to review tribal external relationships.

EXTERNAL RELATIONS

White-Indian relations in the Basin are characterized by attitudes of antipathy and distrust. Most of the whites live in small, closed communities with a social and political structure centered around the Mormon church. They have competed with the Utes for what meager resources the Basin has had for over seventy years. Like small farmers everywhere, they have not been able to survive the trend of mechanization and increasing scale of agro-business. Nearly half of all the farmers have had to seek either full-time or part-time employment in other local industries or migrate to urban centers. Being politically conservative, they naturally resent the Ute for having received so much financial and technical assistance from the government. As the tribe has become increasingly more competitive in all sectors of Basin industry, antipathy has given way to animosity. Where the Indian behavior was once considered a joke or child-like, it is now viewed by the whites as threatening.

The Ute have not been passive to this change in white attitudes. Confrontation over alleged mistreatment or injustice has become more frequent. Only four years ago, most Ute individuals tended to accept such conditions as a fact of life. In the past eighteen months they have challenged the local school board on treatment of Indian children, demanded changes in State Family Service's policies, and have prevented local off-reservation police from jailing tribal members. Some conflicts have been resolved by threatening white-owned businesses by the use of boycotts. Hence, the Utes as a group have begun to realize their potential as a force in local political and economic issues.

Ute relations with the government are not as desperate as that reported in the press for Indians nationally. Blessed with an unusual number of talented and aggressive leaders, the tribe has been able to manipulate its manipulators in federal agencies. These leaders have innovated at crucial times to prevent the loss of reservation resources (water rights, hunting privileges, and so on) to state agencies. Instead of investing their own capital for development, they have searched outside the BIA for funding. When private companies, particularly those notorious for exploitation of low-skill labor, have made liberal offers to locate on the reservation, the tribal leaders have refused. In some cases the refusal has been contrary to the desires of the BIA superintendent.

At present, the Utes have greater access to Congress than any other racial minority in the state. It is not uncommon for tribal leaders to personally contact their U.S. senators on issues relating to the reservation and Indian programs. They have been able to turn this political capital into economic opportunity. On two separate occasions they submitted proposals for funding only to have the request increased by several thousand dollars. The BIA has recently designated them as one of ten tribes in the Accelerated Change Program, which makes them eligible for unlimited funding for development projects.

Although tribal members will frequently malign their leaders and the BIA, there is a general consensus on the desire to maintain current federal legal status. They may wish to restrict BIA hiring to Indians, but they do not hold any desire to see it dissolved. As one young Ute put it, "We would be nowhere without the BIA." Without this special federal bureaucracy the Ute would lose much of their political leverage locally and their access to Washington.

Moreover, the Utes have observed firsthand the difficulties experienced by the mixed bloods in their termination of federal status. The money they received for dissociating with the tribe was spent in a few weeks. The stocks issued each individual in a corporation established to administer the 29 percent of reservation land and mineral rights were quickly converted to cash. Today, over 60 percent of these shares are owned by non-Indians and are paying generous dividends in oil royalties. The mixed bloods received only a fraction of their value when they were sold. In some cases stocks were exchanged for cheap used cars. Today, this segment cannot claim any of the advantages of being a legal Indian, such as tax benefits and medical care in the Public Health Service. Nor does it carry any political influence in either the white or Indian community.

Perhaps it was the mixed blood dilemma that prompted the tribal chairman (Ute Tribal Report 1968:37) to write:

> And for the future, we want to remain in the Uintah Basin, identifiable as Ute Indians. . . . We want to keep the resources we now have. We feel we are doing a good job right now in using the resources available to us. We are searching for new and better ways to use our resources. . . . But it is in the finding of these ways to better use what we have that we fear the word 'termination.' Will our future progress mean the abandonment of us by the Bureau of Indian Affairs? As we become more capable, will not the help that made us capable be withdrawn? Some of our membership would like to see a reexamination of our agreements with the government, to be

sure that old obligations are being met. We, of the Business Committee, feel that the Congress and the Bureau of Indian Affairs should give us assurance that the development of our capabilities does not also mean the withdrawal of Bureau services, the opening of avenues through which we will again lose, as we have in the past, more of our land and resources.

Thus, the Utes, from the Chairman on down, are apprehensive about the reservation's political future once economic parity is achieved. Therefore, the Utes are determined to maintain their ethnicity as a device for their continuing defense of their reservation and their desired life-style.

NOTES

[1] The data reported in this paper were collected as part of a wider research project over a four-year period from 1968 to 1972. A variety of methods was used in this project, including both department interviewing and extensive interviewing. A random sample of eighty-eight Ute households and fifty-four white households on or near the reservation was surveyed during the winter of 1969. The general research objective was to document behavioral change using baseline data obtained in early work by Stewart (1942; 1948) and Lang (1953).

LITERATURE CITED

Bruner, Edward M.
  1956   Primary Group Experience and the Processes of Acculturation. American Anthropologist 58:605–623.

Cohen, Abner
  1969   Custom and Politics in Urban Africa: A Study of Hausa Migrants in Yoruba Towns. Berkeley: University of California Press.

Gans, Herbert J.
  1967   Culture and Class in the Study of Poverty; An Approach to Anti-Poverty Research. *In* On Understanding Poverty. Daniel Moynihan, Ed. New York: Basic Books.

Glazer, Nathan, and Daniel P. Moynihan
1970   Beyond the Melting Pot. Cambridge: MIT Press.

James, Bernard J.
1961   Social-Psychological Dimensions of Ojibwa Acculturation. American Anthropologist 63:721–741.

Jones, John A.
1955   The Sun Dance of the Northern Ute. Bureau of American Ethnology Bulletin 157. Anthropological Papers 47:207–263.

Kupferer, Harriet J.
1962   Health Practices and Educational Aspirations as Indicators of Acculturation and Social Class among the Eastern Cherokee. Social Forces 41:154–162.

Lang, Gottfried O.
1953   A Study in Culture Contact and Culture Change: The White-rocks Utes in Transition. University of Utah Anthropological Papers No. 14. Salt Lake City, Utah.

1954   The Ute Development Program: A Study in Culture Change in an Underdeveloped Area within the United States. Cornell University: unpublished Ph.D. dissertation.

Levy, Mark R., and Michael S. Kramer
1972   The Ethnic Factor. New York: Simon and Schuster.

Spindler, George D.
1955   Socio-Cultural and Psychological Processes in Menominee Acculturation. University of California Publications in Culture and Society, Vol. 5. Berkeley and Los Angeles: University of California Press.

Stern, Theodore
1966   The Klamath Tribe: A People and their Reservation. Seattle: University of Washington Press.

Stewart, Omer C.
1942   Culture Element Distributions 18. Ute-Southern Paiute. Anthropological Records 6:4. Berkeley: University of California Press.

1948   Ute Peyotism: A Study of a Cultural Complex. Boulder: University of Colorado Studies Series in Anthropology No. 1.

Suttles, Gerald D.
1972   The Social Construction of Communities. Chicago: University of Chicago Press.

Ute Tribe
    1968   Annual Report. Fort Duchesne, Utah. MS.

Voget, Fred
    1952   Crow Socio-Cultural Groups. *In* Acculturation in the Americas.
            Sol Tax, Ed. Chicago: University of Chicago Press.

Wax, Murray
    1971   Indian Americans: Unity and Diversity. Englewood Cliffs, NJ:
            Prentice-Hall.

Willie, Gertrude C.
    1971   I Am an American. Utah Historical Quarterly 39:194–195.

6

The Same North and South: Ethnicity and Change in Two American Indian Groups*

GEORGE L. HICKS

Brown University

With a few notable exceptions (e.g., Murphy and Steward
1956), American Indian acculturation studies during the past two decades have tended to emphasize locally bounded circumstances. Even
in a 1956 Social Science Research Council summer seminar, participants
failed, at least in the published results (Spicer 1961), to come up with
regularities that hold across localized situations. The concept of "con-

* Fieldwork on the Catawba was done in the summer of 1963, with the assistance of Linné H. Hicks, and partially supported by funds from the Department
of Anthropology, University of Illinois at Urbana. (Most of the funds came
from the author's pocket and friendly banks.) Fieldwork on the Monhegan
was done primarily in the summers of 1968–71, with less intensive research in
the intervening months, with the assistance of David I. Kertzer. Financial
support came from the Doris Duke Foundation, administered through the Department of Anthropology, University of Illinois at Urbana.

tact community," developed in that publication, aptly reflects this stress on situational uniqueness. A previous lack of attention to local variation in Indian-white relations, so ably demonstrated by Mason (1955) in sixty-five specific studies, formed the background against which these twenty years of work can best be appreciated. Yet significant similarities in geographically separate situations can be masked, in some cases, by more obvious differences. This is, of course, the argument put forth in Murphy and Steward's study of Mundurucú and Montaignais "acculturation" (cf. the commentary on this study in Murphy 1964).

In this paper, I point out regularities in the process of adaptation among two American Indian groups, the Catawba of South Carolina and the Monhegan of New England.[1] Differentiated linguistically and culturally in the precontact period, the two groups nonetheless have faced a deep-seated and pervasive aspect of Anglo-American culture: racism. I hope to demonstrate that, in their attempts to establish satisfactory relationships with whites, members of the two groups have applied different tactics to achieve essentially the same end. After a brief description of the history of each group, I argue that a single "ideology of race" (Nash 1962) influenced their adaptation to surrounding peoples.

THE CATAWBA

At least by 1700, the Catawba were part of a four-tribe confederacy in the Carolina Piedmont (Lawson 1967:49–50). As the British swept westward in the eighteenth century, the Catawba absorbed the remnants of smaller tribes and acted as a buffer for European expansion. Until the Revolutionary War, they maintained an alliance with the British against the Cherokee and other tribes. (Their participation in the Yamasee uprising of 1715–16 is the single exception.) After the war, they continued their position as middlemen in the trade with coastal South Carolina and Virginia. ·

In 1763, a treaty between the Catawba and South Carolina resulted in a grant of fifteen square miles for the group, in what is now York and Lancaster counties. During the ensuing decades, most of the land was leased to whites, and in 1841 the Catawba sold all their land save one square mile to the state. Their population had declined from an estimated 5,000 in 1600 (Swanton, 1952) to less than 100 in 1840 (Scaife 1896:11). Throughout the nineteenth, and well into the early twentieth century, the Catawba made a meager living by fishing, collecting wild fruits and berries, and selling firewood and pottery. A state reservation of 652 acres was augmented in 1943 by an agreement reached between the state of South Carolina and the federal government. About 3,500 additional acres, in several tracts, were purchased with the expectation that the Catawba would put the land to agricultural use. This was expected to reduce the amount of financial aid for the group previously granted by the state legislature. Since the 1880s, the Catawba had periodically petitioned the state legislature for compensation for the land ceded in 1841.

What remained of Catawba aboriginal cultural and social patterns by the twentieth century was scant. Not quite 100 people remained on the reservation in 1910, and of these, less than one-third spoke Catawba (Bureau of Census 1910:274). Indeed, the language was almost extinct, "for although remembered by the older Indians and many of those in middle life, it is rarely spoken, English being the language of daily use" (Harrington 1908:400). They had long since "abandoned the old dances and ceremonies," and only pottery-making, of the crafts of the Catawba, was still carried on. Pottery, made by women, was sold to local farmers and constituted a major economic resource for the group. Little use was made of pottery by the Catawba. It was almost entirely produced for sale or barter, and most traditional pottery forms had disappeared, "sacrificed to the demands of the trade" (Harrington 1908:401–402). Men of the group worked as day laborers on the farms of nearby whites and made a small amount of cash by peddling firewood cut from the reservation (Bureau of Census 1910:274). They had become rural slum dwellers; so much that their economic condition was described in 1896 as "generally a little below the standard of the average southern negro" (Scaife 1896:12).

Intermarriage of white and Catawba was already well established by 1900 and usually involved white spouses of low economic status— "white trash, believe me! I mean trashy scum," in the words of one white informant who lived near the reservation community from 1915 to 1940. (For similar judgments, see the *Charlotte Observer*, August 12, 1928.) Whites seldom married into the tribe alone. Sisters would marry Catawba men and live on the reservation, or cousins would take Indian spouses at about the same time. Sometimes an in-marrying white would bring a kinsman to live with him on the reservation and the kinsman would later marry a Catawba.

Intermarriage with Negroes was disallowed. From white or Catawba informants, no comment was more frequently volunteered to me than "the Catawbas marry whites but never colored people; there's not a drop of Nigra blood in the whole tribe." Over the past half-century, this has been the standard compliment paid by whites to Catawba respectability; it echoes through almost all documents (newspapers, books, legislative reports), and is partly supported by a recent study of the physical anthropology of the group (Pollitzer et al. 1967).

Not only have the Catawba refused intermarriage with blacks; they have long regarded them with disdain. As an observer wrote in 1896, "They do not mix blood with the Negroes, for whom they entertain the strongest antipathy, and it is said that a Negro can not be induced to go on the Indians' land" (Schaife 1896:12).

This attitude received official encouragement, as a means of controlling black slaves and potentially hostile Indians, as early as 1750. It remained a firm policy of colony and state throughout the eighteenth and most of the nineteenth centuries. For the earlier period, Willis provides this interpretation:

> The picture in the Colonial Southeast was this: a frightened and dominant White minority faced two exploited colored majorities. To meet the Negro danger, South Carolina devised a harsh slave code; the police control of slaves was comprehensive, specific, and brutal. To meet the Indian danger, the province had a system of trade regulation that was less brutal than the slave code but of approximately equal thoroughness. That Indian tribes were still independent and had some freedom of choice necessitated their being dealt with somewhat like equals. . . . In meeting each danger, South Carolinians were plagued by the discrepancy between what they willed and what they could actually do. This discrepancy became greater with time. It did not take much imagination on the part of whites to put the two dangers, Indians and Negro slaves, together. As early as 1712, Governor Alexander Spotswood, of Virginia, juxtaposed them (1963:160–161).

With the adoption of Mormonism by most of the Catawba in the late nineteenth century, their separation from blacks was greatly strengthened. The beliefs about race and racial categories embodied in Morman theology lent moral justification to the aversion for blacks, and the emulation of whites, that had become characteristic of the Catawba. Morman belief includes an explicit racial hierarchy amply buttressed by theological explanation. Caucasians are supreme among the three races recognized in the Book of Mormon, while Negroes are despised as "an idle people, full of mischief" (Smith 1958:61). Until the late 1960s, Negroes were forbidden to hold office in the Mormon church organization. American Indians occupy a special position in the Mormon hierarchy. Indeed, Mormons consider it their peculiar mission to convert American Indians, and the writings of the church extend a promise of eventual absorption into the Caucasian category for Indians who obey church law. The obedient, says the Book of Mormon, will become "white and delightsome" (Smith 1958:102). Mormonism provided a supernatural basis for explaining the relation of Catawba to whites and Negroes. The promise of a transformation from Indian to Caucasian was already gradually being fulfilled by 1900, and even in 1963, many Catawba tended to interpret this as a result of spiritual good behavior rather than the influence of heredity and intermarriage with whites.

Although the Catawba were apparently never classified together with blacks, their position in the local social hierarchy was considerably below that of whites. It was a measure of their distance from blacks that a Catawba leader could make a public complaint about the sexual exploitation of Catawba by whites: in a letter to the local newspaper in 1905, he protested the "white men coming in the nation [reservation] to ruin our young girls. . . ." (*Rock Hill Herald,* April 5, 1905). With some exceptions, Catawba men met no violent reprisals when they married white women (cf. Hicks 1964:118). Most such marriages were consensual unions; as an elderly Catawba said in 1895, "They just take up with one another" (Brown n. d.).

Yet there were limits to the association of Catawba with whites. Around the year 1910, a Catawba woman and her Oneida husband (they had met as students at Carlisle School) tried to enter their six-year-old daughter in a local white school. The child was refused admission and was taught at home by a white tutor. This family lived in a white neighborhood in the town of Rock Hill, nine miles from the reservation school, and the husband worked as a railway clerk. Racial segregation in both educational and industrial activities was directed by state law, but no objections were raised to their residing among whites, or to his employment in a job usually reserved for whites. Nonetheless, Catawba men were hired, beginning in the late 1920s, as textile mill workers and construction laborers. White employers were aware of the legal restrictions; a prominent white businessman testified in 1930:

> I am in the cotton business and under the law as it stands now we
> are not really permitted to employ them [Catawba]. We don't

object to them, but if a white employee in that building raised the
question we would simply have to obey the law . . . we
couldn't work an Indian in the same room with white people if
anybody in that mill raised the question (U.S. Senate 1931:7540–
7541).

By 1930, in violation of state law, several Catawba children were attending the local white high school. After the federal reservation opened in 1943, regular transportation from the reservation to Rock Hill became available for Catawba high school students. Minor incidents of insults and taunts occurred, but there was no organized attempt to forbid Catawba attendance at white schools after about 1935.

Even while some activities were open to Catawba on a basis of equality with whites, distinctions continued to be made among whites, Indians, and blacks. The wife of a local textile entrepreneur explained in 1930:

Note this distinction—the negro always comes to your [whites']
back door; the Indian will come to your front door, even if he is
an Indian. And when the Indian comes around to your front door
asking you to give him something to eat he . . . doesn't want
charity doled out to him, he wants to give you something in exchange for giving him something to eat. That is one of the characteristics that distinguishes an Indian from a colored man (U.S.
Senate 1931:7537).

Nevertheless, local whites did not see in Catawba behavior the respected traits assumed to be found among whites. The Indians were described as "like children. They must be taught to farm, to provide for themselves, and to take care of what they make" (Columbia, *SC State*, January 22, 1921) or as "somewhat shiftless and people in neighboring towns do not like to employ them" (*Charlotte Observer*, August 12, 1928). At least part of the explanation for these opinions lay in the whites' inability to demand from Catawba the kind of deferential behavior and obedience they received from blacks:

Unfortunately, white people can't control them just like they
would like to control a [black] laborer because the Indian considers himself the equal of the white man and a white man is likely
to get into trouble if he curses an Indian. Therefore a white man,
rather than take that chance of getting into trouble, will seldom
hire an Indian. That is an unfortunate condition, of course
(U.S. Senate 1931:7543–7544).

For many years after their conversion to Mormonism, the Catawba continued to receive paternalistic treatment at the hands of whites.

In the early years of this century, they saw themselves as far closer in status to whites than to blacks. As a folk saying, current on the reservation about 1910, expressed it: "First comes the white man, then the Indian, then the Indian's dog, and then the nigger." The Catawba lacked sufficient power to enforce deference toward them on the part of blacks, and they kept as much physical distance from blacks as possible. Even in 1963, there was an informal but firmly enforced rule in the local area that blacks could not go afoot on reservation land.

Intermarriage with whites was by 1963 the predominant pattern. Of seventy-three households on and near the reservation, forty-seven included a white spouse. In 1960, an enterprising newspaper reporter uncovered a state law, dating from 1879, that forbade marriage between individuals of different races (*Rock Hill Herald*, January 1, 1960). To replace this outdated rule, the proposal for a new law encountered no significant opposition, and legislators' comments indicated that they were simply remedying an oversight (ibid., Feb. 10, 1960). By the revised statute, marriage between Caucasians and *Catawba* Indians was legalized and made effective retroactively. The specificity of the law demonstrated the nearness of Catawba and whites and the distance still existing between Catawba and other South Carolina groups— mestizos or "triracial isolates" (Berry 1963; Beale 1957) claiming to be Indian. When a court clerk was asked why he had been issuing licenses for Catawba-white marriages, he stated the case for Catawba status succinctly: "I considered the Indians one of us" (*Rock Hill Herald*, January 1, 1960).

Encounters of Catawba with other legal agents at this time were similar. An informant told of applying for a driver's license in 1959. She had neglected to state her race on the application, and offered to fill in the blank. The clerk remarked, as he wrote "white" in the space, "it don't make no difference nohow; we're all the same."

Of over eighty-five Catawba families contacted in 1963, none, including those who were physically indistinguishable from whites, appeared to resent being referred to as Indian. One frequently heard jocular and romantic comments about their Indian origins. Children with much Catawba blood, they said, behaved better than white children. At regular Saturday afternoon baseball games, when a crowd of Catawba and related whites gathered to watch the Catawba team perform and to gossip with kinsmen, there were many bantering remarks about behavioral traits assumed to be due to "Indian blood." A middle-aged woman, describing her pleasure in fishing and in going barefoot, told me, "I guess it must be the Indian in me, the way I like to be out of doors." Even color differences, an awkward subject for members of other racially mixed groups (Johnson 1939), are the basis of joking comment here. The Catawba president of the Mormon church remarked to me, "These dark brown Catawba, I always tell people, are just born in the dark of the moon." And, looking over the yard at her ten children, a young mother spoke admiringly of the wide variation in their skin color.

Their Indianness worn lightly, the Catawba nevertheless remain distinctive as a localized group. They have long been recognized by whites for their importance in local historical traditions; this has assumed even greater significance in the past two decades. Many whites think the Indians have not been adequately paid for the land taken from them and hope the state government will make a generous, if belated, settlement with the group. For a number of years, the county historical commission has planned to build a museum of the Catawba Indian on or near the reservation. The project is justified by Catawba and whites as a means of preserving historical tradition and as a magnet to draw tourists off the busy highway nearby (Columbia, SC *State*, September 25, 1962).

A remarkable expression of the whites' concentration on the Catawba as the central feature of their own history appeared in 1960. An elaborate historical drama, written by an instructor in the local college, was staged by townspeople. The plot of the play dealt with events of the late eighteenth century, giving special attention to the aid extended to early white settlers by the Catawba. Several members of the tribe appeared in the drama, and the state governor attended the opening night performance. Like the museum project, the affair had double intent. An editorial in the local newspaper unambiguously phrased the aims:

> This is the drama of the most colorful era in the history of the Catawba Indians. . . . Besides having obvious financial possibilities, it is a tribute to the Catawba Indians, who meant much to the survival of the early white settlers. As the drama points out, the Catawba helped protect the settlers from other Indians and later fought side by side with the settlers against the British. In return, the Catawbas were often inadvertently mistreated. There is much drama in the Catawba Indians' history and the pro-

duction opening tonight will attempt to capture and portray it (*Rock Hill Herald*, September 21, 1960).

The belief of Indian and white that the Catawba are already thoroughly assimilated to the white social stratum and that they will soon vanish as a distinctive group probably contributes to the sentimentalizing of the group and the history of Catawba-white relations.

Another more subtle aspect of Catawba distinctiveness is found in their classifications of themselves. They identify themselves differently in different contexts; by their own account, they are variously Americans, American Indians, Catawba Indians, Southerners, and South Carolinians.

With the exception of three elderly members of the group, the Catawba most frequently put themselves into two local categories, Catawba and white. Their expressions of identity as white are similar to expressions of identity among local whites—American, Southern white, local white. For Catawba and white alike, an expression of identity as Southern or local white usually appears in a discussion of racial relations. This is precisely the context, of course, in which distinctions between Southern and Northern whites is considered most clear-cut and significant. In this crucial respect, the Catawba are well adapted to the local social milieu.

THE MONHEGAN

At the time of their first regular contact with Europeans, in the early seventeenth century, the Monhegan had already established themselves as one of New England's most powerful tribes. They had conquered neighboring groups and controlled several hundred square miles of territory. Like the Catawba in this respect, they continued to absorb the remnants of smaller groups who had been weakened by epidemics or warfare.

During the first fifty years of English settlement in their territory, the Monhegan remained generally peaceful, with only occasional outbreaks of violence directed against the English and adjacent tribes. Many Monhegans were employed by the English as laborers; others served as middlemen in a widespread trading network. "They were considered," in the words of an eighteenth century historical writer, "as a commercial people, and not only began to trade with the English for goods for their own consumption, but soon learned to supply other distant nations at an advanced price. . . ."

These amicable relations ended abruptly in the last quarter of the seventeenth century, when the Monhegan joined with other tribes in an all-out effort to repel the English. The English retaliated in large force, and the Monhegan were decimated; many hundreds died of wounds or starvation, their towns were burned, and most of their land taken from them. Large numbers of those who survived were sold into service as indentured servants and some were transported to the Caribbean as slaves.

This bloody episode marked the end of Monhegan dominance, and brought on a period of rapid adoption of European customs and, over the next half-century, an increasing dependence on the English colonists. By the early 1700s, the colonial government had reduced their tribal lands to a reservation of sixty-four square miles. In the following 150 years, this was lost through sales to whites, and by 1875, only 1,500 acres remained as tribal property.

The Monhegan rapidly exchanged their aboriginal tongue for English; by 1800 probably only a few words of Monhegan remained. Their religious ceremonies soon disappeared, and in the 1750s, a Baptist church was built. Following the ill-organized efforts of Christian missionaries to educate Monhegan children, the colonial government established a regular school for the tribe in 1765.

Political organization, too, soon was modeled on the colonists' usage. The traditional chieftainship, while it continued until the late 1700s, was under the direct supervision of the colonial government and was finally abolished in favor of an annually elected president and four-man council. Even this body, however, held little authority, its primary duties being to manage tribal lands and provide for the indigent.

From the mid-1600s, Monhegans had intermarried with whites and blacks, a trend that greatly accelerated after their defeat late in the century. Monhegans who found themselves sold into servitude worked alongside black servants and slaves, and for many purposes Indians and blacks were classified together. A law of 1750, regulating the sale of alcoholic beverages, for instance, mentions "Negroes, Indians and other impudent persons," and forbids the sale of liquor to "any Indian, Mulatto, or Negro servant or slave."

Intermarriage with members of other racial categories had, by the 1830s, resulted in a broad range of physical types. A report of the state Indian commissioner in 1835 declared that only 7 persons, all "aged females . . . were of genuine Monhegan blood," in a total population of 200 Monhegan. Relying on physical appearance as an indication of the extent of racial mixture, the commissioner went on to observe that "less than [80 Monhegan] were . . . probably more than three-fourths of the African Negro race." The report of 1860 noted that "there is not an Indian of full blood remaining."

The prevalent view of the Monhegan was as a morally degraded people. Despairing of the loss of aboriginal customs, a 1856 report of the condition of the group stated:

> From that high position which they occupied [in the seventeenth century], they have fallen; their limits have become circumscribed; they have gradually wasted away; and the Monhegan of the present day can boast of little else than the name, without exhibiting any of the traits of character that distinguished his ancestors.

Attempts by state politicians to terminate the Monhegan reservation and abolish the legal existence of the tribal organization were continuous from the 1850s until 1885, when the aim was finally accomplished. Throughout the period, the Monhegans were charged with not being industrious, a claim vigorously rejected by the Indians. They could not obtain decent jobs because, as a Monhegan spokesman declared in 1870, of the prejudice of whites. Speaking to state legislators, he demonstrated an acute awareness that Monhegan and black, in the eyes of whites, belonged to the same category:

> We wish it understood that we fully appreciate our position. Poor, despised, uneducated though we be, still we know our rights. We come to your workshops and ask permission to learn trades. You tell us, "We can't take Indians or niggers in our shops." Until very lately the school houses were closed against us. And yet we are met by the assertion that we are ignorant and degraded. . . . Every trade, almost, has its representative among us, and in everything but the color of the skin we claim an equality.

A few years after termination was complete, a sanguine report of the results was rendered to the legislature:

> Since the passage of the act dissolving the tribal relations and admitting the members of the Tribe to all privileges of citizenship of this State the Indians have almost completely assimilated themselves with the body of surrounding citizens without disturbance or ill effect.

If, as was confidently assumed, the Monhegans existed only as a legal fiction, then termination of their reservation—erasing their legal status as a corporate group—should bring about their speedy demise as a distinctive group. This is the view put forth by newspaper accounts over the several decades following termination. In an 1899 obituary for a well-known Monhegan, his death was said to have severed the "last link that bound the Indians of the present day to the traditions of their days of strength and power. . . . The Monhegan Indian, pure and simple, has become extinct."

The Indian church still stood on land held in common by Monhegans, and the Annual Meeting was still held in August. Services in the church were held only on this day in August. The Annual Meeting, with apparent roots in precontact ceremonies, resembled an exuberant country fair with dances and games, meals of clam chowder and corn on the cob, and, perhaps most important for the participants, a reunion of local Monhegans with kinsmen who had moved away from the local area. Early in the century, in newspaper reports of this event, it was described as "one of the biggest days of the year for the colored population of that section of the State" (1910), but declining in popularity.

The prediction of extinction was made for the Annual Meeting, too. It was declared in 1910 to "be one of the last of the kind to be held . . . the 'Indian meeting' is now but a shadow of what it was a decade ago." Although it never entirely disappeared, attendance at the Annual Meeting did continue to decline through the years from 1885 to the early 1930s. Then, aided by the Indian Reorganization Act of 1934, the Monhegans reestablished their existence as a corporate entity. Receiving a charter from the state government, the Monhegan set up an elected tribal council and sachem. Membership in the reorganized "tribe" was to be through proof of a "blood tie" to any member listed at the time of termination.

The council began publishing a Monhegan magazine that, although it survived only a few years, is still considered a major part of the reorganization effort. In its pages appeared a wide range of opinion, exhortation, and self-congratulation.

The most significant aspect of reorganization, however, was the change wrought in the Annual Meeting. Rather than allow it to continue as a family reunion attended by dwindling numbers, the group decided to turn it into a public spectacle, a Monhegan Powwow. By the mid-1930s, the Meeting had become, according to documentary sources and informants' memories, a drunken, disorderly gathering. Whites rarely attended, as they had in large numbers around 1900, and violence had become an inevitable part of the day's activities. New rules for the powwow, with this reputation in mind, included a ban on the sale of alcoholic beverages on the grounds and the appointment of tribal officers to enforce the rule. The Monhegan magazine reported on the 1934 Powwow with pride:

> About 200 of hitherto unacquainted tribal members, from four states, conversed, ate, played, swam, and socialized in a very dignified, congenial manner. Not one bottle of liquor on the grounds! The modern idea of a booze party was put to shame, by this respectful group of Monhegans. The tribe can collect without firewater and enjoy themselves, yet there are those who still believe a Monhegan August Meeting is a drunken brawl.

By the 1960s the Powwow had become the predominant feature, in the public view, of modern Monhegan life. It steadily increased in the elaborateness of presentation; in the number of visitors attracted, both Indian and tourist; and in the amount of favorable coverage in newspapers and on television.

In *New York Times* advertisements designed to attract summer visitors to the local area, Monhegan history plays a prominent part. The 1969 version read in part:

> Legendary figures like [Chief Brewster] are woven into the history of [Wilson] County. You'll hear all kinds of stories about them as you travel through the area. There's even one about an Indian ghost who is still haunting the county. It's said that he had a habit of mislaying his head as he went from place to place.

Such sympathetic treatment is indicative of some success gained by the Monhegan in presenting a public image as Indian. Contemporary news accounts of the Powwow, as well as other, less regular, ceremonies staged by the group are invariably laudatory.

Yet doubts about the authenticity of Monhegan status as Indian still linger. Members of the group wage a constant battle to justify themselves as "real" American Indians. Arguing that their identity as Indian does not depend upon physical appearance, the Monhegan frequently point out that there is a wide range of physical types among the group's members. Whenever questions are raised about the Negro appearance of some individuals among them, the standard response is a reference to particular individuals who acknowledge themselves as Monhegan and who are blond, of light complexion, and blue-eyed. If these white-appearing Monhegan remain in the local area, their kinship links to Monhegan of darker hue tend to invalidate any claim they might make to unequivocal status as white. Hence, although they are not often involved in Powwow or Monhegan church activities, they usually identify themselves as Monhegan rather than white.

In the past, relations have sometimes been tense between those Monhegans who have married blacks and those who have married whites. Tension is most apparent between Monhegans who, having married whites, have tried to claim status as white and Monhegans married to blacks who have relied on genealogical evidence to validate their position as Indian. One informant remembered that, before the 1930s,

> some members of [a particular] family might intermarry into the Negroes. Other members, a brother or a sister, would intermarry into the whites. And the ones that intermarry into the whites maybe wouldn't associate with the ones that intermarry into the Negroes, and of course this split up whole families.

There is considerable variation among Monhegan individuals in regard to their assertions of Monhegan and Indian status. Some members of the group project a Monhegan identity in most aspects of their life; others take on this self-identification only at the Powwow, or even less often. Between these extremes stand most members of the group, who vary their identity-claims according to situation and audience. That is, most Monhegans have at hand a number of expressions of identity and tend to vary them according to different situations. Perhaps the least problematic are those Monhegans who announce their claim to Indianness only by their yearly attendance at the Powwow and, for the rest of the year, melt back into the urban black ghettos of the region. Even here, individual differences are pronounced, as this incident from the 1971 Powwow illustrates:

> A Negro-appearing man of about fifty years, attired in street clothing, was asked by a Negro-appearing girl of about thirteen whether he was an Indian. With a sweep of his hand to indicate a cluster of Negro-appearing people dressed in Indian costumes, he replied: "I'm as much Indian as any of *them* are!"

A vivid reminder of the multiple self-identification of many Monhegans appeared on several automobiles at the 1970 Powwow. The drivers and passengers were all participants in the dances and calumet ceremonies, but their cars displayed large metal plates inscribed "Soul Brother."

CATAWBA—MONHEGAN SIMILARITIES

In spite of the considerable differences in their respective postcontact histories, the circumstances of the Catawba and Monhegan groups had become, by about 1900, remarkably similar. Members of neither group spoke an aboriginal language; English was in use in both groups. In neither group was the maintenance of precontact culture significant. The Catawba still made pottery in much the same way as before, but local marketing conditions determined pottery shapes and among the Indians, pottery had fallen into disuse. The Annual Meeting of the Monhegan, although held every August, had taken on the style of a New England country fair or family reunion: old rites were forgotten, costumes not worn.

Both groups were Christian, and no member of either held to traditional religious beliefs or practices. Christianity, indeed, had become traditional for both. Occupationally, members of each group were restricted, by law in the Catawba case, by local custom for the Monhegan. Industrial jobs were, for the most part, closed to members of both groups. The educational and economic status of Monhegan and Catawba were quite similar: their local neighborhoods were rural slums; opportunities for upward mobility were limited in either case. Each group had lived on state reservations, the Monhegan until 1885, the Catawba until the present time, and this tended to reinforce their isolation from urban industrial life. Both lived within a few miles of small urban centers.

From 1900 to the present, there have been a number of significant parallels in the history of these groups. Under the terms of the Indian Reorganization Act of 1934, both underwent a renewal of organizational enthusiasm and adopted new constitutions. And, in the era after World War II, each found itself being used by local white promotional agencies as a potential attraction for tourists. Catawba and Monhegan accepted the image of themselves as historical curiosities and aided, by participation in a locally staged drama and by tailoring the Powwow for white spectators, the sometimes fanciful presentations of their pasts. In both cases, this has led to sympathetic publicity in the news media, and provided a favorable public image.

Differences between the two groups appear in patterns of intermarriage and in ideologies of race that are closely related to the adaptation of Monhegan and Catawba to local social and cultural conditions. Although both groups have a long history of intermarriage with non-Indians, the Monhegan have married members of both black and white categories, while the Catawba—insofar as can be ascertained—have intermarried only with whites. Very early in the postcontact period, the Monhegan were thrown into close, daily contact with black people, particularly through enforced servitude to whites. At least by the mid-eighteenth century, they were explicitly classified with blacks, a tendency that seems to have been quite general for New England Algonkians. Whites in New England "instigated their [blacks' and Indians'] interracial mixing" (Brasser 1971:81). Laws discriminatory to both blacks and Indians placed persons of both categories together.

The Catawba, on the other hand, were constantly encouraged by colonial and state government, as well as the prevailing rules of "racial etiquette," to regard themselves as distinct from blacks. Even when their claims to status equality with whites were refused, as was the case until the past two decades, they were never relegated to the same category as blacks.

These social patterns were supported, for the Catawba, by a convergence of traditional racial ideas with the more elaborately formulated doctrines of the Mormon Church. There was little, if any, disjunction between their social relationships—emphasizing the avoidance of interaction and especially intermarriage with blacks—and the ideology of race provided by their white neighbors and, from the late 1800s, Mormonism.

Monhegan ideas about racial categories, while less unambiguous, tend to treat blackness as inferior. As one informant remarked, in questioning the authenticity of one family of Negro-appearing Monhegan, "Now, that's people with a . . . very highly pigmentated epidermical quality." In the same vein, those Monhegan who become drunk and rowdy at the Powwow are generally considered to be those with the greatest degree of "Negro blood." That is, behavior that lacks respectability and moderation is ascribed to Negro racial inheritance.

CONCLUSIONS

In establishing and maintaining their identity as American Indian, both Monhegan and Catawba have been confronted with a bipolar model, or "two-category system" (Daniels and Kitano 1970:1–28), of race relations.[2] Whether lumped together with blacks, as the Monhegan have been, or treated as a separate category, as the Catawba have been, members of either group have adapted to situations in which their own status is subordinate to that of the dominant whites. Members of both groups, in attempting to overcome the disadvantages of this classification, have used various means of marking themselves off as distinctive. Mormonism, with its special position for Indians as potential whites, has been the primary means for Catawba in justifying their status as one of progressive upward mobility.

For the Monhegan, whose position is more likely to be contested than that of the Catawba, the risks are high in their effort to establish and protect a category that is neither white nor black. If they convince local whites and the general public that they are a distinctive people, they can be reasonably assured of privately stated moral judgments giving them superiority over blacks. Assignment to an intermediate category —American Indian—is clearly more desirable, in most circumstances, than inclusion in the black category.

Assertions of identity are, for members of both groups, to a large extent situationally determined. The Catawba meet little opposition to their usual inclusion of themselves in the category of white. It can be argued, indeed, that they so easily accept their Indianness because it is not incompatible with claims to high status. What is most important for them, it seems, is that they are widely praised for their avoidance of association with blacks.

The Monhegan, given the appearance of some of their number as black, face the same general cultural classification system—the bipolar model—but are forced to acknowledge intermarriage with whites *and* blacks. In order to make a good case for their claim to a separate category as Indian (neither white nor black), they must maintain a group membership that spreads across the phenotypical spectrum from black-appearing to white-appearing. In other ways than with reference to biology, they disparage the black appearance of some of their group. Behavior generally regarded as characteristic of the Afro-American stereotype—drunkenness, rowdiness, slovenliness—are, by the whiter-appearing Monhegan, attributed to blackness.

To describe these two groups as isolates reacting to an acculturative situation—the dominant white society—would ignore the regional and

historical variations that makes their condition at the present time seem
so different. By comparing the two, we can observe the influence of
racial ideology in the dominant society in shaping similar processes of
adaptation.

NOTES

[1] Monhegan is a pseudonym: Catawba, of course, is not. I have tried to protect the Monhegan from what could be, for them, potentially embarrassing results of these paragraphs. Some dates (of reports, events) have been slightly
changed for the same reasons. Finally, it is part of this effort at anonymity
that no references for the various quotations are given. The Monhegan case
is taken up at greater length in Hicks and Kertzer 1972.

[2] Winder has used the term "bipolar" society to refer to portions of West
Africa (1962:317), and Banton considers the American South to once have been
"a two-category system" (1967:118). I intend bipolar model to refer to cultural, rather than social, phenomena. Bipolar is preferred to "two-category,"
since the former allows more scope for consideration of the hierarchical nature
of subcategories. That is, to apply the concept of "two-category" system to
the entire United States, with the categories being labeled white and nonwhite,
is less useful than to make the imagery of continuum explicit. This makes
allowances for regional variation in the ranking of different subcategories of
white and nonwhite.

LITERATURE CITED

Banton, Michael
    1967   Race Relations. London: Tavistock Publications, No. 36.

Beale, Calvin L.
    1957   American Triracial Isolates. Eugenics Quarterly 4:187–196.

Berry, Brewton
    1963   Almost White. New York: Macmillan.

Brasser, T. J. C.
    1971   The Coastal Algonkians: People of the First Frontiers. *In*
           North American Indians in Historical Perspective. Eleanor
           Burke Leacock and Nancy Oestreich Lurie, Eds. New York:
           Random House. pp. 64–91.

Brown, D. S.
n.d. Notes for a History of the Catawba, MS. in Rock Hill, SC Public Library.

Bureau of the Census
1915 Indian Population in the United States and Alaska: 1910. Washington, DC: Government Printing Office.

Charlotte, NC *Observer*
1928 August 12.
1938 April 13.

Columbia, SC *State*
1921 January 22.
1962 September 25.

Daniels, Roger, and Harry H. L. Kitano
1970 American Racism: Exploration of the Nature of Prejudice. Englewood Cliffs, NJ: Prentice-Hall.

Harrington, M. R.
1908 Catawba Potters and their Work. American Anthropologist 10:398–407.

Hicks, George L.
1964 Catawba Acculturation and the Ideology of Race. Proceedings of the spring meeting of the American Ethnological Society. Seattle: University of Washington Press, pp. 116–124.

Hicks, George L., and D. I. Kertzer
1972 Making a Middle Way: Problems of Monhegan Identity. Southwestern Journal of Anthropology 28:1–24.

Johnson, Guy B.
1939 Personality in a White-Indian-Negro Community. American Sociological Review 4:516–523.

Lawson, John
1967 A New Voyage to Carolina. Edited with an introduction and notes by Hugh Talmage Lefler. Chapel Hill: University of North Carolina Press.

Mason, Leonard
1955 The Characterization of American Culture in Studies of Acculturation. American Anthropologist 57:1264–1279.

Murphy, Robert F.
1964 Social Change and Acculturation. Transactions, New York Academy of Sciences, Ser. 2, Vol. 26. 7:845–854.

Murphy, Robert F., and J. H. Steward
1956 Tappers and Trappers: Parallel Process in Acculturation. Economic Development and Cultural Change 4:335–355.

Nash, Manning
1962 Race and the Ideology of Race. Current Anthropology 3:285–288.

Pollitzer, William, D. S. Phelps, R. E. Waggoner, and W. C. Leyshon
1967 Catawba Indians: Morphology, Genetics, and History. American Journal of Physical Anthropology 26:5–14.

Rock Hill, SC *Herald*
1905 April 5.
1960 January 1.
1960 February 10.
1960 September 21.

Scaife, H. Lewis
1896 The History and Condition of the Catawba Indians of South Carolina. Philadelphia: Indian Rights Association. *Reprinted in* U.S. Senate, Document No. 92, 71st Cong., 2nd sess., 1930.

Smith, Joseph, Jr.
1958 The Book of Mormon. Salt Lake City: The Church of Jesus Christ of Latter-Day Saints.

Spicer, Edward H., Ed.
1961 Perspectives in American Indian Culture Change. Chicago: University of Chicago Press.

Swanton, John R.
1952 The Indian Tribes of North America. Bureau of American Ethnology Bulletin 145. Washington, DC: Government Printing Office.

U.S. Senate
1931 Hearings of the Subcommittee of the Committee on Indian Affairs. Survey of Conditions of the Indians in the United States. Pt. 16: North Carolina, South Carolina, Florida, Mississippi. Washington, DC: Government Printing Office.

Willis, William S., Jr.
1963 Divide and Rule: Red, White, and Black in the Southeast. Journal of Negro History 48:157–176.

Winder, R. Bayly
1962 The Lebanese in West Africa. Comparative Studies in Society and History 4:296–333.

7

Ethnicity and Ethnic Group Relations in the British Virgin Islands*

ROBERT DIRKS

Illinois State University

INTRODUCTION

The mistaken tendency to create homologies between population aggregates and ethnic categories has been brought to the attention of anthropologists several times within the past few years. Contributions on the part of Lehman (1967) and Barth (1969) have been particularly outstanding in drawing attention to the dynamism present in the process of identification between peoples and their ethnic categories. Ethnic

* Much of the data reported in this paper were collected in 1969–70 with the support of a Hokin Fellowship for Ecological Research. Fieldwork was conducted under the auspices of the Caribbean Research Institute, College of the Virgin Islands. I wish to thank Kay Mitchell Calavan, Leo A. Despres, James W. Green, and Virginia Kerns for their comments on a previous draft of this paper.

95

categories appear to be subject to manipulation and selective use, more so it seems than those categories that have reference to age or sex criteria. This degree of freedom in creating an identity between a people and an ethnic category has repercussions in the field of ethnic relations.

Following Linton's classic distinction, it is clear that an ethnic identity as a kind of imperative status (Barth 1969:17) can be generated on the basis of achievement or ascription. Many times self-assumed identities and those ascribed by others are in complete agreement. However, such a happy coincidence does not always occur. This appears to be especially true in complex societies and in situations highly charged with competition for scarce resources in which ethnic membership confers an advantage. Here identities themselves may be in dispute. Ancestries, phenotypes, and behaviors may be scrutinized and challenged. Whether identification with a category is attempted on the basis of one's own efforts or is acquired from others on the grounds of their ascriptive criteria, there is no guarantee that the identification will be a matter of consensus. Instances in which either self-identification or identification by others has been rejected as legitimate in the face of criteria that elsewhere and at other times have been acceptable clearly suggests that ethnogenesis is more than a matter of displaying some objectively sufficient quantity of cultural contrasts. A certain amount of subjectivism appears to have a place in ethnic determinations.

This same subjective component may allow some latitude in imputing ethnicity from a range of sources. Certainly, there is no reason to assume that ethnic claims are always genuine in the sense that they are deeply rooted in ancestral traditions. To the contrary, there is reason to doubt that ethnicity need be founded upon a genuine native tradition at all (Lehman 1967:109). In this connection, a case in which ascription into an ethnic category is based upon situationally specific or environmentally modified behaviors that are subjectively interpreted as a traditional life-style presents a theoretical possibility. Indeed, this paper documents such a case.

In the following account, one of the many interethnic lines that segment Virgin Island communities is described. In general, I am concerned with the ethnic boundary that exists between the native black population of the Virgin Islands and the Afro-West Indians who migrate to the Virgin Islands in search of employment. More specifically, I will focus on British Virgin Islanders who alternatively find themselves on either side of this ethnic boundary: (1) as the native hosts to aliens working in the British Virgin Islands (B.V.I.) or (2) as aliens themselves often employed in the nearby American Virgin Islands (U.S.V.I.). Whether the British Virgin Islander is in the position of native or alien, the ethnic identity applied to aliens is the same. Characteristically, it is neither an identity that is embraced by those to whom it is ascribed nor an identity that is supported by cultural contrasts emanating from native sources. In order to delineate how such an ethnic identity may be generated, I will describe what appear to be the outstanding structural and processual features that bear on the formation of the nature-alien relationship in the Virgin Islands. These include (1) certain aspects of the natural environment and the regional political economy that together constitute a framework of opportunities and constraints for the various island work forces, and (2) the pattern of competition that applies between these work forces within the context of the local-level labor markets.

THE VIRGIN ISLANDS

The Virgin Island archipelago constitutes the geographic setting for an open-ended social field located immediately to the east of Puerto Rico. The islands are divided into three national administrative units: American (St. Croix, St. John, St. Thomas), British (Anegada, Tortola, Virgin Gorda), and Puerto Rican (Cuelebra, Vieques).

With the exception of picturesque sandy beaches, a plentitude of sunshine, and fecund human populations, the Virgin Islands are not well-endowed with salable natural resources. None of the islands contain commercially significant mineral deposits. In view of opportunity costs, all but St. Croix have been either too arid or too mountainous for large-scale crop production. For the islands' proletarians, available opportunities typically have called for migration to both near and distant labor markets. The export of labor has been a major source of income for the peoples of the Virgin Islands since the abolition of slavery. Nevertheless, the islands have attracted some capital investments as well.

The American islands, under Danish jurisdiction until their sale in 1917, have long been the hub of commerce in the archipelago. For the most part, this activity has centered on St. Thomas, once an important trade and transshipment depot for the Eastern Caribbean. In the years since World War II, St. Thomas has led the other islands toward becoming a major tourist center. Over one million travelers, whose local expenditures totaled more than sixty-five million dollars, were visiting the U.S.V.I. annually by the mid-1960s (Gray 1970:42). The history and present magnetism of the St. Thomian economy has attracted a multiethnic agglomeration of peoples that include Afro-American Virgin Islanders, Afro-British West Indians, "continental" Americans—both white and black, Puerto Ricans, Europeans, native Jews, and creole French "Cha-Chas."

Situated several miles to the east of the U.S.V.I., some 10,000 British Virgin Islanders stand on the economic margins of the archipelago. Residing within the hinterland of St. Thomas, the predominantly black inhabitants of these islands have traditionally tapped the produce and labor markets of their more prosperous neighbor as a principal source of livelihood. First as dockers, petty hucksters, and coal carriers, later as construction workers and hotel staff, British Virgin Islanders migrated the eight miles to St. Thomas, remitting or returning with cash incomes far greater than could be earned at home. Over the years, the opportunities available in St. Thomas regularly attracted from 10 to 15 percent of the total population of the B.V.I. Often this migration began as a temporary expedient aimed at raising the cash required for undertaking a project at home, perhaps starting a herd of cattle or building a dwelling house. In many cases, however, migration to St. Thomas was in fact only the first stage in what proved to be a two-staged movement (Harrigan n.d.: 165). British Virgin Islanders, in an attempt to upgrade their status and increase their security in the American labor market, often applied for and sometimes received permanent resident visas or citizenship papers. These documents allowed them to move on to the continental United States. For those islanders either unwilling or unable to move on themselves, the birth of their children on American soil often carried this second stage into the next generation.

In 1963, a small counter-flow to the export of B.V.I. produce and labor began. The construction of a luxury tourist resort, financed with American capital, was initiated at Virgin Gorda. Several less ambitious ventures followed on Tortola. In view of their success, large-scale British-financed development schemes were begun at Road Town, Tortola and on Anegada. Thus, within sight of the nearly urbanized St. Thomas, the unspoiled B.V.I. were discovered. Land prices soared. With government grants and private capital suddenly pouring into the islands, construction was undertaken at an unprecedented pace. These developments created a demand for labor far surpassing the local supply. Alien workers, most from the Leeward Islands, were recruited. By 1969, 1,486 aliens were registered for employment in the B.V.I.

In effect, during the 1960s the B.V.I. experienced what the U.S.V.I. had been experiencing for many years: a simultaneous immigration and emigration of labor. While British Virgin Islanders departed for work in the U.S.V.I., the vacuum created by their departure was filled by other British West Indians who were unable to gain access to the more rewarding American labor market. In the U.S.V.I., British Virgin Islanders and others from the islands to the south found places vacated by natives who either had moved to the continent or out of the lowest-paying sectors of the local economy. Invited by a liberal temporary immigration policy to fill the least desirable positions in the American islands' labor force, the West Indian alien population grew to more than 16,000 individuals (S.E.R.D. 1969:13) by 1970.

MARGINALITY AND COMPETITION

The outstanding feature of life as an alien temporarily employed in the Virgin Islands is economic and social marginality, despite the fact that during periods of rapid economic escalation both American and British Virgin Island labor markets have proved dependent on alien workers for their supply. This marginality manifests itself in the differential structure of rewards and tenures allocated to the islands' work forces.

Relatively high pay, security, and mobility distinguish native working conditions from those of aliens. In the U.S.V.I., 27 percent of the native population is employed by the government (U. S. Bureau of the Census 1972). Given a choice, the remaining natives do not select manual labor. This relatively unrewarding work is left to aliens on temporary visas. Aliens are typically found in the lowest-paying categories of the construction, service, and domestic sectors of the economy (S.E.R.D. 1969:1–4). Until recently, most occupied the position of bonded laborer.

The bond system, the last in a series of regulatory tactics aimed at migratory labor, allowed an alien to reside in the U.S.V.I. only as long as he held a job with an employer who would attest to his inability to recruit a U. S. national for the position. If the alien quit or was discharged, he was then subject to immediate deportation. This system conferred tremendous power into the hands of employers. They could,

Bennett Am.Ethnological Soc.–CTB—8

and often did, withhold pay or neglect minimum wage payments, over-
time increments, social security contributions, retirement plans, or health
coverage.   Since complaints were likely to bring deportation, alien
workers generally remained silent.   These conditions being favorable
to business interests, alien workers were hired at every opportunity.
In the B.V.I., where a similar system of bonding prevailed, small employers were quite frank with me in stating their preference for aliens
who were willing to work for considerably less pay than natives.   The
result in both the American and British islands was depressed wages
and working conditions throughout the entire economy (S.E.R.D.
1969:28).

With the tourist economy in serious decline during the 1969–70
season, the negative effect of alien labor on wages and working conditions became abundantly clear to native Virgin Islanders.   As the employment picture began to lose its promising glow, the popular attitude
toward aliens moved from simmering resentment to boiling animosity.
Brutal police roundups of illegally entered aliens were undertaken in
response to public outcries in both the U.S.V.I. and the B.V.I.   Local
political pressure was exerted in favor of more stringent enforcement
of immigration and employment laws.   In the U.S.V.I., the bond system
was abolished and alien immigration all but terminated.   Thus, under
the stimulus of economic recession, relations between natives and aliens
assumed the stance of lopsided competition, with the latter in full re-
treat from the islands that once welcomed them.

Though not always direct and open, competition has been the hallmark
of native-alien relations in the Virgin Islands for many years.   At least
within modern times, the stage for this competition has been set by
international enterprise, most recently the travel industry.   The periodically expanding and contracting sales markets of industries such
as travel call for respective increases and decreases in labor supplies.
In the Virgin Islands, as elsewhere, the supply of labor can be regulated by the government through the manipulation of immigration codes
and policies.   These manipulations occur in response to the economic
conditions facing the islands' interests groups.   Native labor and business concerns both have a voice in the determination of Virgin Island
immigration codes and policies, though their positions are often in
opposition.   Alien labor has no power in this regard.   Because of this
powerlessness, in the early 1950s, and again at the onset of the recent
decline in tourism, authorities have had an easy time in curtailing immi-

gration and in routing temporary workers from the niches that they previously occupied. On this basis, aliens would seem an unlikely threat and certainly no serious competition to native labor, particularly during periods of full employment when aliens occupy jobs not sought after by native workers. Such, however, is not the case. During periods of relative prosperity, alien migrants are aligned against native Virgin Islanders in a form of indirect competition.

By virtue of his very entry into the Virgin Islands, the alien becomes involved in the fundamental opposition between employer and worker interests that characterize class-structured industrial societies. As a part of what essentially is an oversupply of unskilled labor introduced into the islands by administrative policy, the alien represents an ever-present threat to the native. This threat is not simply implied; it is realized through the slow but persistent process that allows aliens to acquire permanent status and thereby inflate the ranks of those who have first call on desirable employment opportunities. The threat of the alien is further realized by his employment in work above and beyond formal job descriptions, work that has the effect of reducing the demand for individuals in the more costly occupational categories. Powerless by virtue of his jural status, and unable to negotiate an independent position in the economy, the alien becomes the unwitting ally of employers. He is placed in a partisan position with respect to the collision of class interests. As an environmental feature of pervasive importance, the structure and organization of the Virgin Islands' political economy precasts the boundary that separates the native from the alien worker in a competitive mold. The competitive relationship that exists between natives and aliens in the Virgin Islands calls for behaviors that provide the basis for the ethnic differentiation of these social categories.

THE GAROT

Virgin Islanders, both British and American, distinguish themselves from the Afro-West Indian peoples to the south, whom they refer to as "down-island" people. Those down-island people temporarily working in the Virgin Islands are commonly called "Garots." Distinctive behavioral features and value orientations are cited as distinguishing Garots from Virgin Islanders. Garot behaviors and values are thought to have cultural sources in their native communities. These sources are not precisely defined. Nevertheless, it is quite clear that any

alien coming from down-island to work temporarily in the Virgin
Islands can be and usually is seen as displaying Garot behaviors.
Insofar as these behaviors and the values that are thought to under-
lie them are presumed to be part of the Garot's traditional way of
living and can be used to identify him with respect to an imperative
status, the Garot identity is an ethnic identity. The characteristics of
this identity will be considered directly. But, first, it should be emphasized that the characteristics of a Garot are not always extended to
down-islanders at large. There is a tendency on the part of some
Virgin Islanders to use the categories interchangeably when discussing
the behaviors and values of other West Indians. However, most
distinguish between Garots and other down-islanders, citing the former
as a particularly different and undesirable kind of down-islander. In
any case, all down-islanders visiting the Virgin Islands are not identified
as Garots. Businessmen, professionals, and students are immune from
such identification.

The Garot category glosses over numerous social and cultural differences that apply to down-island workers resident in the Virgin Islands. Garot peoples do not originate from a single native society.
The term *Garot* seems to have been applied first to Antiguans and later
extended to include immigrants coming from such places as Anguilla,
Dominica, St. Kitts, Nevis, and Trinidad.[1] Cultural differences between these peoples, though minimal, do exist. Garots themselves tend
to stress these differences. Although they are aware that Virgin Islanders are categorically "prejudiced against we of their color" (cf.
Star 1970:18), migrants emphasize their various insular origins rather
than their unity as aliens. Associational solidarity is far stronger on the
basis of island nativity than it is on the basis of shared alien status.
The common Garot identity applied by Virgin Islanders ignores all such
distinctions.

The content of the ethnic identity placed on down-island immigrants
is phrased by Virgin Islanders in negative, pejorative terms. From the
point of view of British Virgin Islanders, the Garots are "dirty" people.
Their personal appearance and the appearance of their dwellings is often
offered as proof of this assertion. In terms of their social lives,
Garots are viewed no better. As spouses, Garots are believed to have
no respect for one another. The men are said to beat their wives
often. Garot women are considered "natural whores." It is said that
Garots think nothing of living together under the most crowded con-

ditions, as many as a dozen to a room, using the beds in shifts in order to save a cent.

Alien laborers are considered fundamentally dishonest. They are thought not to consider it wrong to cheat or steal. Every crime calls for a discussion of the "alien problem." Garots are seen as posing a threat to Virgin Islanders who contend that the down-islanders will conspire to take all of the available jobs and eventually attempt to "rule" the area in which they settle. During the course of my fieldwork, I listened to numerous tirades by British Virgin Islanders urging their neighbors to keep Garots out lest they "take over."

In general, Garots are said to have "hard heads" and are viewed as unintelligent and difficult to educate. Their dialects are judged inferior. Their religious practices are also appraised negatively. Down-island people are noted as prone to magic. They use such means to harm the members of their host community. Garots' frequent interest in "shouting" sects rather than the more conservative church organizations is offered as further proof of their lack of Christian respectability. Thus, citing traits ranging from unmannerly dinner table habits to improper ethics, Virgin Islanders ethnicize those down-island peoples with whom they come into most close contact; they assign to them a culture seen as significantly different and inferior to their own.

Many of the traits attributed to Garots should have a familiar ring to anthropologists. The list of negative traits bears a striking resemblance to that associated with the so-called culture of poverty: essentially an attempt to ethnicize the world's poor that emphasizes the intergenerational transmission of certain behaviors and values. Since Garot status is typically transitory due either to return migration or to integration into local Virgin Island society, one lacks the stable personnel required for framing a theory of intergenerational trait transmission. This raises a question having to do with the etic reality of the ethnic identity ascribed to the Virgin Island Garot. Are the cultural differentia considered typical of his identity pure collective fantasy used to justify economic and social discriminations? Or, are they based upon reasonably accurate emic representations of etically demonstrable material and behavioral facts? My analysis shows the latter to be the case.

There are two fundamental criteria for the inclusion of alien West Indians in the Garot category. One basis for identification is the jural status conferred by a temporary work visa. The respective statuses of native and temporary alien differentially define rights with regard to employment opportunities, rewards, and tenures. As previously indicated, alien visitors to the Virgin Islands who fall outside of the status defined by a work visa are not generally identified as Garots. A second basic criterion for Garot identification is a situation of social marginality: effective isolation from the day-to-day activities of the native networks and groups internal to Virgin Island communities. By gaining access to native community life, a Garot identity can be lost. Provided with close sponsorship by a long-term resident of the islands, a newly arrived immigrant can avoid Garot identification entirely. Most often, however, assignment to the category is shed gradually. Jural status, economic position, and social penetration all advance slowly over the years until invidious distinctions are seldom, if ever, applied.

As a group, British Virgin Islanders have done extraordinarily well in escaping the low-grade status of temporary alien and the Garot identification that accompanies it in the U.S.V.I. In a recent survey that included more than 400 interviews with temporary aliens in St. Croix and St. Thomas, less than 6 percent of the sample were British Virgin Islanders (S.E.R.D. 1969:37). On the other hand, slightly more than 2,000 British Virgin Islanders with both temporary and permanent visas made up about one-half of the total alien West Indian population in the U.S.V.I. as recently as 1960 (U.S. Bureau of the Census 1963).[2] Furthermore, as Harrigan (n.d.:157) documents, more than 1,300 permanent residence visas were issued to British Virgin Islanders through the years 1963–67. Over the years, the British Virgin Islanders' success in crossing the legal boundary that separates them from U.S. Virgin Islanders has occurred hand in hand with the social integration of the islands through extensive intermarriage and the creation of interisland kinship networks. Other West Indians have been far less successful in this regard.

Relegated to a jural status that consistently defines his rights as inferior to others and without much by way of influential social contacts, the Garot is able to exert little control over the individuals and groups with whom he comes into contact. Employers, companies, and agencies rule the life of the alien worker, who has no power in the determination of their policies and directives. This places the alien migrant in a situation with little day-to-day security and an uncertain employment future, particularly in view of the highly competitive and cyclical nature of the Virgin Islands' labor markets. Without the wealth or the social capital necessary to invest in a long-range campaign for advantage within the political economy, a strategy that optimizes short-term interests is called for on the part of Garot peoples.

The behaviors entailed by such a strategy do not escape the notice of Virgin Island natives. In this connection, their use of the term *garot* is interesting. It calls to mind the garot bird, a creature that flies from its home to other islands, stripping them clean of food before moving on again.[3] Ecologists classify such behavior as "exploitation."

Exploitation is a competitive strategy, in which the rapid utilization of resources is the key to success (Miller 1967:12). Once access to resources is gained, the competitor scrambles to obtain and use the largest quantity of resources in the shortest possible time. Little effort is devoted to defense as a competitive strategy. Thus, elaborate forms of social coordination and group organization would seem to have minimal value in overall strategic terms. My suggestion is that Garots employ a kind of exploitive strategy within the framework of the Virgin Island socioeconomic system.

Uncertain concerning their tenure as residents of the Virgin Islands, down-island workers attempt to minimize their long-term outlays and maximize their short-term gains. Minimization includes relatively little expenditure on individual housing and other symbols of respectability. Very few aliens accumulate assets that cannot be liquidated immediately (S.E.R.D. 1969:5). Migrants typically do not journey to the Virgin Islands with spouses and children. Such ties might encumber mobility. Carefully calculated balanced reciprocity characterizes locally contracted social relations. Here, flexibility is valued over solidarity. Mating alliances are entered into and terminated in terms of immediate economic objectives. For example, in 1950, under pressure from U.S.V.I. authorities who were attempting to close the door on aliens, marriages between B.V.I. and St. Thomas or St. John individuals rose from a constant annual figure in the neighborhood of 12 percent to 34 percent of all B.V.I. marriages (Harrigan n.d.: 168).

As in the case of marital bonds, other dyadic links are pragmatically created and maintained as a source of intelligence and to assure access to employment while investments in group relations are cut to a minimum. Maximum effort is bent toward the rapid obtainment and full exploitation of income-earning opportunities, even if the conditions of employment are substandard. In some cases, the oversupply of labor, the resulting low wages, and the high cost of living contribute to the pursuit of illegal tactics, including theft and violation of immigation laws. On the basis of such minimax behaviors, alien workers are able to accummulate cash surpluses, much of which is sent to their home islands. The alien West Indian population of the U.S.V.I. is responsible for the export of approximately three million dollars annually (S.E.R.D. 1969:5).

Clearly, the foregoing is a highly generalized portrayal of the Garot strategy. Firsthand observation reveals a great deal of tactical variation. Nevertheless, the economic and political constraints faced by alien down-islanders limit their options and thereby shape a discernible pattern. This pattern is observed by Virgin Islanders who represent it in an idiom of behavioral and value differences which they consider threatening. Their response to this threat further reinforces the assignment of negative ethnic contrasts.

Virgin Islanders, in both American and British island communities, respond to the alien threat with an interference strategy. Interference refers to any activity that either directly or indirectly limits a competitor's access to useful resources (Miller 1967:8). Solidary, group-organized means would seem highly valuable as part of such a strategy.

In the Virgin Islands, interference includes a range of intimidating and excluding activities. Intimidation is achieved through subjecting the Garots to a continuous series of insults and threats, occasional outbursts of personal violence against individual aliens, and terrorist policing of the alien community. Garots are excluded from schools, public housing, welfare services, and political participation. In one B.V.I. village, where I resided for many months, I was able to observe interference tactics on the local level that excluded Garots from social relations useful in securing economic betterment. Garots were rigorously excluded from any contact with local females. Garots were not taken into the local round of male conviviality that characterizes open dyadic bonds. Garots were not approached by church members concerning congregational membership. In other words, virtually all locally available sources of power and prestige were denied to temporary immigrants. In this way, interference further widens the gap between alien behavioral patterns and those of the host community.

CONCLUSION

I have described what might be considered to be a somewhat special case of ethnicity and ethnic relations. In this case, an ethnic identity is ascribed to an alien category of people on the basis of the belief that their behaviors and values originate from down-island native sources. In reality, the identity ascribed to aliens ignores both similarities and differences that emerge from traditional cultural backgrounds. Therefore, from one point of view, this ascription might be considered to be of a spurious nature (cf. Lehman 1967:109). From another point of view, it might not be considered a case of ethnicity at all, since Garots lack the "internal complexity" of many ethnic groups (e. g., Barth 1969:31). In response to such objections, it must be kept in mind that Garots are identified as members of a cognitive category that has an emic reality for Virgin Islanders. Internal considerations aside, Virgin Islanders behave as if Garots comprised a distinctive ethnic cultural unit. The interference behaviors of native islanders contribute to the maintenance of a well-defined line between Virgin Islanders and aliens that displays an essential characteristic of an ethnic boundary; the people on either side of the boundary appear to behave and hold values according to a different set of rules and standards.

The fact that Garot identity is not based on a genuine cultural heritage that has been passed down from one generation to the next makes the Virgin Islanders' representation of it nonetheless real. Rather than deriving from native cultural contrasts, the collective representations that adhere to the identity derive from the observation of the strategic reactions of marginal peoples to their assignment to an alien status offered within the context of a particular political economy. This tends to confirm Barth's (1969:31) assertion that ethnic minority relations are shaped by supervening institutional frameworks. It further suggests that special jural statuses erected without cultural reference may at times serve as the basis for the genesis and maintenance of behaviors liable to interpretation as ethnic.

In the Virgin Islands, as elsewhere, the legal categories that serve to define a social macrostructure often limit the opportunities that otherwise might be available to individuals and groups. As the grounds for constraining pressures, these categories become a part of a local-level environment and stimulate the development of coping behaviors aimed at negating or minimizing their impact on individual pursuits. What makes the case of the Garots extraordinary is the fact that such coping behaviors provide the sole foundation for the ascription of an ethnic contrast between what otherwise might be considered a relatively homogeneous—though legally differentiated—population of Afro-West Indians. The extent to which strategic adaptations to the constraints of "outsider" statuses contribute to the genesis and maintenance of ethnic differentiation in other ethnographic cases is problematic. Nevertheless, in cases where environmentally modified behaviors are systematically distinguished from culturally inherited behaviors, I suspect that the contribution of macrostructural pressures will emerge as an important consideration in the understanding of ethnic groups and boundaries.

NOTES

1 In the B.V.I., one informant who employed several Nevisians insisted that the Garot category is most properly reserved for Antiguans. I could not find any other British Virgin Islanders in the area where I was conducting research who shared this opinion. Professor James Green (personal communication) indicates that the term was reserved originally for Antiguans on St. Croix as well but has been extended in recent years.

2 Comparative data from the 1970 census is not yet available.

3 The origin and/or the species reference of the term *garot* is as yet unclear to me. While in the islands, I neglected to seek an identification of the bird from informants since the topic was of peripheral interest to me. However, it is interesting to note the fact that the term *Garrulinae* is used with reference to a subfamily of birds that includes both magpies and jays. These, of course, are omnivorous and predatory. Reference might also be made to the *Garuda*, the gigantic bird of prey found in Hindu mythology and perhaps carried to the West Indies in the course of East Indian migration.

LITERATURE CITED

Barth, Fredrik, Ed.
    1969   Ethnic Groups and Boundaries. Boston: Little, Brown and Co.

Gray, H. P.
    1970   International Travel. Lexington: Heath.

Harrigan, Norwell
    n.d.   A Study of the Interrelationships between the British and United States Virgin Islands; Mimeographed. St. Thomas: Caribbean Research Institute.

Lehman, F. K.
 1967   Ethnic Categories in Burma and the Theory of Social Systems. *In* Southeast Asian Tribes, Minorities and Nations, Vol. 1. Peter Kunstadter, Ed. Princeton: Princeton University Press.

Miller, Richard S.
 1967   Pattern and Process in Competition. *In* Advances in Ecological Research, Vol. 4. J. B. Cragg, Ed. London: Academic Press.

Social, Educational, Research and Development, Inc. (S.E.R.D.)
 1969   A Profile and Plans for the Temporary Alien Worker Problem in the U.S. Virgin Islands. Report submitted to the Office of Economic Opportunity, Washington, DC.

Star, Jack
 1970   Virgin Islands: Shame in the U.S. Tropics. Look, Vol. 34, No. 5.

U.S. Bureau of the Census
 1963   U.S. Census of the Population: 1960, Vol. 1, Pt. 55. Washington, DC: Government Printing Office.

 1972   U.S. Census of the Population: 1970, Vol. 1, Pt. 55. Washington, DC: Government Printing Office.

8

Patterns of Dominican Ethnicity

NANCIE L. GONZALEZ
Boston University

INTERNAL HETEROGENEITY AND ETHNICITY

As I have indicated in an earlier publication, (Gonzalez 1970a, 1970c), the people of the Dominican Republic have diverse origins, and it is difficult, if not impossible, to outline any truly distinctive traditional Dominican ethnic configuration (see also Wiarda 1969:114). In terms of phenotype, the range is from purest Negroid to apparently pure northern European Caucasoid types, with every imaginable kind of inter-mixture. The picture is further complicated by an unknown number of genes from the aboriginal Indian population, with a dash of Japanese and Chinese thrown in for good measure. Thus, it is clearly impossible to identify a Dominican on the basis of the way be looks.

The national language is a New World dialect of Spanish. Here again, the picture is complicated by a good number of Arawak (Taino) loan words which have become a part of the local expression and which help to characterize it as Dominican. But even here, many of the words, phonetic patterns, and other elements leading to a distinctive "accent" are closely paralleled by speech patterns in parts of Puerto Rico and in Cuba.[1] It does make some sense, perhaps, to define a Caribbean Spanish dialect in which these three units share more with each other than they do with other Spanish-speaking areas of the New World or elsewhere.

In terms of religion, over 90 percent of Dominicans count themselves as Roman Catholics, and there is a continuum of beliefs and practices ranging from old European folk traditions to modern church teachings and ritual. This in no way, of course, sets them apart from other Latin Americans. Indeed, this is true for most Dominican culture content, even in the case of some that have recently been held to be symbols of the modern nation. Some of these symbols, furthermore, have quite recently been introduced there. Thus, among food items that Dominicans feel "belong" to them is included the *quipe* (a kind of fritter, made of cracked wheat and stuffed with meat, raisins and spices, then fried in deep fat; originating from the Middle East). Another specialty, *sancocho* (a stew made of meat boiled together with a variety of roots commonly found in the area), is actually a more generalized Caribbean dish. The *merengue* is often said to be "the national dance" and is extremely popular among Dominicans. It cannot be said, however, to be peculiar to this nation or culture (cf. Simmons 1955). Hoetinck (1971:76) indicates that the *merengue* was introduced as late as 1890. The accordian, a favorite instrument among peasants, may be traced either to a German or an Italian origin, but in either case was probably introduced during the nineteenth century.

Indeed, part of the difficulty in defining Dominican ethnicity has to do with the very diversity of origins mentioned above. As I have suggested elsewhere, one of the characteristics of a neoteric society such as this is that it readily accepts and incorporates not only peoples, but a variety of foreign cultural baggage (Gonzalez 1970a). There has been a relative lack of "tradition," and it may be that the Dominican Republic is only now in the process of forming a distinctive ethnicity out of its diverse components. I will return to this notion further on in the paper, but first I would like to review and briefly describe the components to which I refer. That is, I will not only mention the visible and identifiable ethnic components of the present population, but will also mention those which have apparently been quite thoroughly assimilated.

When Dominicans speak of ancestral origin, race seems to be more important than other aspects of ethnicity.[2] Thus, European or North American ancestors may be claimed in an effort to call attention to or emphasize one's Caucasoid characteristics. Thus, there have been considerable numbers of immigrants from the United States, France, England, Germany, and the Netherlands, the descendants of whom are blended today, along with some other stocks, into what we might call a "white Dominican" type. It is, however, important to note that persons with such backgrounds are not confined exclusively to the upper classes, but the latter are composed almost entirely of such "whites." In a perusal of a Dominican yearbook, published in 1906, I viewed photographs of what were described as "typical Dominicans" and found, to my surprise, that only 3 out of the total 108 showed any clear evidence of having other than a perfectly white skin, and all 3 of these were prominent literary persons. Needless to say, the book was published by and for white Dominicans, apparently in an effort to encourage immigration of more European and North American peoples (Deschamps 1906). Many other works had similar goals (see Courtney 1860). In the lower social ranks, there is a noticeable clustering of persons of Negroid background.

Nevertheless, Dominicans, as some other Latin American peoples, like to think of themselves as being without race prejudice. They pretend that a person of color can rise to any social rank, and they would be embarrassed if caught verbalizing any other kind of value. On the other hand, an interesting dodge has developed, which allows Dominicans to deal with race without actually seeming to. By this I mean that an extreme prejudice against Haitians has been institutionalized, to the point that references to supposed Haitian personality characteristics (blood-thirstiness, stupidity, laziness, and so on) have become part of the national ideology. Interestingly enough, this distinction is often made as though it were cultural rather than racial. Especially at the folk level, however, there are many clear cultural parallels between Haiti and the Dominican Republic, a fact which is denied by most Dominicans with whom I have spoken.[3]

In addition to Haitian blacks, the Dominican population has been swelled by migrants from the various West Indian islands, many of whom have come to work in the sugar industry, or whose parents or grandpersons came for the same purpose. In some localized spots about the island, there are dark-skinned persons whose ancestors go back many generations to the early slaves brought in by the Spanish. One might, then, also speak of a basic Dominican "black" type, which is phenotypically indistinguishable from Haitian and other West Indian blacks. For all of these blacks, the ability to speak Spanish like a Dominican becomes the ultimate symbol by means of which they establish their Dominican identity. Blackness per se then, is admissible, although less desirable than having a lighter skin. On the other hand, the spectre of the Haitian black "monster" is constantly there, but the psychological effect for the black person is one of rejection on the basis of nationality rather than skin color.[4] Thus, a black Dominican sees no contradiction in cursing the Haitian for his negritude (Hernandez 1973).

Another more common Dominican type is the mulatto, who probably considers himself more white than black and is by far the most prevalent type in the country. A Dominican (and Caribbean) joke suggests that the eighth wonder of the world would be a white Dominican (*un Dominicano blanco*), thus recognizing the large Negroid genetic component in the total population and also poking fun at the upper classes who often consider themselves to be pure Caucasoid. Indeed, even the basic white Dominican type to which I refer throughout this paper is not without admixture.

The nineteenth century brought to the shores of the Dominican Republic not only most of the European elements noted above, but also a large number of Near Easterners, many of whom were from Lebanon, Turkey, and other Arabic nations. Today, even though actual origins may have been more varied, persons of this category, who are distinguished by their surnames, are referred to as Lebanese.[5] Phenotype alone probably is not sufficient to distinguish them from other Dominicans. Part of the reason for this is that many of them have intermarried with other Dominicans, most especially with the whites and lighter mulattos. What distinctive cultural patterns they may have brought with them have now for the most part either disappeared or have been blended into the larger national pattern (for example, the *quipe* as noted above). The Lebanese seem to be especially well-represented in the middle ranks of society and earn their living as white-collar workers, teachers, merchants, accountants, lawyers, pharmacists, and medical doctors. A few of the merchants and professionals have become wealthy, and many have achieved considerable status both locally and nationally. In fact, they have come very close to what might be called total assimilation.

Jewish components include the Sephardim, who, like the Lebanese, are almost totally assimilated. I do not have good evidence as to when the Sephardim first arrived in the Dominican Republic, but it is safe to guess that some of them came as early as the sixteenth century. Others came from Puerto Rico, Cuba, or Curacao as late as the nineteenth century. Some of these will self-identify on occasion, and they may recognize kinship links and maintain contacts with other Sephardic families in the larger Caribbean. However, most of them have intermarried, or are products of marriages, with persons of non-Jewish ancestry, and they may be included in what I am here calling white Dominican.

Ashkenazi Jews are represented primarily in the colony on the north coast at Sosua. This colony was established after World War II by refugees from Austria who were subsidized by Trujillo. The effort was an economic success though the colony has failed to perpetuate itself. Most of the children of the original settlers have emigrated and many of the older people are currently selling their land and retiring to Europe. There are also a few recent immigrants, who have established themselves primarily in Santo Domingo and who are for the most part not consciously set apart by other Dominicans. Although there is a synagogue in Santo Domingo, the Jewish component is apparently not large enough to be visible as a distinctive minority. It is possible that many of the persons in this colony are actually merely resident businessmen from other countries.

In the rather isolated Constanza Valley is a small group of Japanese, almost all of whom are engaged in truck farming. The group is relatively small and invisible. Most Dominicans, even if they are aware of their presence, would not consider the Japanese to be "real Dominicans." Not having done fieldwork in that area, I am unable to state how the Japanese view themselves, or what is happening to the younger generation, although it is said by some Dominicans that most of the original colony has now left the Constanza Valley—they know not for what destination. If the situation is at all comparable with that in Brazil, one might predict eventual assimilation with the larger Dominican population (see Walker 1973).

There is a relatively small, culturally isolated, geographically scattered, but easily distinguishable group of Chinese in the Dominican Republic at the present time. Most of them seem to be concentrated in the restaurant and hotel business, and some of them also run houses of prostitution in connection with the hotels. In 1904, a small group of Chinese laborers was brought in to introduce wet rice technology (Consular Reports 1904:M–93, roll 11). In 1932, according to the Chinese Minister in Havana, who was visiting the Dominican Republic, there were no more than 400 in the latter country, of whom about 160 were unemployed, being maintained by their compatriots (Dominican Customs Receivership Records, R. 6.59:839.55/24). Although I have no specific data concerning the Chinese, casual observation indicates that today they may be found in almost every city and town of any size in the Republic. I believe that they are bound together by a network of kinship and business ties, and I also suspect that there is a constant, although very small, increase in their ranks through immigration. In Santiago, the city's most elegant and popular restaurant is owned by a Chinese. He and his wife appear to be somewhat acculturated, and may sometimes be guests in upper- and middle-class Dominican homes. He belongs to the Rotary Club and seems active in city affairs in general. However, this type of participation for a Chinese seems unusual. The group is easily distinguishable by the distinctive phenotype, which seems to be maintained by endogamy. In recent years, this has begun to break down because of an increasing number of marriages with other Dominicans—both black and white. The continued use of an esoteric language also sets them apart and helps maintain the ethnic boundaries. Aside from Chinese foods, which are popular with Dominicans in general, I am not aware of other elements of Chinese culture which have survived, though I think it likely that much of the traditional domestic culture pattern remains intact.

Finally, I would like to discuss the various Spanish-surnamed and Spanish-speaking components. First of all are the Spaniards, who can be generally classified according to period of immigration. The early (sixteenth and seventeenth century) Spanish immigrants obviously contributed heavily to the basic white Dominican stock. This is true not only for the upper classes, but also for many of the more isolated peasant populations. Many of the earlier immigrants were further distinguished by region. The eighteenth century brought a major immigration from the Canary Islands, with many of the settlers going to the ports of Monte Cristi, Puerto Plata, Samaná, Sábana la Mar, Baní, and probably elsewhere (Hoetinck 1971:55–58). These, too, have blended into the basic white Dominican stock, and are distinguishable only when an individual claims such ancestry, as I suggested above, perhaps to stress his Caucasian origins.

During the nineteenth and twentieth centuries, additional Spaniards arrived, some of them having come as soldiers in the army of occupation between 1860–65. A distinction was made between Spaniards and Catalans, both of whom, however, suffered a certain amount of discrimination at the hands of "native" Dominicans. Immigrants from Spain have continued to arrive during the twentieth century up to the present. Most of these have gone into some aspect of merchandising, although there is also a small agricultural colony in Constanza (Walker 1973) and scattered persons in the professions. Some Spaniards, or descendants of Spaniards, have become very wealthy and are today to be found in the upper ranks of society and government, especially in Santo Domingo and other cities. One of the primary supporting institutions for this immigrant group is the Spanish Club, which serves its members as a recreational, cultural, and mutual aid society. It corresponds to other upper-class nonethnic clubs, which are to be found in every Dominican city and which provide a means of exchanging information and arranging marriages or other personal ties among members of the middle and upper classes.[6] A certain amount of prejudice still exists toward those who maintain their Spanish citizenship and/or ethnic separateness.

As the Spaniards have become more acculturated (most typically the second-generation Spaniards), they tend to drop out of the Spanish Club and become generally indistinguishable from other basic white Dominicans.[7]

DOMINICAN NATIONALISM AND ETHNICITY

The history of what is now called the Dominican Republic has been checkered, the territory having been governed by seven independent national entities at different times. There has been considerable movement of the population, with periodic migrations, especially to Puerto Rico and Cuba. Indeed, one of the striking facts about the history of the Spanish Caribbean is the tremendous amount of interaction that has occurred among these three units. Each time any kind of crisis has developed in any one of the three islands, large numbers of the population have fled, usually to one of the other two countries. As I have suggested above, there are many cultural similarities amongst the three nations today. Dominicans commonly try to escape the vigil of United

States customs officers by pretending to be Puerto Ricans, and thus United States citizens, for purposes of immigration to what they call New York (by which they mean the entire nation). Yet, it is also true that there is great jealousy and sometimes great animosity among Cubans, Dominicans, and Puerto Ricans. Although these have probably been in existence for the past 100 years, I think there is evidence that the animosity has increased during the past 10 or 15 years. I believe that recent political events in the three home areas, plus the massive migration to the eastern seaboard of the United States, have been causative factors. I will discuss each of these briefly in turn.

In terms of the political situation, it is clear that the Dominican nation first became truly welded together during the era of Trujillo (1930–61). Despite the excesses and authoritarianism of this dictatorship, it is true that Trujillo emphasized Dominican nationalism and was effective in publicizing his tiny island-nation to the rest of the world. It cannot be said that the majority of Dominicans were opposed to Trujillo during the bulk of his regime. To the contrary, I believe there are still thousands of Dominicans who wish that he might return tomorrow. Many informants from all social classes have expressed these thoughts to me personally.

On the other hand, the events in Cuba of the past twelve years are seen by most Dominicans as tragic in the extreme. Although a small leftist minority has always extolled the Cuban solution, and although there have been attempts to move in that direction, these have failed both because of intervention by the United States and because of the power of the local elites. The fear of being taken over by Cuba or by persons who "think like Castro" remains a real one in the minds of many Dominicans today, as well as in the minds of many U.S. State Department officials. As has occurred in earlier crises, many Cubans have sought refuge on Dominican soil. Although these tend to be middle-class, professional persons, with a political view not too different from that of the majority of Dominicans, there is a definite undercurrent of antagonism towards these outsiders, many of whom are seen as possible revolutionaries in disguise, or (as is more probable) as economic competitors. Many of the Cubans are in business, and they seem to do very well in the Dominican Republic, as they have in Miami. Although on an individual level Cubans tend to relate well and often intermarry with Dominicans, there tends to be a generalized national feeling against them.

Puerto Rico presents still a different picture. That island is often envied for the economic advantages it enjoys through its peculiar political relationship with the United States. Dominicans of all classes have been to Puerto Rico (the round-trip air fare is only fifty-six dollars), and they often speak of it as a kind of wonder-world, second only to New York itself. Indeed, odd-jobbers are able to make five or six times what they can at home, and many have spent some time there as a stepping stone to eventual migration to the mainland itself.

But in spite of this envy and eagerness to visit and even live in Puerto Rico, there is also a certain feeling of disdain towards the island because of its loss of sovereignty to the United States. Although at various points in history the Dominican Republic has sought annexation to the United States, this solution to their problems has not been a popular one since the United States occupation of 1916–24. Dominicans today tend to be very proud of their de jure political independence, and even while they seek closer economic ties with the United States, they imagine that they are totally independent. Yet, I suggest that there is an ambivalence in their attitude, for at the same time that they scorn Puerto Rico, they also want to be more like her.

Those who have migrated to the mainland itself find themselves frequently in contact with immigrants from Cuba and Puerto Rico. In the past, many Dominicans tended to blend in with the generalized Puerto Rican population, especially in New York. However, as their numbers have increased, and as more of them have become American citizens through birth or through naturalization, they have more often insisted upon differentiating themselves from Puerto Ricans. Indeed, there have been outbursts in both New York and Boston, and perhaps elsewhere, of open hostility between the two peoples. In Boston during the Independence Day celebration in 1972, a small riot broke out because a float bearing a Dominican flag won an award in a presumably Puerto Rican parade.

Dominican immigrants, for the most part, have not become a public burden. Indeed, statistics uphold their own perceptions of themselves as independent, hard-working, and nonindigent souls. Of course, since many Dominicans have come illegally to the United States, they are often unable to seek welfare or unemployment compensation without being subject to deportation (Gonzalez 1970b). Unlike Cubans, who are here as political refugees and are often given public assistance until they can find some kind of paying job, and unlike Puerto Ricans, whose nationality gives them a right to all forms of welfare, Dominicans have enjoyed no such rights. They have turned this exclusion, however, into a point of national pride.[8]

One final point is worth mentioning. Within the present confines of the United States society, ethnicity per se is an important means of classifying people. Indeed, it seems to have become more fashionable recently in both governmental and social scientific circles. Other kinds of evidence include the burgeoning of studies of various ethnic groups by anthropologists, sociologists, political scientists, historians, and others. Although most of these are concerned with ethnicity and ethnic groups in the larger metropolitan areas of the United States, there is also an increasing interest in rural ethnic enclaves (see Chrisman 1973). Federal, state, and municipal officials are increasingly concerned about ethnic mix on boards and agencies representing the populace. Indeed, efforts to ensure minority participation and representation have permeated nearly every aspect of our public life today. Though not all ethnic groups and categories classify as "minorities" in the sense of being deprived, it has become clear that ethnicity is one means of successfully pressuring public officials to take action on behalf of certain groups. Certainly, this element has long been important in city politics in places such as New York, Boston, and Chicago. Nina Glick (1972) has documented the process by means of which one ethnic group developed and established its identity as such in New York City. It appears that to be poor and without ethnicity in the United States today is to be handicapped.[9]

I suggest that the Dominican presence in New York has itself contributed to an intensification of Dominican ethnicity vis-à-vis non-Dominicans, while at the same time the diverse elements within the Dominican Republic itself are becoming more increasingly bound together in a common ethnic identity, because a solid political front in the United States requires a firm symbolic and social unity. Although the two processes have somewhat different historical antecedents and functional effects, they support and reinforce each other.

On the other hand, if we consider it in a broader, international context, we might speak of two stages in the evolution of ethnicity in a complex society. We are witnessing the development of a melting pot concept within the Dominican Republic while, ironically, Dominicans in the United States are becoming caught up in the apparent move to deny or oppose the process of assimilation in that country by encouraging the perpetuation of ethnic differences. This issue bears further consideration and analysis.

The process that John Murra has referred to as ethnogenesis (Open Session on Ethnicity, AES Symposium, Wrightsville Beach, March 1973) is one that has occurred and is occurring in many new nation-states. In some ways, it might better be thought of as "ethnotransformation" rather than ethnogenesis, since it seems likely that part of the process involves a breaking down of earlier loyalties and a merging of old symbols from diverse cultural patterns into a new and self-conscious ideological framework that glorifies and crystallizes the new collectivity. We call the resultant configuration "nationalism" in those new nations where there are exerted strong pressures for people to abandon earlier regional, tribal, or in the case of immigrants from other countries, national loyalties. In other words, in such cases cultural assimilation takes on a positive value. The United States went through this process in the nineteenth and early twentieth centuries, and many other countries are undergoing it now. Examples are numerous, but I point especially to the new African states and to many developing nations in Latin America.

It may be, however, that cultural and social assimilation in the classic sense is no longer possible or desirable in a highly developed society such as the United States today. Large and dense populations demand some mode of internal differentiation, not only because of the necessity to accomplish the diverse tasks of production, distribution and administration, but also in order to preserve the mental health of citizens. Recent analyses emphasize the importance of neighborhood and ethnic organizations in avoiding the pitfalls of *anomie*, once thought to be an inevitable concomitant of urbanism as a way of life. Many descriptions of rural-to-urban migrants stress the natives' tendency to value continued association with persons from their own homeland, whether through voluntary associations, neighborhood clustering, or other means.

Thus, we might think of ethnogenesis as a process that may also occur as a means of creating diversity and, thus, a higher level of organization in an otherwise apparently amorphous and impersonal environment. Ethnicity is certainly not the *only* possible basis for classifying people in large societies. We are also familiar with segmentation based on sex, age, occupation, religion, wealth, region, and so forth. However, as Delmos Jones recently suggested, these other criteria have usually resulted in ranked classes with unequal access to resources and prestige (Jones 1973).

Ethnicity, on the other hand, may turn out to be a criterion which does not lead to such discriminatory ranking. It has in the past, to be sure, but there is some evidence of change in this regard. The continued development of an ideology which places high value on ethnic diversity may be seen as a response to the increasing size and complexity of the postindustrial society in which we live.

NOTES

[1] This is not to say that a trained linguist or a native with considerable experience could not tell the difference among the speech patterns of these three units. Indeed, sometimes a mere twist of a word can be quite revealing when one wishes to distinguish Dominicans from the other two (see, e. g., German 1967).

[2] I am here using a definition of ethnicity which includes the notion of common origin, and thus of race (see, e. g., Shibutani and Kwan 1965). I am perfectly willing to accept other definitions of ethnicity for other circumstances in which race is isolated and/or held a constant (Barth 1969).

[3] There are a few exceptions to this among the younger intelligentsia. Indeed, there is recent evidence that a thrust is being made to reinterpret history and to strive for closer cooperation and greater understanding between the Dominican Republic and its western neighbor (see Hernandez 1973; Cordero Michel 1968).

[4] In a recent study of a small rural village, Dr. Susan E. Brown found that darker skin color and marital arrangements of a loose, unstable type were correlated. The sample group was also assigned lower status than other, lighter-skinned members of the village who also happened, not coincidentally, to live according to more stable kinds of marital patterns. The implications of this correlation have not been thoroughly discussed in the literature. Dr. Brown and I are currently engaged in a collaborative examination of the question, and hope to publish our thoughts and findings soon.

[5] Regardless of the country of origin, Near Easterners tend to be classified together in common parlance. At the turn of the century, the terms "Arabes" and "Turkos" were in common usage.

[6] My data indicate that club participation is greatest among persons who are upwardly mobile or who feel insecure in their assigned social position. Indeed, the offices of the clubs are often used as springboards for improving status. Historically, the parents and grandparents of today's most influential families were active in these clubs, but their descendants are not necessarily involved. As one informant told me, the only reason he belonged to the club was so that his children would have a place to play pool, to dance, and to associate with other children of their class. He rarely, if ever, visited the club. Thus, it seems clear that contacts made within the clubs may be instrumentally impor-

tant for the nonelite upper classes during the younger, formative years when they may meet and become friendly with children of the elites. This subject is too involved for this paper and will be described in another publication.

[7] Personal communication from Dr. Susan E. Brown, who is more acquainted with this population component than I am. On the other hand, I have been told by Dominicans that one can always spot a Spaniard and that they do not assimilate readily. This may merely reflect the national prejudices mentioned above.

[8] A recent (June 1973) trip to New York City resulted in new information on this point which suggests that Dominicans are fast "learning the ropes" and are increasingly to be found on various types of welfare lists, including ADC, unemployment, disability, and so forth. My informant suggested that "most" Dominicans she knew in New York had at one time or another received United States government assistance. I have no quantitative data to confirm or refute this statement, but it seems quite likely that as the total numbers of Dominicans in the United States increase, and as experiences and information are gathered and shared, every opportunity will be taken to make a better way of life by these people. My own informant, currently on ADC, pointed out that she was living like a "rich woman." Knowing her background and having personally visited the homes of her relatives and friends in the Dominican Republic, I had to agree with her assessment, even though her New York living conditions were poor by United States standards.

[9] Even the nonpoor may get caught up in the trend. Paul Bohannan remarked to me a couple of years ago that affluent WASPS in the North Shore areas of Chicago were turning their country clubs into ethnic societies.

LITERATURE CITED

Barth, Fredrik, Ed.
    1969   Ethnic Groups and Boundaries. Boston: Little, Brown and Co.

Chrisman, Noel J.
    1973   Ethnic Persistence in an Urban Setting. *In* Urban Socio-Cultural Systems (forthcoming). R. Lincoln Keiser and David Jacobson, Eds.

Cordero Michel, Emilio
    1968   La Revolucion Haitiana y Santo Domingo. Colección Historia y Sociedad. Editoria Nacional. Santo Domingo, República Dominicana.

Courtney, Wilshire S.
    1860   The Gold Fields of Santo Domingo. New York: A. P. Norton.

Deschamps, Enrique
    1906   La República Dominicana: Directório y Guía General. Santiago de los Caballeros, República Dominicana (Barcelona, Impr. de la vda. de J. Cunhill).

German, A., Consuelo Olivier Vd. de
1967   De Nuestro Lenguaje y Costumbres. Santo Domingo.

Glick, Nina Barnett
1972   The Formation of a Haitian Ethnic Group. Columbia University. Ph.D. dissertation. Ann Arbor. University Microfilms.

Gonzalez, Nancie L.
1970a   The Neoteric Society. Comparative Studies in Society and History. 12(1) :1–13.
1970b   Peasants' Progress; Dominicans in New York. Carribbean Studies. 10(3) :154–171.
1970c   Social Functions of Carnival in a Dominican City. Southwestern Journal of Anthropology. 26 :328–342.

Hernandez, Frank Marino
1973   La Inmigración Haitiana en la República Dominicana. Eme Eme: Estúdios Dominicanos (Santiago) 1(5) :24–56.

Hoetinck, H.
1971   El Pueblo Dominicano: 1850–1900. Apuntes para su Sociología historia. Universidad Catolica Madre y Maestra, Santiago, República Dominicana (agosto).

Jones, Delmos
1973   Personal communication.

Shibutani, Tamatsu, and Kian M. Kwan
1965   Ethnic Stratification: A Comparative Approach. New York: Macmillan.

Simmons, Ozzie P.
1955   The Criollo Outlook in the Mestizo Culture of Coastal Peru. American Anthropologist 57 :107–117.

U.S. Consul in Santo Domingo
n.d.   Consular Reports. Microfilm. National Archive of the U.S., Washington, DC.

Walker, Malcolm T.
1973   Politics and the Power Structure: A Rural Community in the Dominican Republic. New York: Teacher's College Press, Columbia University.

Wiarda, Howard J.
1969   The Dominican Republic in Transition. New York: Praeger.

*

ETHNICITY AS STRATEGY IN RESOURCE COMPETITION

*

9

Ethnicity and Ethnic Group Relations in Guyana*

LEO A. DESPRES

Case Western Reserve University

Among the most difficult to analyze and fundamentally important consequences of recent developments in Guyana have been the emergence and, at the same time, the submergence of ethnic groups as viable entities of sociocultural reality. The existence of ethnic populations is a fact of Guyanese history.[1] The persistence of such populations is deeply rooted in the colonial fabric of Guyanese society.[2] Their emergence as corporately organized political factions have attended the pre- and postindependence struggle for national power.[3] On the other hand, coupled with a common history of exploitation and colonial rule, these

* I wish to thank Professor Melvyn Goldstein, Case Western Reserve University, for having read and criticized earlier drafts of this paper. Some of the data used in this paper were collected with the support of a postdoctoral fellowship provided by the Social Science Research Council in 1960–61. Thanks to the support of a Fulbright Fellowship, additional data were collected over a twelve-month period in 1970–71.

same developments have served to submerge ethnic populations so that their boundaries lack clarity as a unit of analysis.[4] Part of the difficulty we encounter in this regard derives from the ambiguities surrounding our conventional analytic framework.[5] However, whether one proceeds according to the institutional emphasis of "plural theory," or from the more subjectivist framework suggested by Barth, ethnicity remains a fact of life in Guyana, and ethnic phenomena contribute substantially to the overall structure of Guyanese society.[6]

With a view toward drawing out a few tentative conclusions for purposes of discussion, I shall briefly describe what I consider to be some of the more salient features of ethnicity and ethnic group relations in Guyanese society. In so doing, I will focus attention mainly on three levels: that of the overall social system, the level of ethnic group relations, and the level of individual ethnic encounters within varying situational contexts. Although related, each of these levels may be dealt with separately.

At the societal level, it should be noted that Guyana constitutionally subscribes to what M. G. Smith (1969:434–435) has called a "universalistic" or "uniform" mode of incorporation. As citizens, individuals are directly incorporated into the public domain on identical conditions of civic and political status. In law, their rights are not to be infringed by reference to such sectional identities as may derive from racial and/or cultural origins. Accordingly, within the limits proscribed by law, differences of institutional belief and practice as regards family, religion, education, politics, associational memberships, and the like are private options of equivalent indifference in the determination of civic status. These norms are officially proclaimed by the government, by political parties, and by every group and association with which I am familiar. They are articles of faith to which all Guyanese subscribe. From these derives the motto on Guyana's coat of arms: "One People, One Nation, One Destiny."

One must also take note of the obvious and much-discussed problem of census classification at the societal level. Guyana is said to be a land of six peoples: Africans (31.3 percent), East Indians (50.2 percent), Portuguese (1.0 percent), Chinese (0.6 percent), Amerindians (4.6 percent), and Europeans (0.3 percent). A mixed residual population (12.0 percent) is also recognized. Numerous students of Guyanese society have proclaimed the ambiguity and empirical invalidity of these cognitive categories. Guyanese who count other Guyanese sometimes give note to subjectively asserted ethnic identities for purposes of classification. In other instances, attention is drawn to cultural diacritica that are assumed to be generally standardized, such as dress, religion, house form, or style of life. In still other instances, persons are counted in reference to socially recognized phenotypical variations, particularly skin color, facial features, and hair texture. All of this underscores the fact that in the final analysis such categorizations are stereotypic.

Following Barth (1969), the critical question is whether or not imperative statuses attach to these ethnic and/or racial categories within the overall social system. There is substantial evidence to suggest that this is the case. Unofficially and sometimes officially, these ethnic categories are the focus of differential planning and consideration within the public domain. One recent example of this is provided by the 1965 inquiry into the problem of racial imbalance in the public services. The rather exhaustive study made of this problem was commissioned by the government of British Guiana and carried out by the International Commission of Jurists.[7] Concerning this inquiry, quite apart from its procedures and findings, I should like to emphasize three points.

First, there can be no doubt that the Burnham government of 1965 felt constrained to undertake this inquiry to alleviate political pressures arising from the widespread belief that an imbalance, particularly among Africans and East Indians, existed in the public service. Second, the measure of that imbalance was made explicitly in reference to population ratios that were derived from the application of the stereotypic ethnic categories previously mentioned. And third, implicitly if not explicitly, the investigation itself gave expression to a set of norms very different from those expressed in Guyana's constitution. Contrary to the latter, a great many Guyanese, including some who are important members of the government, are inclined to support the view that within the all-inclusive public domain, the structure of Guyanese society should disclose what M. G. Smith (1969:434–435) has called a "consociational" form of incorporation.

In other words, many Guyanese are inclined to see their society as one composed of diverse ethnic and/or racial collectivities of unequal status and power. To mold from these one people with one destiny, if I may paraphrase a title borrowed from the prime minister's recent book (Burnham 1970), many Guyanese would maintain that these collectivities need to hold equivalent corporate entitlements and status in the common public domain. Therefore, regarding recruitment into government departments, agencies, and undertakings, some consideration needs to be given to ascribed ethnic and/or racial criteria in addition to criteria of individual achievement. At the very least, achievement criteria should not be allowed to contribute further to the corporate inequalities that are perceived to obtain among ethnic populations as a consequence of their former colonial domination. It follows from these views that Africans and East Indians should be given entitlements not only in reference to their numbers, but also in relationship to the inequalities of their assumed corporate status in the overall social system.

Although official census classifications have sharply curtailed the public use of ethnic categories in the last decade, ethnic data continue to be compiled by political parties and various departments of government. These data are extensively used for purposes of establishing developmental priorities and policy decisions affecting the allocation of public resources. Accordingly, numerous examples can be marshalled in support of the thesis that ethnic categories do, in fact, enjoin imperative statuses. To cite one instance in 1961, the cooperative movement was the main vehicle by which the Jagan government promoted the status of East Indians to the virtual exclusion of Africans in regard to land settlement schemes (Despres 1967:246–248). Between 1957 and 1964, East Indians achieved parity in employment in almost every department of the public service. Also, during this period, the interests of East Indian businessmen and professionals were supported by the government in numerous and subtle ways.

Since the Burnham government assumed office in 1965, the situation has been reversed. East Indian rice farmers have been displaced from a whole section of the Black Bush land-settlement scheme that was developed by the Jagan government. Their homes have been bulldozed and their leasehold lands have been given over to an agricultural cooperative organized by Africans. The new settlement is officially known as Zambia. Cooperatives are now being organized by government to settle Africans on new lands in the interior. One settlement alone has received in excess of $4 million (Guyana dollars) in developmental support, and it has yet to produce a profitable crop. Similarly, market and consumer cooperatives are being organized by the government among Africans in the commercial sector. Legislation giving the government complete control of imports has been combined with a policy of price control to secure competitive advantage for these co-ops vis-à-vis shops owned by East Indians, Portuguese, or Europeans. Even the educational system has not completely escaped these developments. In 1971, the government was exerting financial pressure in an effort to get the University of Guyana to modify its achievement-based recruitment criteria in favor of ethnic considerations.

Of course, the definition of inequalities among ethnic populations in Guyana is somewhat relative to the ethnic population with which one happens to be identified. However, ethnic identities are not entirely subjective. They combine both cultural and socially perceived physical diacritica. The former can be subjectively altered; within more restricted limits, the latter cannot. Notwithstanding the fact that many Guyanese might subjectively reject identification with one ethnic population or another in favor of asserting other socially relevant statuses, they are often accorded an ethnic status in reference to phenotypical features. Thus, in Guyana, the complexity of ethnic phenomena is compounded by elements of racialism. Quite apart from all of this, in the overall social system, empirically observable status inequalities do exist among populations that Guyanese identify as ethnic and/or racial.

The only relatively unambiguous measure of status inequality is that which discloses the relationship of individuals and groups to material resources. In Guyana, even the most cursory review of the data available on this account discloses an inequality of status among ethnic populations and a pattern approximating differential incorporation (M. G. Smith 1969:433–434) within the inclusive social system. That is to say, in relationship to the material resources they own, control, or otherwise manage, a definite order of inequality exists among ethnic populations.

To illustrate this point, it should be noted that in Guyana six industries generate approximately 78 percent of the Gross Domestic Product (GDP) and also contribute 78 percent to the employed labor force. The six include: sugar and sugar processing; mining; distribution and trade; rice agriculture and mixed farming; financial services (mainly banking); and government. Directly and indirectly, these six industries exploit and produce most of the material resources presently available to the Guyanese population. How that population stands in relationship to these resources reveals not only an order of inequality among individuals and groups, but more important for our purposes, the individuals and groups so ordered cluster significantly within the ethnic and/or racial boundaries which Guyanese themselves recognize.

The status of Europeans is derived from their ownership and control of those industries that dominate the economy: sugar, mining, banking, and distribution. Together, these four industries contribute 57 percent to the GDP and only 37 percent to the employed labor force. Except for that part of the distribution industry which is in the hands of Portuguese and East Indian merchants, practically all the firms operating in these core industries are subsidiaries of foreign-owned corporations.[8]   In response to recent political changes, the employment of Guyanese by these firms has reduced the number of Europeans in the overall population.   Still, there can be little doubt that these enterprises remain firmly in the control of Europeans.   By virtue of this control, Europeans in Guyana disclose the characteristics of a corporate economic elite rather than those of a population element in a generalized social-class structure.   Regarding recruitment into this elite, ethnic and/or racial criteria continue to be important.   A variety of epithets—some racial, some ethnic, and some denoting social class— are applied by Guyanese to other Guyanese who work on the fringes of this elite.

An undetermined but marginal proportion of the resources exploited and produced by these four industries are made available to Guyanese, mostly by way of taxes, duties, and wages.[9]   As marginal as their share of these resources is, it still serves as the basis for the differential incorporation of ethnic populations.   Bauxite mining, for example, is the business of Africans.   Although it only contributes 3 percent to the employed labor force, in excess of 95 percent of all bauxite workers are Africans.   The sugar industry, on the other hand, is mainly a concern of East Indians.   While sugar processing contributes 18 percent to the employed labor force, approximately 85 percent of all sugar workers are East Indians.   As previously noted, the distribution industry is largely in the hands of Europeans, Portuguese, and East Indians.   Even the stalls in the Georgetown markets are predominantly owned and operated by East Indian merchants.

By way of contrast to these four industries, rice agriculture and mixed farming, including processing for market distribution, contribute approximately 11 percent to the GDP and 21 percent to the employed labor force. In 1955, East Indians comprised 71 percent of all farm operators, a category that includes rice farmers. It is more than apparent, however, that the overwhelming majority of rice farmers are East Indians. Africans, on the other hand, are normally mixed farmers. As such, they occupy some of the most fragmented and least productive agricultural lands in the country (Despres 1969:33–37). Moreover, while underemployment is a problem affecting the agricultural industry in general the problem is much more critical among mixed farmers than among rice cultivators.

In view of the contribution these industries make to the employed labor force, and considering the imbalance of Indians and Africans employed in these industries, it is not surprising that Africans comprise a majority of the unemployed in Guyana. It also is not surprising that Africans define their interests corporately and with particular reference to the government. As an industry, the government generates approximately 11 percent of the GDP, and it contributes 19 percent to the employed labor force. Thus, apart from agriculture, the government is the largest single consumer of labor in the country. While all elements of the Guyanese population look to the government for various kinds of support, the majority of Africans view their control of it as an absolute prerequisite of their economic survival.

To state this in another way, Guyana has an economy which is encapsulated within the sphere of European, Canadian, and American influence. Its core industries are foreign-owned and controlled. Only a marginal share of the country's material resources remains unexpropriated by these industries and available to Guyanese. Over the years, the competitive allocation of these unexpropriated resources has served to order ethnic populations in an arrangement of unequal status and power. Amerindians, who have not been mentioned previously, are marginal to the whole economy and rank at the bottom of this stratification structure. Africans comprise a population holding little land and having practically no investment in commercial enterprises. Outside of the bauxite industry, part of which has been recently nationalized, Africans have little security of employment. Thus, in consideration of their numbers, they have looked and continue to look to the government for status. Made up as it is of businessmen, merchants, shopkeepers, rice farmers, and sugar workers, and in view of its size, the East Indian population is perceived by the

Africans as a major threat to their material well-being. East Indians, of course, express reciprocal views. Enough racial diacritica attend ethnic identities that most of the mixed population has little choice but to align themselves with the Africans. And the Portuguese, because of their small number and their racial identity with Europeans, are of their own accord leaving the country.

Inevitably, this structure of inequality among ethnic populations has promoted the organization of a variety of special-interest groups and associations which, in turn, define much of the interface of interethnic relations. Most notable among such groups have been Guyana's ethnically based political parties. These, it may be reported, are alive and well. Also important in this regard have been business and professional associations, labor unions, religious associations, and such ethnic associations as the League of Coloured Peoples and the East Indian Association. The latter two organizations are no longer alive. Most of these associations have been described elsewhere (Despres 1967:121–176). Thus, it will more suitably serve the purposes of this analysis to focus attention briefly on the kind of interface which three relatively new groups have provided.

One of the most dynamic and influential associations to emerge in recent years is ASCRIA (African Society for Cultural Relations with Independent Africa). First organized as a black separatist movement (the Society for Racial Equality) in the early 1960s, under the leadership of Sidney King (now known as Eusi Kwayana), it has subsequently supplanted the League of Coloured Peoples and has been reorganized into a black power movement with loose ties to similar movements in North America. To describe ASCRIA simply as a black power movement, however, is to distort its complexity. To be sure, it is militantly black, but in defining black, it combines elements of race, social class, and cultural elements that are visibly African. Membership rules are rigid and proscribe a six-month course of black studies as prerequisite for full membership status. Thus, a black who does not think black is a "redneck" and cannot belong to ASCRIA. A light-colored African who thinks black can belong. Of course, East Indians, Portuguese, Chinese, Amerindians, or Europeans cannot belong at all.

ASCRIA, in one dimension, is an ethnic organization dedicated to the revitalization of African culture. In this effort, it maintains a surprisingly extensive educational program, importing materials and often teachers from Africa and North America. It encourages the adoption of African names, values, and dress. It uses what are considered to be African rituals in religious practices, weddings, funerals, and other celebrations. If ASCRIA were simply a cultural revitalization movement, it would not be of such concern to other elements of the population. Of equal significance, however, is the fact that ASCRIA is also an economic and a political movement with considerable muscle. Many of its members are prominently placed in government, in the National Bank of Guyana, and the National Cooperative Bank. ASCRIA's coordinating elder, Eusi Kwayana, in 1970–71 chaired the National Land Settlement Committee and the executive board of the National Marketing Corporation. In addition to these and other positions, he served as a close advisor to the prime minister.

One ranking member of ASCRIA described the situation in the following terms: "Burnham is ASCRIA as much as Eusi Kwayana is ASCRIA. ASCRIA is Burnham's right hand and the PNC [Peoples National Congress] is his left." He continued: "ASCRIA is the cultural and economic arm of the government: the PNC is its political arm. We have two prime ministers. Burnham is the political prime minister. He is a public figure and a point of contact with the outside [meaning outside of the black community]. Kwayana is the economic and cultural prime minister. He is not public. He works on the inside."

Needless to say, this informant's statement is somewhat exaggerated. In 1970–71, however, there appeared to be relatively few Amerindians, Portuguese, and East Indians who would not have considered it a statement of fact. Charges of ethnic and racial discrimination on the part of the government were both prevalent and believed. Thus, in November 1970, another new movement came into being. It called itself the Anti-Discrimination Movement. Organized primarily by East Indian businessmen and professionals, its leaders held public meetings at which they proclaimed themselves opposed to "gross acts of discrimination and corruption at all levels of the government." Apparently well-financed, the ADM published a weekly, called the *Liberator*, and distributed it freely in all parts of the country. By the spring of 1971, many Africans believed that ADM was in the process of giving birth to a new East Indian political party.

This type of interface among ethnic groups can be found in most areas of the country and among virtually all elements of the population. As illustrated by a final example, it can be found even among university students. At the end of the 1970 academic year, three groups contested the elections for student government at the University of Guyana. One was an all-Indian slate of candidates, another an all-African slate, and the third represented a carefully balanced slate of Africans and East Indians. To assure the honesty of the elections, the retiring student government requested that the elections be supervised by the university administration. So supervised, the all-Indian slate won. Soon after, Africans from the mixed slate accused the East Indian members of their slate of having secretly campaigned in favor of the all-Indian slate. The national political parties were also accused of having invested funds in the campaign. Subsequently, a petition was circulated to have the vice-chancellor of the university declare the election null and void. In the following academic year, 1970–71, this issue divided the student body for the entire year and in respect to every activity sponsored by the student government. By February 1971, the African faction threatened to strike the university unless the vice-chancellor voided the election. This dilemma was averted by factional disputes among the members of the all-Indian slate in regard to finances. Some of the officers resigned, and in the end, the vice-chancellor was forced to call a university-wide meeting of the student body, at which time he removed the president from office and invested full responsibility for student government in the hands of the university administration until the books could be audited and new elections held. Needless to say, a great many students considered this whole affair ludicrous. Still, the situation was sufficiently charged with emotion that jokes about it among the students were confined to exclusively ethnic circles.

Thus far, we have focused attention on the imperative statuses attached to categorical ethnic and/or racial identities within the overall social system and on the interface of interethnic relations as it tends to be defined by corporately organized groups and associations. These dimensions of the problem are largely structural. As such, they disclose the more permanent alignments that obtain in regard to power and status in Guyanese society. There remains to be considered the level of individual ethnic encounters. Viewed from this vantage point, ethnicity and ethnic relations assume dimensions that do not make readily apparent the structural dimensions that have been described.

More to the point, from the flow of ordinary everyday affairs in Guyana, one has the impression that ethnic and/or racial identities, to the extent that they are obvious, do not enjoin imperative statuses affecting the interactions of persons of apparently different ethnic categories. Such interactions are commonplace. In the markets and shops, at workplaces everywhere, in the schools, at parties in private homes, one can observe Guyanese of virtually all ethnic categories interacting with one another and it does not appear immediately that their behavior is in any way modified by differences in their ethnic or racial origins.

Gradually, as one takes a deeper look, this general impression begins to change. At the seawall, where people gather to enjoy the evening breezes, or in the Botanical Gardens, where afternoon walks may be taken, it can be observed that Africans and East Indians sit separately and seldom join in conversation with one another. At the lunch counters in the cafeterias they form separate clusters. Friends who greet friends at the weekly band concert always seem to be of the same ethnic category. The peer groups that collect after school seem to be ethnically composed. At the barber shop or some other casual setting where one may engage in semiprivate conversation, one also notices the ease with which the subject of conversation may swing, without prompting, to matters having to do with ethnic groups and their differences. On these occasions, one may also detect how the substance of such discussions changes according to who the speaker is and what other persons happen to be in hearing distance. Similar episodes may be experienced at the filling station, the dry cleaning establishment, the market stall, or in the faculty lounge. A few social visits to the Police Officers Club, the Army Staff Mess, or the Civil Service Association Club, reinforce these less generalized impressions. The parties one attends are not spontaneous affairs. When planned by ordinary people as an occasion for merriment among close friends, they are inclined to be ethnically exclusive. However, when planned by intellectuals, important public figures, or foreigners, their ethnic composition is carefully mixed.

The occasions of individual encounters, then, are not only episodic, but are also extremely variable in respect to situation, circumstance, and personnel. This makes their structuring difficult to discern. Nevertheless, as observations are drawn together and given systematic attention, a pattern emerges. A few selected examples may serve to illuminate the characteristics of this pattern.

First, in most situations involving non-Guyanese and Guyanese of different ethnic origins, the Guyanese of virtually every ethnic and/or racial origin will tend to obfuscate or submerge their respective ethnic identities in favor of asserting a common national identity. The imperative status that becomes operative in these situations incorporates all Guyanese in a manner as to suggest that as a people, Guyanese think and behave in ways that set them apart from nonnationals, especially Europeans, Americans, and Canadians. Even other West Indians are given to understand that the Guyanese are nationals to be differentiated from Jamaicans, Trinidadians, or Barbadians.

In other situations—for example, a meeting at the Critchlow Labour College where the initial topic of discussion happened to center on the problem of unemployment and what the labor unions might do about it—it may be observed that Guyanese of different ethnic origins will merge their respective ethnic identities in opposition to other Guyanese, also of different ethnic origins, who are epithetically labeled as "white niggers," "house slaves," or "red people." This latter group may include East Indians, Afro-Guyanese, Guyanese of mixed ancestry, Portuguese, and Chinese. Collectively, they form a special status category because of their relationship to Europeans or because of their style of life. This group is thought to discriminate against other Guyanese not only in terms of employment practices but also in terms of their associational proclivities.

What emerges in this instance is the definition of an imperative social-class status. Because it seems to combine certain phenotypical and cultural diacritica in its definition, this social-class status is reminiscent of the color-class continuum, a stratification structure that many observers consider to be pervasive in West Indian societies. However, when it is observed that the distribution of resources is more perfectly correlated with generalized ethnic identities than with specifically defined racial identities, it seems rather difficult to attribute pervasive structural significance to a color-class continuum. For example, at the meeting referred to above, there were Guyanese of mixed ancestry and two Portuguese who most definitely were not identified as "white niggers" or "red people" by the rest of the group.

More precisely, it would seem that elements of a color-class differentiation are functional primarily in situational contexts where the submergence of ethnic identities facilitates interaction among persons who have in common something more important than their differences. In the instance provided, ethnic identities were submerged by the assertion of a more generalized "white–non-white" dichotomy, which is thought by many Guyanese to correspond to an historically derived economic differentiation. This facilitated interaction among Guyanese who shared a relatively low economic status quite apart from their ethnic differences. In other situations, these very same individuals will assert their African, East Indian, or Portuguese ethnic identities rather than a generalized identity expressive of their economic status. Thus, in this instance, the elements of a color-class continuum were operative only to the extent that phenotypical images (such as "red people") attach to cultural differentiations that give specific focus to important economic experiences.

In some situations, usually involving encounters among persons of only two ethnic groups, ethnic identities are asserted to lay claim to special status consideration. The indirect effect of this is to declare the opposition of the group with which one identifies to a third group, no member of which is participating in the encounter. For example, it frequently may be observed that when one or two Africans, or alternatively, one or two East Indians, are interacting with non-Guyanese, they seize the opportunity to assert their African or, as the case may be, their Indian identity. What appears to be involved here is a declaration to the effect that Guyanese are not to be considered alike in the way they comport themselves; that Guyanese differ particularly according to their ethnic origins. Typically, such declarations are accompanied by a stream of negative stereotypes in reference to ethnic groups not included in the encounter. Similarly, when East Indians have encounters with Portuguese, negative references may be made to Africans. The variations on this type of episode are endless, but they always seem to involve a special status claim for the collectivity with which one identifies.

Invariably, status claims arising from one ethnic identity serve to diminish the claims arising from another. Thus, less commonly observed are situations in which individuals of different ethnic origins counterpose their respective ethnic identities. When confrontations of this nature do occur, they generally occasion a verbal or a physical quarrel. The exception is when one party to the encounter simply ignores the claims asserted by the other, often in a joking manner. However, an increasingly common variant on this pattern is when members of militant ethnic associations seize opportunities to express their militancy. This usually occurs in contexts that are somewhat organized and formal, and therefore under control. Under such circumstances, the assertion of conflicting ethnic claims are more often ignored than rebutted by persons who might otherwise rise to the offence.

From these few illustrations, it is evident that sensitivity to ethnic and/or racial differentiations tends to be pervasive in Guyanese society. Therefore, it should not be surprising to learn that a rather elaborate code of etiquette has developed in respect to interethnic encounters. This code has not received systematic research, and its details are imperfectly known. Nevertheless, it soon becomes apparent to even the most casual observer that on most occasions of interethnic encounters it is simply impolite to assert ethnic identities. As previously noted, such assertions almost always involve claims which diminish the status of one group or another. As these claims can be a source of embarrassment to others, unless the situation is appropriate, they also can be a source of embarrassment to those individuals who assert them. Therefore, unless observation is more than superficial, it would seem that ethnic and/or racial identities are more apparent than real; that such identities do not enjoin imperative statuses affecting the interactions of persons of different ethnic categories.

Regarding encounters among persons of apparently different ethnic and/or racial origins, the question remains: what kinds of situations tend to evoke, without embarrassment, the assertion of their respective ethnic identities? To answer this, one must keep in mind that the assertion of such identities effects a status claim which establishes a mode of competitive opposition between one ethnic group and another. Invariably, when such a mode of competitive opposition is effected, it reflects upon the very real status inequalities that have been previously described. Thus, regarding individual encounters, situations which call into question the rights, privileges, and entitlements that are thought to attend the status inequalities exising among ethnic populations, or situations that give issue to the resource allocations from which these inequalities derive, appropriately call forth ethnic identities and claims.

To continue, the pattern that emerges from the variety of these interethnic episodes seems to be one of segmentary opposition. That is to say, some situations evoke national claims which override ethnic identities. In these, the status claims of all Guyanese are inclined to be joined in opposition to Europeans, Americans, Canadians, and even other West Indians. Some situations bring into focus claims which serve to join Africans and East Indians in opposition to other ethnic and/or racial elements. Still other situations evoke identities that place individual Africans and East Indians in opposition to one another. In fact, when some Africans refer to other Africans as "red people," an epithet which combines racial and cultural criteria to define a social class status, it needs to be recognized that some situations evoke identities that serve to divide Africans among themselves. On the whole, this pattern of segmentary opposition corresponds to and reflects both the continuities and discontinuities which the differential incorporation of ethnic and racial populations enjoins in the overall structure of Guyanese society.

In view of these data, the description of ethnicity and ethnic group relations in Guyana may be concluded as follows.

First, at the level of ideology, Guyanese have declared themselves in support of a political constitution that defines the rights and obligations of citizenship without reference to ethnic and/or racial considerations. However, for reasons that are historical, this pattern of universal incorporation does not obtain. Rather, in relationship to those material resources that Europeans and others have not expropriated, there exists an order of inequality according to which primarily ethnic, rather than racial or social class, populations are aligned in competitive opposition. Over the years, this structure of inequality has been productive of considerable tension and conflict. In response to this, and in an effort to achieve stability, Guyanese governments have generally conceded to ethnic populations corporate, but equal, entitlements in the overall public domain. In other words, they have accorded such populations consociational status at least until such time as universal incorporation can be approximated. However, the definition as to what in fact constitutes equal entitlements is a matter on which there continues to exist a great deal of ethnic dissension.

Second, between this overall structure and the level of individual encounters, a variety of associations and groups exist which seek to secure and promote the corporate interests of ethnic populations. These include political parties, ethnic associations, business and professional associations, religious organizations, and in some instances labor unions. These groups and associations have served simultaneously to define and maintain the interface of interethnic relations. That is to say, the political and economic activities of such organizations as ASCRIA or the Anti-Discrimination Movement bring into sharp focus the corporate interests of ethnic populations quite apart from the fact that only small numbers of these populations may belong to the groups in question.

Third, ethnic identities and status claims enter selectively into the domain of individual transactions. In other words, such identities and claims tend to be asserted only in those situations which bring into focus the status inequalities that exist among ethnic populations. The range and variety of these interactional episodes discloses a pattern of segmentary opposition. In general, this pattern corresponds to and reflects both the continuities and discontinuities which the differential incorporation of ethnic populations enjoins in the overall structure of the society.

Based on these conclusions, suggestions of a more general nature are in order. I present three for purposes of discussion. First, ethnic identities and status claims obviously contain a subjective component. However, the data presented here underscore the fact that these subjective elements are situationally specific in their expression. Only when we understand that ethnic identities are informed by considerations of a more material nature do we begin to understand also the structural significance of these identities. It is precisely in regard to their structural significance that ethnic identities reveal themselves as not being primarily subjective in their determination. Thus, it would seem that if generalizations of invariant order are to be established in respect to ethnic phenomena, we need to look much more carefully into the material conditions that give rise to these phenomena.

A second suggestion has to do with the problem of stratification and, more specifically, the color-class continuum. The view is current in the literature that ethnic differentiation in the Caribbean is largely a by-product of a social-class system which incorporates elements of racism. The data presented here controvert this view: it is much too simple and one-dimensional in its conception to accurately describe the complexity of stratification in Guyana. It fails, for example, to explain how in some situations Europeans could consider Portuguese as one with themselves and then consider them differently in other situations; or how in some situations Africans, Indians, and Portuguese may submerge their racial and ethnic differences and assert an identity that places them in opposition to other Africans, Indians, and Portuguese. To be sure, elements of racism are evident in Guyana. They are evident whenever such phenotypical images as "red people" are employed to summarize differences that are essentially cultural. When the distribution of resources is considered, however, the predominant order of inequality in Guyana obtains among ethnically defined populations and not socially defined persons.

It is not inconsistent that the social definition of persons is often at variance with the inequality that obtains among ethnic groups. As has been noted, in some instances racial images are combined with cultural criteria for purposes of joining individual Africans and Indians in a way that is not expressive of the inequalities that obtain between their respective ethnic groups. In other instances, as when Africans of different socioeconomic statuses are joined in opposition to Indians, the social definition of persons tends to be at variance with the economic considerations according to which Africans and Indians are inclined to define their status inequalities in the first place. These discontinuities are real and to dismiss them as the illogical attributes of a simple color-class continuum is to ignore their significance.

Furthermore, in Guyana, ethnic identities engage imperative statuses in reference to populational groups that are ordered by an unequal distribution of resources. However, within the groups so ordered, there also exists an unequal distribution of resources. Not all Africans are without land, secure positions, or precluded from business enterprises. Nor do all Indians have land, good incomes, or shops. Some Portuguese have very limited access to resources. At the same time, the criteria according to which Guyanese make categorical identities are not so one-dimensional or compelling as to be impervious to modification as the occasion may warrant. These discontinuities are part of the system and because of them situationally defined social identities need not always correspond in one-dimensional fashion to the order of inequality that, in general, obtains among categorically defined ethnic populations.

It follows from these discontinuities that social identities can and do vary according to circumstance and situation. This variance, however, is not without pattern. More precisely, it is this variance which imparts to the system its segmentary character. Thus, whenever interactional situations engage status inequalities arising from the overall distribution of resources, the social definition of persons engages identities that are relative to that order of inequality. Although the point cannot be further developed in the present context, it is suggested that this pattern of segmentation very well may be an essential feature of any stratification system based on the differential incorporation of categorically defined groups. Were social identities similar to group identities in respect to resources, instead of a hierarchial arrangement of ethnic populations, we would have more nearly a system of social classes.

Finally, it should be noted that if ethnicity and ethnic group relations in Guyana are to be treated as stratification phenomena, it follows that these phenomena cannot be understood apart from the problem of exploitation and its relationship to the larger issue of international inequalities. More specifically, it appears that the competitive alignment of ethnic populations in Guyana is very much a function of the conditions affecting the quantity, quality, and technological accessibility of resources. Why ethnic, rather than alternative strategies, are operative in these circumstances is a matter to be considered in another paper. When it is considered how much Guyana's resources are diminished by economic dependency and external control, the question of internal inequalities must turn upon the question of international inequalities. The one type of inequality cannot be dealt with completely apart from the other. All of this suggests that the problems of ethnicity and nationalism may be subsumed within the same general framework. It suggests also that more systematic research attention must be given to the way in which societal structures are affected by international and supranational economic and political developments.

NOTES

1 For a general history of Guyana, see A. R. F. Webber (1931). N. E. Cameron has related the history of the Negro (1934). First published in 1950, Dwarka Nath (1970) has up-dated his history of the East Indians. A summary of historical materials is provided in Despres (1967:30–67). For a more general treatment, see R. T. Smith (1962).

2 See Despres (1967:30–67); and (1969:14–44). See also Jayawardena (1963); and R. T. Smith (1956).

3 See Despres (1967:177–267); Newman (1964); and R. T. Smith (1962).

4 This problem is discussed by R. T. Smith (1962:98–143); Despres (1964: 1051–1077); and Cross (1968:381–397).

5 M. G. Smith (1965:18–74) presents a review of the conventional analytical frameworks that have been employed in Caribbean research. For a brief but critical review of the conceptual problems attending the study of racial and ethnic populations, see P. L. van den Berghe (1967:1–41). For a more general review of the literature dealing with ethnic relations, see R. A. Schermerhorn (1970) and Tamotsu Shibutani and Kian M. Kwan (1965).

6 See Barth (1969:9–38). An extensive bibliography has developed regarding plural theory. An excellent review of the literature on this subject may be found in Leo Kuper and M. G. Smith (1969), especially articles by Leo Kuper, M. G. Smith, and P. L. van den Berghe.

7 The memoranda from this study have been presented in five volumes by the Government of British Guiana. A summary report is presented by The International Commission of Jurists (1965).

8 The data presented here in reference to GDP have been abstracted from Wilfred David (1969:1–42). Data in regard to employed labor force have been abstracted from various tables found in the British Guiana Report On A Survey of Manpower Requirements and the Labour Force, vol. 2, *Human Resources in Guiana* (1965).

9 How marginal the Guyanese share of exploited resources can be is illustrated by the bauxite industry. According to one generous estimate, over a fifty-year period, Guyana realized 39 percent of the sale value of bauxite by the Demerara Bauxite Company in the form of taxes, duties, and wages. However, the prime minister has noted that this amount is less than 3 percent of the total profits realized from the bauxite extracted by the Demerara Bauxite Company and its parent firm, Aluminium Ltd. of Canada. The first figure reported here may be found in the August 27, 1970 edition of the *Guyana Graphic*. The second figure was presented in a speech by the prime minister, as reported in the February 25, 1971 edition of the *Guyana Graphic*. Because bauxite prices are fixed by the parent company according to its own calculations, the true value of the bauxite extracted by this firm may never be known. The Demerara Bauxite Company was finally nationalized in July 1971.

LITERATURE CITED

Barth, Fredrik, Ed.
  1969 Ethnic Groups and Boundaries. Boston: Little, Brown and Co.

British Guiana Ministry of Labor and Social Security
  1965 Human Resources in Guiana: Report on a Survey of Manpower Requirements and the Labour Force, Vol. 2.

Burnham, Forbes
  1970 A Destiny to Mold. London: Longman Carribbean Ltd.

Cameron, N. E.
  1934 The Evolution of the Negro. 2 Vols. Georgetown, B.G.: Argosy Co.

Cross, Malcolm

1968 Cultural Pluralism and Sociological Theory: A Critique and Reevaluation. Social and Economic Studies 17:381–397.

David, Wilfred

1969 The Economic Development of Guyana, 1953–64. London: Oxford University Press.

Despres, Leo A.

1964 The Implications of Nationalist Politics in British Guiana for the Development of Cultural Theory. American Anthropologist 66:1051–1077.

1967 Cultural Pluralism and Nationalist Politics in British Guiana. Chicago: Rand-McNally.

1969 Differential Adaptations and MicroCultural Evolution in Guyana. Southwestern Journal of Anthropology 25:14–44.

International Commission of Jurists

1965 Report of the British Guiana Commission of Inquiry into Racial Problems in the Public Service. Geneva, Switzerland.

Jayawardena, C.

1963 Conflict and Solidarity in a Guianese Plantation. **London:** Athlone Press.

Kuper, Leo, and M. G. Smith, Eds.

1969 Pluralism in Africa. Los Angeles: University of California Press.

Nath, Dwarka

1970 A History of Indians in British Guyana. London: Thomas Nelson and Sons.

Newman, Peter

1964 British Guiana: Problems of Cohesion in an Immigrant Society. London: Oxford University Press.

Schermerhorn, Richard A.

1970 Comparative Ethnic Relations: A Framework for Theory and Research. New York: Random House.

Shibutani, Tamotsu, and Kian M. Kwan

1965 Ethnic Stratification: A Comparative Approach. New York: Macmillan.

Smith, M. G.
  1965 The Plural Society in the British West Indies. Los Angeles:
        University of California Press.
  1969 Some Developments in the Analytic Framework of Pluralism.
        In Pluralism in Africa. Leo Kuper and M. G. Smith, Eds. Los
        Angeles: University of California Press. pp. 415–458.

Smith, Raymond T.
  1956 The Negro Family in British Guiana. London: Routledge and
        Kegan Paul, Ltd.
  1962 British Guiana. London: Oxford University Press.

Van den Berghe, Pierre L.
  1967 Race and Racism. New York: John Wiley and Sons, Inc.

Webber, A. R. F.
  1931 Centenary History and Handbook of British Guiana. George-
        town, B.G.: Daily Chronicle.

10

When Indios Become Cholos: Some Consequences of the Changing Ecuadorian Hacienda[*]

MURIEL CRESPI

Hunter College, CUNY

This paper considers traditional ethnic relations in the context of the changing economy of a preindustrial hacienda. More specifically, it discusses some factors giving rise to a class of "surplus" Indians who are denied access to traditional occupational roles on the hacienda and, at

[*] Some ideas expressed here were mentioned in a paper read in Toronto at the 71st annual meeting of the American Anthropological Association. I appreciate the comments Jacquetta Burnett, Joseph B. Casagrande, George L. Hicks, and Erica McClure made on an earlier draft of this paper. Data were collected under the auspices of a Public Health Research Grant which supported work from January 1964 through March 1965, and during the summer of 1970. Fieldwork during the summer of 1968 was sponsored by Joseph B. Casagrande, of the University of Illinois, as part of his comparative study of ethnic relations in highland Ecuador. A Faculty Research Grant from the City University of New York supported work in the summer of 1969. Additional data were collected during the summers of 1965, 1966, and 1972.

the same time, become potential recruits to an existing category of socially dominant non-Indians. This category embraces Cholos (often referred to as Mestizos elsewhere) and whites, known everywhere in Ecuador, correctly or not, as the co-opters of power and prestige. Conceptually, allowance is made for achieving the elevated non-Indian status. Actually, a rigid stratification system based on ascription forestalls mobility and consigns "surplus" Indians to a kind of ethnic limbo, or forces them from the hacienda in search of economically more viable environments that offer the possibility of ethnic redefinition.

The exodus of poor, rural Indians to cities and coastal plantations is a familiar pattern in highland Latin America. Such Indians often assume stereotypically non-Indian dress, speech, and mannerisms and manage to become redefined as members of the non-Indian category (cf. Miller 1967; Greaves 1972). The local view, racial labels notwithstanding, that Indians and non-Indians are not members of discrete categories identified by color or other physical characteristics as much as members of sociocultural categories (Harris, 1964), facilitates ethnic redefinition under some conditions. But persons judged non-Indian outside their rural locale frequently remain categorized as Indians in their natal communities despite the newly acquired sociocultural trappings (cf. Burgos 1970). Colby and Van den Berghe (1969:91) suggest this local situation is due to "the existence of a strongly cohesive Indian culture. . . ." Wagley (1959:539) attributes local constraints on ethnic redefinition to tense interethnic relations. In the latter case, the Indians' birth-ascribed status takes precedence over sociocultural criteria. The rural dimensions remain somewhat elusive, particularly with respect to the factors that account for tense interethnic relations and the migrant's anomalous position in his natal community.

Dealing with the rural situation, this paper analyzes the overlapping ethnic and occupational role structure of Hacienda Atahualpa (pseudonym). Ethnic categories and identities are viewed, like other role systems, as associated with certain constraints on the things people may do and as implying a bundle of more or less conventionalized attributes (cf. Lehman 1967; Barth 1969). In this case, occupational attributes are regarded as "pivotal" to ethnic identities—"pivotal" in Nadel's (1957:32) sense of attributes whose presence validate a more general role (here, an ethnic one) and whose absence invalidate other attributes. *Indian,* in local usage, does not merely refer to persons who assert their distinctive heritage in ceremony, dress, and speech; it also refers to estate laborers who play unequivocably subordinate occupational roles. This ethnic-occupational role merger reflects a pattern characteristic of traditional societies, in which, Gould notes (1971 :7), "occupational role and role occupant were regarded as being identical." Where this merger is found combined with ascribed statuses, as occurs at the hacienda, the resulting stratification system approximates the Indian caste or European "estate order" in its rigidity (cf. Salz 1955). By considering ascription in terms of hacienda stratification and economic requirements, some of the structural stresses and strains that preclude local ethnic redefinition and encourage city-bound migration are thrown into relief.

In the following pages, I shall briefly describe the traditional hacienda context of Indian and non-Indian interactions and then consider the traditional ethnic system. Finally, I will discuss ethnic assignments at the hacienda in terms of changing economic requirements.

THE SETTING

Hacienda Atahualpa is located in the northern highlands, in cantón Cayambe, a county of prized farmland dominated by estates producing foodstuffs for the domestic market. Although profit oriented and exploiting more than 2,000 hectares of valley land, Atahualpa, like its traditional neighbors, relies primarily on a simple technology and abundant Indian labor paid more in kind than in cash. In order to conserve scarce capital, the estate uses its superfluous resources in lieu of cash to reimburse otherwise landless laborers (*huasipungueros*). Usufruct rights to a combined housesite and subsistence plot (*huasipungo*), usually located on agriculturally marginal land, and access to under utilized pastures, are among the most significant perquisites laborers receive. These productive arrangements result in a dualistic structure, similar to that of a company town, in which a commercial enterprise and a subordinate community of Indian laborers are mutually dependent, but the latter is economically disadvantaged.

Until Atahualpa was reorganized along the lines mandated by the 1964 agrarian reforms, it was among those haciendas controlled by the government's social welfare agency (*Asistencia Social*) and either managed by government bureaucrats or leased to private individuals and corporations for renewable eight-year periods. These upper-level jurisdictional matters can profoundly bear on the community, but on a daily basis they are practically inconsequential. White managers, whether the de facto or surrogate patrons representing the government or the lessees, exercise immediate control over commercial operations and the estate community; in 1964, that meant control over some 1,509 persons, most of them members of Indian families.

An integral component of the local system is the nearby town of some 825 whites (so-called by themselves and by Indians). Hacienda Atahualpa, almost exclusively geared to agriculture, whether for the market or subsistence, offers its residents few specialized goods and services. Consequently, although Indian social networks are comparatively circumscribed, alliances are formed with white occupational, administrative and religious specialists in town. But because Indians are chronically short of cash—miniscule wages are usually paid at intervals of several months [1]—they cannot readily utilize town services unless townsmen extend credit and loans. When these prove inadequate, Indians mortgage their incoming crops to townsmen or permit the latter to rent and sharecrop the small subsistence plot. Regardless of the form economic arrangements take, townsmen claim so sizable a share of the Indians' future incomes as to make town shops the functional equivalents of "company stores." These arrangements often flagrantly exploit Indian ignorance, but they do not necessarily make townsmen wealthy. The ubiquitous haciendas prevent the town's physical expansion, and so generally constrain its economic growth that some townsmen lead as precarious an existence as their Indian clientele.

THE ETHNIC SYSTEM

The ethnic system, which reflects the ecological facts of hacienda life, is the fundament of local social organization. In the local purview, society is grossly stratified into *gente* (people) and *señores* (gentlemen). These named social categories correspond, respectively, to the distinction between Indian and non-Indian, and distinguish the latter as enjoying privileged access to the material and nonmaterial assets that are valued by both sectors. In hacienda parlance, *señores* are "those in command." They claim the social capital—education or "civilization" (education in its broadest sense), wealth, and occupations—that bring esteem, power, and material rewards; reciprocally, *gente* lay claim to no such capital, but are subservient to those who do. The non-Indian stratum is internally differentiated into white and Cholo categories, both of which are further divided on the basis of descent. In ascending order, the overall ethnic hierarchy is conceived as built up of Indian,

Cholo, and white categories, each associated with a bundle of roles—occupational ones being crucial—personality attributes, and symbolic markers or diacritica such as speech, dress, and general demeanor.

Explanations for this hierarchy combine alternative rationales. One stresses a mystique of alleged biological factors, or descent, which ultimately justifies ascribed social inequality, and the other acknowledges the acquisition of social capital as leading to achieved high status. Circumstances determine which rationale is invoked. Indians reject the judgment, made by some whites, that they are intellectually "degenerate" or even "childlike," but concur that "heavy" blood inherently equips them for arduous agricultural chores and partly accounts for their inferiority. In contrast, "light" blood vests whites with superior leadership and intellectual abilities and makes them natural candidates for responsible positions. These candidates form a numerically small elite stratum within the white category. Even townsmen reluctantly admit that only *legítimo* or "legitimate" whites (whites by the blood of both parents) can incontrovertibly claim unique biological advantages and the esteem automatically accrued to it. The Atahualpa patron who periodically titillates a local audience with tales of his venerable ancestry, and so reinforces the stereotype, is acknowledged to be among the few *legítimo* whites. By implication, other whites are nonlegitimate and come by their status without the necessary blood qualifications.

Thus persists, in attenuated form, the colonial tradition of ascribing ethnic status not in terms of either parent's category, but in terms of both parents' categories. Inasmuch as Spanish-born "pure" whites were viewed as superior, the degree of white blood determined the relative rank of any other category. Cevallos comments (1889:82–84) that nineteenth century Ecuadorians categorized offspring of Indian and white parents as Mestizo, but the offspring of Indian and Mestizo parents as Cholo. Cholos were a step down from Mestizos with respect to blood, and consequently were a socially inferior order. Still, as Harris (1964:37) notes, colonial efforts to socially categorize the offspring of interracial unions were little more than legal fictions. In the Atahualpa area, Mestizo, which is rarely used, and Cholo are telescoped into a single category collectively called Cholo. "Legitimacy" here is contingent on having an Indian and a white parent. Actually, the category is numerically insignificant in the area, although there may be more such Cholos than people could comfortably admit.

The "nonlegitimate" Cholos, who are becoming increasingly significant locally, are regarded as persons born of two Indian parents; achievement, rather than ascription, is at play here. Cholos are commonly defined as people who were "born Indian" but are in the process of "becoming white." This subcategory is viewed as consisting of upwardly mobile, educated Indians whose Western dress, familiarity with non-Indian speech and mannerisms, and wide-ranging social experiences, enable them to adeptly handle encounters with whites. Conceptually, then, Indians and whites concede a nongenetic route to membership in the dominant category. In effect, ethnic categories, with their associated ranks and roles, are construed as being given at birth, but becoming somewhat mutable with the accumulation of social capital. Nevertheless, Atahualpa area residents irrevocably allocate persons to their respective categories at birth.

The dichotomy between *señores* and *gente*, or non-Indians and Indians, and an overlapping differentiation of persons in terms of control over natural resources, skills, or manual labor organize the estate social heirarchy. The arrangement is well-described by the three role strata Gould (1971:6) distinguishes as concomitants of preindustrial agrarian society, namely, power-elite roles, technical implementation roles, and menial roles. White de facto patrons preempt the few power and prestige-bearing roles. The ethnicity of technical and supervisory employees is ambiguous to the extent that role occupants define themselves as white, whereas patrons regard them as Cholos, but in either case, these specialized roles are non-Indian ones. Because estate employees maintain direct and continuing contact with the labor force and the patrons, they occupy a critical interface between the two, and derive their own limited power from this position. Among other things, they relay and enforce the patrons' instructions to the Indians and transmit information upward. They, therefore, have it in their power to transmit, or withhold, information prejudicial to the Indians' welfare—for example, the Indians' encroachment on commercial fields or pastures—or to intercede with the patron on the Indians' behalf. Specialized roles (both estate and town) are certainly respected, because they are believed to reflect something positive about the role occupant's superior native abilities and tend to be financially more remunerative than manual labor. But they are also respected because specialized personnel impinge on the Indians' security in very real and direct ways. Positioned at the bottom of the hierarchy, Indians have no formal power. Decisions regarding hacienda operations tend to be the patron's exclusive prerogatives. Yet, they ultimately bear on the community subsystem. For example, Indians live dispersed on hillsides overlooking the level, fertile valleys devoted to commercial farming. The location of these plots, their size and arability, heirship, the number and types of grazing animals permitted, and ultimately, the Indians' overall economic situation and even household organization, are unilaterally determined by the hacienda management.

The patron's dominion over the community has traditionally implied more than authority to dictate the terms of hacienda living, although that itself carried considerable weight. As the once commonplace phrase "owned Indian" (*indio propio*) [2] succinctly put it, Indians are the patrons' property, as much as any field, team of oxen, or piece of agricultural machinery. Until very recently, jurisdiction over the community and the labor force automatically accompanied the lessee's right to exploit the estate's natural resources. A replenishable labor force of subordinate and unambiguously defined Indians has been vital to protecting the landholder's investment and ensuring the productivity of the estate.

A docile labor force is not taken for granted. Patrons are not misled by the annual festivities in which costumed Indians pay them ceremonial homage, no more than Indians are misled by the patrons' reciprocal gestures of noblesse oblige. Although traditional estates do not formally provide for Indian participation in decisions regarding the labor community, the numerically overwhelming Indian sector can influence minor policy decisions by the implicit or explicit threat of physical violence. Work stoppages or slowdowns during critical harvest periods bring the same results. Moreover, although the Indians' political mobilization is effectively hindered by, among other things, threatened eviction from the estate, Atahualpa has a militant labor union which sporadically asserts itself. Sensitive to the potentially hostile Indian sector, patrons in the Atahualpa area keep rifles at their bedsides. Establishing and maintaining dominance over the labor force is crucial to the well-being of the small group of controlling whites. In this respect, ethnic roles and rules stressing the Indians' passive nature function as systems of social as well as economic control. Molding Indians into a docile labor force is a burden many patrons accept as inherent in their own roles. As one Cayambe patron depicted it, the making of a "good" Indian is analogous to breaking a horse:

> In order to be tamed, Indians must be held firmly by the reins and shown that any attempt to throw or bite their riders is to no avail. You must never reveal your fear. If the Indian suspects your fear, he will surely attack. But if you are consistently unyielding, he will become trained to your liking . . . softspoken, responsive to your commands, and good.

That old North American adage, "the only good Indian is a dead Indian," which reflected the attitude of colonists more dedicated to claiming land, furs, or mineral wealth than controlling an indigenous work force, is clearly not the "good" Indian Ecuadorian whites have in mind. The only good highland Indians are alive and well and working quietly in the hacienda fields.

Although opportunities for economic advancement are most severely curtailed for menial personnel, restrictions are fairly pervasive at all levels of the heirarchy. Without the requisite social and economic capital, non-Indian supervisors and technical staff can no more reasonably aspire to the patron level than Indians to the supervisory level. Acquiring and holding a technical position is not automatically assured to even non-Indians when candidates for specialized positions are more abundant than can be locally accommodated. Atahualpa readily satisfies its limited demand for specialists by recruiting the offspring of existing personnel, or, alternatively, drawing on non-Indians from the neighboring town. Despite their skills, townsmen are hard-pressed to find an adequate clientele for their services and compete for employment on the surrounding haciendas. As a result, although some Indians may become straw bosses and thereby rise an economic notch above their ethnic confreres, they cannot compete effectively for the few available specialized roles. This, combined with estate needs for unskilled laborers, relegates Indians to a cheap labor reserve. Nor do Indians ordinarily control the necessary skills. Atahualpa does have a school, but it barely imparts the rudiments of reading, writing, and arithmetic, and these usually languish with disuse. Consistent with hacienda efforts to sequester Indians from potentially disruptive influences, technological training has not been provided.

The rules governing interethnic relations reflect the expectation that Indians be unobtrusive socially and physically. Ethnic boundaries are maintained by prescribed endogamy, and social distance regulated by proscriptions against commensalism, residential integration, and the symmetrical use of first names and familiar Spanish pronouns. The markedly asymmetrical nature of intergroup relations is further exemplified by the etiquette requiring Indians to remove their hats when addressing whites, yield their seats to whites on public conveyances, and use rear seats, or the floor, of the town church.

Acquiescing to the rules has ordinarily assured the Indians' survival in the system; it is, in Casagrande's terms (1970) an adaptive strategy devised to make the best of the situation within the limitations imposed by a dominant group. Socialization to this strategy begins early in life. As one informant recalled:

> I was always very polite and made sure to remove my hat and quietly greet the patrons "good morning" or "good evening" whenever they approached. I learned by jobs well and by the time I was 12 or 13 years old . . . I was such a good worker and so honest that the patrons always like me. They came to confide in me and gave me important jobs like riding on the hacienda truck to guard the potatoes from theft.

Indians commonly boast of the patrons' high regard for them, and by implication, their own success at playing the Uncle Tom game. With their continuing stay at the hacienda and good favor with town entrepreneurs contingent on playing this game, Indians observe the rules closely enough to protect their positions. Despite their private indignation and sporadic militancy, even "bad," or militant, Indians are prudent enough to moderate overt opposition with frequent shifts to "good" dimensions of the Indian role.

Whites are likewise constrained to minimize their abusiveness and maximize their expected generosity and benevolent paternalism for the sake of critical social and economic relationships. Ritual kin ties between townsmen and Indians, and estate employees and Indians, superimpose compadrazgo norms of mutual trust and cooperation on those of socioeconomic interdependence. This does not produce egalitarian relationships, but it does result in the more cordial application of interethnic rules. Even where ritual kin ties do not obtain, Indians and whites adjust their interactions in terms of one another's special attributes and accordingly bend the rules. The rules are not broken, however, so that Indians become non-Indians.

ETHNIC ASSIGNMENTS AND CHANGING
ECONOMIC CIRCUMSTANCES

Inasmuch as most residents were born in their respective communities, and, in any event, information regarding parentage is readily accessible, nearly everyone can be located on at least a partial genealogical map. The few hacienda employees born elsewhere are classified as non-Indians in accord with their occupation. Otherwise, residents are either Indian or white, depending on their parents' category. One's self-identity and that assigned by others tend to be in agreement.

The category of some hacienda residents is ambiguous. These are the would-be Cholos, the upwardly mobile offspring of Indian parents. This predominantly young male population meets the specifications for Cholo status in terms of dress, literacy, facility with Spanish, and familiarity with non-Indian institutions. Yet, only the members of this segment define themselves and each other as Cholo; neither Indians nor whites grant them the ethnic change commonly recognized in theory. In the abstract, Indians and whites applaud Indian efforts to become "civilized." In actually confronting such efforts, most whites reward ambitious Indians with, at best, bemused tolerance, whereas Indians tend to disparage and overtly resent the attempted change. To their frustration, aspiring Cholos are locally defined and treated as Indians.

Paradoxically, the ascriptive system continues to recruit personnel to the Indian ethnic category and its associated circumscribed roles, although the hacienda's changing economic requirements have been withholding commensurate occupational roles. Without the appropriate occupation, would-be Cholos are structurally marginal Indians. Until several decades ago, oncoming generations of Indians were provided with a place on the hacienda work force so that a rough balance was maintained between the number of Indians and the available traditional roles. Birth as an Indian automatically recruited one to a menial role, and obligated him to labor on the estate, but this status also gave him automatic access to the subsistence plot which is the basis for surviving as a bona fide member of the estate community. This has ceased to be the case; there are now more Indians than menial roles. The growing category of aspiring Cholos is symptomatic of this imbalance and the consequent new strains on traditional relations both within and between ethnic groups.

Earlier in this century, Hacienda Atahualpa was increasing its cultivated acreage and, correspondingly, expanding its labor force. Soon after marriage, young men acquired their own subsistence plots, with the attendant estate obligations, and established domestic groups independent of their parents'; their youngest brother inherited their father's land and estate role. Between 1920 and 1953, the number of permanent Indian laborers rose from 71 to 132. But the incremental process had begun to grind down even before 1953. Between 1953 and 1961, only three Indians were added to the regular labor force. This same period witnessed the introduction of technological innovations under the auspices of the estate's lessee, one of the nation's leading breweries. New types of seed and breeds of cattle, artificial insemination, chemical fertilizers, tractors, and combine harvesters transformed the estate into what Indians call a "real marvel." But agricultural production expanded without a concomitant increase in unskilled laborers. Specialists were recruited throughout the area and, in an unprecedented move, an Indian became a tractor operator, albeit part-time and temporary. This golden age lasted until the lease expired; except for one tractor, the equipment was withdrawn and the Indian specialist retreated to the unskilled ranks. What remained was a modern orientation with respect to mechanized equipment, with the result that unskilled laborers became supernumeraries.

As already mentioned, the hacienda population numbered 1,509 in 1964. About 90 percent of that number are Indian. Nonetheless, only 26 percent of the Indian males over fifteen years old, or 135 persons, are *huasipungueros*, permanent laborers with subsistence plots. To some degree these plots support 1,237 persons; one-third of them are referred to as *apegados*, the landless dependent kin "stuck on" to the subsistence plots of permanent estate laborers. For the most part, the laborers' married sons or brothers, and their families, whose labor the estate no longer requires, account for the *apegado* category. This new substratum within the Indian community—an object of both Indian and white pity—furnishes the "surplus" Indians who become would-be Cholos.

The principle of ultimogeniture has persisted despite changing man-land relationships. The combined effects of this principle and the hacienda's restricted hiring policy now destine most older sons to be landless and dependent on their brothers' largesse for access to a homesite and land on the subsistence plot. Because Atahualpa offers little more than temporary employment for about a dozen men during the summer harvest and planting seasons, most members of the oncoming generations anticipate only a tenuous future in the estate economy.

Being forced from traditional occupations assumes critical proportions when local negotiations depend on land as collateral. For example, credit and loans from townsmen, or special favors from estate employees, rest on what the estate laborer offers in the way of sharecropping concessions. The *apegado*, or "surplus" Indian, has no bargaining power in dealings with local non-Indians. He fares slightly better with Indians by exchanging his labor for the right to plant on a subsistence plot. But his landless status makes the young *apegado* socially undesirable, and regarded as the worst possible marriage choice. The situation is further aggravated when other Indian-associated roles are unavailable in this area, and whites foreclose specialized niches both at the hacienda and in town. Nor, lacking capital and entrepreneurial experience, can they move into town. On the one hand, this sector has little stake in behaving like traditional Indians. On the other hand, as long as they are restricted from specialized occupational roles, the non-Indian mannerisms they adopt must, perforce, remain vacuous symbols and the Indian category a fixed one. Facing no viable future as either Indians or non-Indians, this disenfranchised population gravitates towards external job opportunities.

Ordinarily these men work as seasonal rural laborers on other highland estates, and less often, on coastal plantations. Cities or the burgeoning oil industry in the eastern lowlands are less attractive.

Regardless of the particular external context, the feined or real ignorance and submissiveness required for hacienda living have little survival value. On the other hand, initiative, assertiveness, non-Indian manners, and inconspicuous Western dress are more adaptive to the competitive and individualistic social environments outside the Atahualpa locale. These attributes do not guarantee the migrant's successful search for stable employment—he competes with scores of others in similar economic straits—but they bring less discriminatory treatment and more options. This is partly due to the "categorical" rather than "structural" nature of relationships associated with the seasonal job exodus. As Mitchell defines these (1966:51–52), the former involves strangers in "superficial and perfunctory" contacts, whereas the latter entail "enduring patterns of interaction. . . ." Where strangers are involved, relationships are necessarily organized according to standardized expectations. As tangible symbols of ethnic category, attire and speech advertise the relative positions of interacting persons and provide a basis for selecting the appropriate mode of interaction by triggering the stereotype. Indians who relinquish the symbols of their customary status and successfully manipulate the symbols identifying a superior category may elicit the greater respect ordinarily accorded non-Indians. How one comes by one's advertised status, that is, whether it is ascribed or not, is irrelevant.

Enterprising Indians who skillfully manipulate their social contacts outside the hacienda stand to convert seasonal wage work to steady employment. Lang (1969:80–118) reports this to be the case at San Pablo, an important coastal sugar plantation that recruits thousands of highland Indians for its annual cane harvest. The permanent labor force, which has been expanding in response to the comparatively dynamic coastal economy, absorbs some migrants, initially at the lowest semiskilled level. As the highlanders begin to resemble *costeños* culturally and move up the occupational hierarchy to more specialized roles, established residents who hold skilled roles are inclined to admit them to their own white category. However, Lang also notes that the plantation's managerial elite reserves white status for itself while relegating lower occupational levels to Mestizo status, the local equivalent of the Cholo.

Several former estate Indians now hold responsible positions in communities within easy reach of Atahualpa. Although the parentage of these men is either known or surmised, their occupationally specialized roles have been sufficient to validate their status aspirations and give them parity in the non-Indian communities and institutions in which they now regularly participate.

As some "surplus" Indians gain permanent status-validating employment, their own objectives are met and the community is rid of disruptive, but potentially innovative persons, and left to those better served by traditional roles. But most aspiring Cholos encounter only seasonal employment and, as a result, remain permanent but periodic hacienda residents. They must come to terms with the dilemma posed by dual but conflicting statuses—the preferred Cholo one superficially accorded outside the hacienda and the disparaged one, which offers the holder no apparent strategic value but which, in its symbolic form, has been the only one locally permissible. To the extent that these ambitious Indians are incongruous with localized patterns of Indian-white relations, hacienda residents also face a dilemma. In adjusting to these misplaced Cholos, traditional Indians and whites unwittingly conspire to safeguard their own respective positions by refusing to acknowledge the aspiring Cholos' claims to superior status.

Indians are disinclined to endorse Cholo claims and thereby admit their own inferiority, as well as reduce their controls over persons who provide labor on their own subsistence plot. More important, Cholos cannot reasonably expect subservience from Indians without having access to the specialized occupational roles, whether those of town specialists or estate employees, and the associated economic power that buttresses status distinctions and commands respect. Without fear of reprisals, Indians opt to ignore what they regard as the pretentiousness of mere ethnic peers.

Aspiring Cholos present a more serious challenge to the structure of traditional authority and influence within both the Indian community and household. Although the rules of interethnic relations stress egalitarianism, age, and the experiential learning that presumably accompanies it, endows older men with respect and influence well beyond the confines of their own extended kin group. But having adopted the attitudinal posture of their new reference group, would-be Cholos disdain the admonitions of "senile old men" along with "Indian ways"; the Cholos' undisguised contempt, and resentment of older men, has often erupted in verbal or physical violence between them.

Authority at the household level is vested in the landholding laborer. In the mature family, he is also the father and a patriarch whose power base is the meager subsistence plot; his authority over the subsistence plot and its inhabitants is equivalent to the patron's over the hacienda. Youngest sons who anticipate succeeding to their fathers' roles tend to conform to the expected subservient filial, and Indian, roles. Rebellious older sons are more prone to dispute parental wishes, particularly, but not exclusively, in the matter of inheritance. Sophisticated men have on occasion successfully challenged their younger brothers' claims to the family patrimony, such as it is, by persuasively petitioning the government bureaucrats installed in Quito (the national capital) to recognize them as legitimate heirs to the estate role.

Their limited identification with Indian interests also reduces the aspiring Cholo's financial and moral support of and active participation in the few communitywide activities. With no obvious advantage to be gained from the Indian role, "good" or "bad," these men are more likely to be onlookers than participants at traditional fiestas involving ritual reaffirmations of Indian status. The militant Indian role dedicated to improving estate working conditions is likewise irrelevant, and hardly worth the risk, for persons with no foreseeable local future. Indeed, the very presence of these jobless men who, by necessity, stand ready to replace recalcitrant Indian laborers is a continuing threat to an already weak labor organization. Aspiring Cholos are, thus, anathema for people with vested interests in the system even at the lowest hierarchical level.

The 1964 agrarian reforms ushered in a new economic phase and a localized reform project designed for Atahualpa. Innovative agricultural practices and social organizational forms which portend new roles and greater wealth for hacienda residents have been introduced. One concrete outcome is a legally constituted cooperative whose members are drawn exclusively from the estate community. If the somewhat utopian plans materialize, the cooperative will be the ultimate owner, manager, and beneficiary of the greater part of estate resources. Meanwhile, under the auspices of the reform agency, responsibility for low-level policy decisions and technical roles fall to elected hacienda residents. An official policy of "protective discrimination" reserves these specialized posts for Indians. Now that skills, literacy, and initiative are prerequisites for filling certain roles, would-be Cholos have a distinct adaptive advantage. As they move into specialized niches, Indians tend to accord them the respect due an elevated ethnic-occupational category; they presently stand to become the new *señores.* However, because they cooperative, like the hacienda from which it emerged, has need for few specialists, and cannot absorb the available males as permanent unskilled laborers, seasonal migration and underemployment are persistent features. For the time being, most aspiring Cholos remain in anomalous positions.

With the passing of the traditional estate economy and its particular labor requirements, playing the ignorant and humble Indian is no longer especially rewarding. The hacienda population at large may well shed the stigmatizing symbols of Indian ethnicity, discard its self-effacing manner, and upwardly revise its image in its own and others' view. Ultimately, the community may redefine its status from Indian to Cholo. Conceptually, this is allowable. But it is also allowable that the townsmen's initial advantages, coupled with the benefits they are themselves deriving from the reforms, will maintain, if not increase, relative status differences. Hacienda residents may indeed be called Cholos, but they will still be "country bumpkins" where townsmen are concerned.

CONCLUSION

An ascriptive basis for ethnic-occupational roles insures the continual and unambiguous allocation of persons to the skilled and unskilled positions crucial to a preindustrial estate economy. An elaborate set of proscriptions, supported by a rationale stressing the biological basis of social inequality, closes ethnic and occupational categories to all but those who belong on the basis of ancestry. These recruitment practices intensify structural stresses when reduced labor needs, or population expansion without increased labor needs, upset a rough equilibrium between the number of persons in ethnic categories and the number of occupations allotted to these categories. The ascriptive system then becomes a regulatory mechanism for controlling competition and strife between members of different ethnic strata. It does so at the cost of new stresses on the system generated by displaced Indians who are expected to play subordinate roles without the occupational base that hitherto supported them. Inevitably, a system predicated on the availability of a passive labor reserve sows the seeds of unrest in the form of necessarily ambitious and increasingly assertive Indians who are structurally marginal men in their natal communities.

In superficial encounters with non-Indians outside the hacienda, "surplus" Indians who adroitly manipulate the symbols of non-Indian ethnicity stand to be provisionally treated as if they were the persons represented by those symbols. But a new ethnic status, where structural relationships obtain, is contingent on acquiring occupational roles involving control over resources more valued than labor.[3] When personnel located at all levels of the occupational hierarchy encounter few opportunities for advancement, an emphasis on ascribed roles protects the non-Indian's favored access to specialized roles, reduces the access to even menial roles, and precludes movement out of the lowest levels. Conceptually, the ethnic system provides for the Indian's movement into specialized roles on the basis of his performance or achievement. Under conditions of economic expansion, when recruitment places greater emphasis on one's own abilities, Indians may, in fact, successfully ascend the ethnic-occupational ladder. As long as the local and national agrarian economy offers few such opportunities, however, ancestry remains a significant factor in role recruitment.

NOTES

¹ Some landholders still manipulate the payment of cash wages into another labor binding device by withholding cash wages but providing advances in kind or in cash during the wageless period. The meager and irregularly paid cash wage rarely balances the outstanding advances, especially if they have been manipulated to the landholders' advantage. Supervisors carefully log the advances and the number of hours worked. But illiterate Indians who are also inept with simple arithmetic cannot verify the tallies that may not only permanently indebt the laborer, but produce transgenerational debt peonage (cf. *Ministerio de Prevision*, 1953:15, 18; CIDA 1965:143).

² The phrase also categorically distinguishes bound hacienda Indians from so-called free landholding Indians (*indio libre*), "so-called," because landholding Indians are frequently forced into hacienda orbits in order to gain limited access to the land and water resources haciendas monopolize (cf. CIDA 1965:173–177). Free Indians recognize estate Indians as a separate and lesser category and regard them as social inferiors as well as undesirable mates (cf. Rodriguez Sandoval 1949:87).

³ I should note that there are exceptional highland Indians who eschew ethnic reclassification as a route to economic mobility. Among them are the well-known weaver-merchants of Otavalo, who exploit their distinctive garb to identify themselves to each other and to their clientele as producers and purveyors of specialized goods. Indeed, on the face of it, they seem presently to be involved in something akin to a "retribalization" process, in Cohen's sense of the term (Cohen 1969).

LITERATURE CITED

Barth, Fredrik, Ed.
   1969   Ethnic Groups and Boundaries. Boston: Little, Brown and Co.

Burgos, Hugo
   1970   Relaciones Interétnicas en Riobamba. Instituto Indigenista Interamericano. Ediciones Especiales: 55 Mexico.

Casagrande, Joseph B.
   1970   Strategies for Survival: The Indians of Highland Ecuador. Paper read at the 39th International Congress of Americanists, Lima, Peru.

Cevallos, Pedro Fermin
   1889   Resumen de la Historia del Ecuador desde su Origen hasta 1845, Vol. 6. Guayaquil, Ecuador.

Cohen, Abner
   1969   Custom and Politics in Urban Africa: A Study of Hausa Migrants in Yoruba Towns. Berkeley: University of California Press.

Colby, Benjamin N., and Pierre L. Van den Berghe
1969 Ixil Country: A Plural Society in Highland Guatemala. Berkeley: University of California Press.

Comité Interamericano de Desarrollo Agrícola
1965 Tenecia de la Tierra y Desarrollo Socio-Economico del Sector Agrícola: Ecuador. Washington, DC: Union Panamericana.

Gould, Harold A.
1971 Caste and Class: A Comparative View. Reading, MA: Addison-Wesley Modular Publications No. 11.

Greaves, Thomas C.
1972 The Andean Rural Proletarians. Anthropological Quarterly 45:65–83.

Harris, Marvin
1964 Patterns of Race in the Americas. New York: Walker and Co.

Lang, Norris
1969 Tradition and Transformation in the Industrialization of an Ecuadorian Sugar Plantation. University of Illinois, Urbana: unpublished Ph.D. dissertation. Ann Arbor: University Microfilms.

Lehman, F. K.
1967 Ethnic Categories in Burma and the Theory of Social Systems. *In* Southeast Asian Tribes, Minorities, and Nations. Peter Kunstadter, Ed. Princeton: Princeton University Press.

Miller, Solomon
1967 Hacienda to Plantation in Northern Peru: The Process of Proletarianization of a Tenant Farmer Society. *In* Contemporary Change in Traditional Societies, Vol. 3. Julian H. Steward, Ed. Urbana: University of Illinois Press.

Ministerio de Prevision
1953 Hacienda Gatazo Grande. Informe 10. Instituto Ecuatoriana de Antropólogia y Geografia. Quito, Ecuador.

Mitchell, Clyde J.
1966 Theoretical Orientations in African Urban Studies. *In* The Social Anthropology of Complex Societies. London: Michael Banton, Ed. Tavistock Publications.

Nadel, S. F.
1957 The Theory of Social Structure. New York: Free Press.

Rodriguez Sandoval, Leonidas
   1949   Vida Economica-Social del Indio Libre de la Sierra Ecuatoriana. Washington, DC: Catholic University Press.

Salz, Beate R.
   1955   The Human Element in Industrialization. American Anthropological Association Memoir No. 85.

Wagley, Charles
   1959   On the Concept of Social Race in the Americas. *In* Contemporary Cultures and Societies of Latin America. Dwight B. Heath and Richard N. Adams, Eds. New York: Random House.

11

Urban Indian Identity in Kansas: Some Implications for Research

C. HOY STEELE

Baker University, Baldwin City, Kansas

Since World War II, American Indians have been migrating from rural to urban areas faster than any other ethnic or racial group. U.S. Census figures reveal that between 1960 and 1970, native Americans moved to cities at a rate four and one-third times that of blacks and eleven and a half times that of whites (U.S. Bureau of the Census 1972:262).[1] Approximately half the nation's Indian population now lives in cities.

Social scientists who have studied this demographic phenomenon have recognized that such an extensive ethnic population shift raises the possibility of significant changes in cultural adaptation and social organization. Many scholars have proceeded on the mistaken notion, however, that the overall result of Indian urbanization is acculturation or assimilation into the larger, non-Indian society.[2] In this paper, I wish to examine briefly and to challenge several assumptions that under-

167

lie this notion. Then, I shall present ethnographic data to suggest an alternative focus to the acculturation/assimilation model.

The first erroneous assumption of many urban Indian studies is that movement from reservation to urban area necessarily or automatically implies a corresponding change from "Indian" to "white," in both consciousness and behavior. The basis for this notion is unclear, but two hypotheses may be offered. The first is the obvious numerical discrepancy between non-Indians and Indians. One scholar, writing about Indians in Spokane, Washington, states, "The assumption made in this study is that the smaller American Indian society will be assimilated into the larger white society . . ." (Roy 1963; see also Price 1968; White and Chadwick 1972). Indians are expected to become absorbed by the dominant society as a teaspoonful of strawberry milkshake becomes absorbed in a large glass of vanilla milkshake.

Secondly, there appears to be an underlying overemphasis in many studies upon the contrast between reservation and urban life. *Reservation* implies both rural and "folk" life, terms frequently placed in opposition to "urban" at one extreme of a continuum in the literature of the social sciences (see Redfield 1947). Furthermore, most reservations are in fact rural by customary standards and probably exhibit as many characteristics of "folk societies" as can be found in this country. These obvious ecological contrasts between reservation and city, however, tend to veil equally important linkages. Joseph Jorgensen (1971) and others (notably Indian political activists) have argued that Indian reservations are totally integrated within the political economy of the dominant society, and thus lie within the sphere of large urban centers. The economic problem of the reservations, therefore, is not underdevelopment—lack or underutilization of resources—but exploitation—lack of control of resources. Jorgensen cites Bureau of Indian Affairs statistics for 1968 to the effect that out of a total of 170 million dollars in agriculture grossed on reservations, Indians received only $58.6 million,

> 16 million of which was derived from rents and permits to non-Indians. This means that 127.4 million dollars, or 75 percent of the gross from agriculture, went to non-Indians who paid Indians 16 million dollars, or roughly 12 percent of their gross, for exploitation of Indian lands (1971:81–82).

One consequence of the fact that Indians do not control the economic resources on their reservations is endemic poverty. A second is that many reservation Indians commute to urban areas to find work. An example of the link between reservation residence and urban work patterns may be found in a study (Steele 1972) that included two small reservations in Kansas, Prairie Band Pottawatomi and Kickapoo, respectively. These reservations are less than fifty miles from a city of 125,000 people, Prairie City (pseudonym). Many reservation residents commute daily to work in Prairie City and in the large industrial plants located just outside the city limits.

Since approximately three-fourths of the 1,000 native Americans residing in Prairie City are Pottawatomi or Kickapoo, much of the social life of the Prairie City Indian community also includes reservation residents. (On Friday nights, for example, one of the most likely places to find a Pottawatomi—young or old, male or female, reservation or urban—is at one of two bowling alleys in Prairie City.) Likewise, residence in Prairie City rarely removes an Indian beyond the influence of the reservation. A high level of locally based tribal participation is maintained on the reservations. This includes, among other things, three active native religious groups, annual powwows, frequent dinners and other events, and a high degree of informal visiting and socializing. The proximity of the reservations to Prairie City facilitates convenient participation in these events on the part of the urban Indians. Indeed, many Indians in Prairie City have indicated a strong preference for reservation life, but feel constrained to reside in the city for economic reasons. In short, the acculturation/assimilation model excludes much of the total environment of both reservation and urban Indians, which encompasses both reservation and city as well as other places mentioned below. Utilization of this model produces a distorted view leading to unwarranted conclusions and generalizations.

The assumption by some social scientists that an Indian moving to a city will alter his identity from Indian to white may also result in a poor research design. One indicator of acculturation or assimilation used for many urban Indian studies is intermarriage. Little attention is paid to the non-Indian spouse, since—the reasoning seems to go—whites are numerically dominant, and therefore it is the Indian partner who will change. This assumption may be valid in many cases; however, the *extent* of its validity is not a priori evident, but is a matter for research. As an untested indicator it probably distorts more than it reveals. Most Indians, reservation or urban, are constantly exposed to non-Indians; for them to marry outside their ethnic group may be no major step. On the other hand, for a white to marry an Indian may require a complete resocialization into a more or less separate subsociety and the internalization of new norms and meanings. Sufficient data were obtained to comment on eighteen interracial marriages between Indians and non-Indians [3] in and around Prairie City. Three couples seem to be entirely non-Indian oriented; in each case both partners appear to have adopted white values, life styles and primary associates. Six couples are split along racial lines—that is, the Indian partner is more or less active within the Indian community while his or her partner is not. Of the remaining nine couples, five are participants in both the non-Indian and Indian communities.[4] The full extent of their participation in the non-Indian society is unknown, but they are fairly active in the Indian community on a primary group level. The remaining four couples present striking examples of *non-Indian* acculturation and assimilation to *Indian* ways.[5] The non-Indian spouses are thoroughly Indian in behavior and values.[6]

If one major assumption of many urban Indian studies is that Indians who move to cities will become absorbed into the white urban mass, a second seems to be that survival in the city is possible by no other means, that assimilation and acculturation are *prerequisite* to successful urban adjustment (e. g., see Price 1968; Roy 1963; White and Chadwick 1972). The subtle but pernicious quality to this point of view is that it places the burden of successful adjustment totally on native Americans themselves. The city—that is, the dominant society—is thus exonerated for any difficulties experienced by Indians within it. The logic employed is of the type that holds that poor people themselves— not the political and economic institutions of the society—are responsible for poverty. Just as liberal social scientists spoke glibly of "the Negro problem" a decade ago, now we have "the urban Indian problem," if on a smaller scale.

Rarely, in urban Indian studies, are urban social institutions subjected to critical scrutiny. What are realistic possibilities for employment at a living wage in the city? How extensive is discrimination, and what forms does it take? What agencies and organizations provide meaningful assistance to low income urban immigrants or residents of whatever ethnic group? Another parallel may be drawn with black-white relations of the volatile 1960s. The Kerner Report (Report of the National Advisory Commission on Civil Disorders, 1968) consisted of bold assertions about the racist nature of the society in its analysis; but its major recommendations amounted to changing black people instead of restructuring the society.[7] Similarly, the chronic poverty and attendant social problems of American Indians are widely deplored; no mistreated ethnic group evokes greater sympathy. Yet our social scientific and social policy ideologies permit us at the same time to require conformity to Anglo, middle-class patterns as the price for inclusion in the rewards of the society.

Even accepting as reality the intransigence of our social institutions and the cultural and class intolerance of the society as a whole, the question must still be asked as to whether acculturation and assimilation *actually* provide the only roads to successful adaptation to the city. This question leads to the internal life of the urban Indian population, which most studies fail to examine. It is my belief that this arena promises to be a far richer source of social scientific knowledge than the investigation of acculturation and assimilation. The latter inquiry, by the very nature of the questions asked, neglects more important questions. For example, are traditional Indian values retained in the city? To what extent are primary relations among urban Indians limited to the ethnic group? Does an urban Indian organizational life exist? Is there such a thing as an Indian "community" within the urban world? My own participant observation study, which lasted over a year, revealed interesting answers to these questions, at least for Prairie City. In the remainder of this paper I shall comment upon Indian values, group life, and community in regard to the Indian population of this city.

Repeatedly, and in a variety of ways, Indian people residing in Prairie City expressed adherence to values that they interpreted as uniquely Indian and that they advanced as credentials of Indianness. These include the legal criteria of Indian identity set forth by the Bureau of Indian Affairs, namely, certifiable membership in a recognized tribal group, which is in turn dependent upon blood descent of specified degree (usually one-fourth) from other members of the group. In addition to the legal requirements, the informal credentials of Indianness include in part an emphasis upon family life and obligations (especially in regard to the extended family), the ethic of mutual aid (especially to kin but also to other tribal members and other Indians), participation in a variety of Indian ceremonies, "Indian" physiognomy and skin color along with a high percentage of Indian "blood," ability to speak a native language, observation of matters of etiquette in personal relationships such as noninterference in the affairs of others, a rejection of what are commonly regarded as peculiarly Anglo traits of acquisitiveness and some forms of competition, and adherence to certain attitudes toward nature.

These and other values have been defined by the community as denoting Indian identity; as such they have become badges or credentials of that identity for those who adhere to them.[8] Of course, no one can fulfill to the maximum all the criteria of Indianness, leaving practically everyone open to the charge of not being totally Indian at some point. This also means, on the other hand, that some flexibility of life-style has to be recognized. (The relevance of this point will be noted presently.)

The people who share the values summarized above come together in a variety of formal and informal activities. I shall mention only the former. They include a Powwow Club, a smaller Indian singing and dancing group, all-Indian bowling teams, softball teams and basketball teams, an Indian (mission) Protestant Church as well as Indian religious groups on the reservations, and an Indian Center with numerous programs that have an impact upon and involve many Indian people within the city. These are Indian activities by virtue of the fact that, with few exceptions, Indian people are the only participants. For many, primary relations in Prairie City are totally restricted to these groups and to other Indians on an informal basis. In short, an Indian subsociety exists within Prairie City.

A portion of the Indian population of Prairie City—approximately 25 percent—remains to be discussed. These people did not come from nearby reservations, but migrated from Oklahoma, Nebraska, the Dakotas, the Southwest, or more distant points. This is a diverse group, but on the whole, it includes a large proportion of individuals who are particularly adept at dealing with white society, and thus who are especially useful to several Indian organizations. On the other hand, these outsiders—that is, non-Pottawatomis and non-Kickapoos, and therefore non-Kansans [9]—tend to possess relatively few credentials of Indianness in the eyes of the local Indian people.[10] The Indian Center, which became the hub of Indian activity in Prairie City while I was engaged in fieldwork there, presents a good example of an Indian organization with both constituencies; its experience also illustrates one way of effectively managing this problem.[11]

The Indian Center entered its second year of existence—the year that determined whether or not it would succeed as an organization—during the fall of 1970. The election of a governing board at that time produced eleven new members, balanced perfectly between the local and nonlocal groups. Four of the new members clearly were outsiders with somewhat dubious Indian credentials, four were local people with rather good Indian credentials, and three were in between. Interestingly enough, these last three comprised the elected officers of the board. The president, a woman in her early forties, was half Pottawatomi, had been raised on the Pottawatomi reservation, and spoke the tribal language. On the other hand, she was also half Seneca and was enrolled in the Seneca tribe in Oklahoma. She was thus able to identify with both the local and nonlocal groups and provided the essential leadership that got the Indian Center off the ground, funded, and growing. The vice-president, a full-blooded Pottawatomi man in his twenties, possessed the liability of having been raised apart from other Indians and of having received a college education.[12] For a while, he seemed able to relate to whites and nonlocal Indians better than to his own tribesmen. He too, however, became a hard worker and provided effective leadership. The secretary-treasurer, half Pottawatomi and half Chicano, married a black man and gradually became more involved in the black community than in the Indian community.[13]

The Indian Center has continued to bridge the gap between local and nonlocal Indians. One of the arenas of this bridging activity has been the struggle of the Pottawatomi tribe to regain nearly 1,400 acres of land lost a century ago to the Jesuit Order of the Catholic Church. After months of negotiation secured promises from the Jesuits to return the land, difficulties emerged with the Bureau of Indian Affairs over who would control it. The conflict—which continues at this writing—has evolved into a major struggle between the Pottawatomis and the Bureau. The point is that in this struggle the Pottawatomis have welcomed aid from Indians of other tribes and from other Indian organizations. Thus, the Indian Center has been able to be firmly supportive of the Pottawatomis without threatening any of its own Prairie City constituency.[14]

A final factor contributing to the sense of Indian ethnic identity and community in Prairie City is the existence of a network of parallel activities in neighboring towns, cities, and states that provide occasions for Indian people to come together from a wide geographical area. All-Indian bowling, basketball, and softball tournaments are held frequently in neighboring cities and especially in Oklahoma. Powwows in the summer and dinner dances during the rest of the year take place throughout the plains states and stimulate frequent travel to distant and nearby places. Every organized group is part of some kind of regional or national network, or both. These networks in addition to the factors already mentioned—particularly ties to local reservations—further contribute to the sense of Indian identity and foster a sense of community within the local geographical unit.

I wish to specify the meaning of the term *community*. It may be defined as "a self-conscious social unit and a focus of group identification" (Theodorson and Theodorson 1969:64) :

> Community also implies a certain identification of the inhabitants with the geographic area, . . . a feeling of sharing common interests and goals, a certain amount of mutual cooperation, and an awareness of the existence of the community in both its inhabitants and those in the surrounding area (Theodorson and Theodorson 1969:65).[15]

According to this definition, not all persons within the Indian population can be considered part of the Indian community. The excluded aggregate consists of all those who, either by choice or circumstance, do not participate in the life of the Indian community—that is, with other Indians. However, the wide range of Indian activities and the possibility of selective participation in them provide considerable flexibility. Flexibility is enhanced further by two facts relating to the earlier discussion of Indian values. First, since no one can fulfill all the criteria for Indian identity, the standards often are not applied rigorously. Second, the sine qua non of Indian identity is participation in the life of the community. This participation, more than anything else, identifies someone as "Indian," for it is a public statement of belonging and pride in belonging.[16]

Prairie City is one of hundreds of urban areas where Indians live in significant numbers. It is clear that in Prairie City, the concepts that have dominated so many urban Indian studies, acculturation and assimilation, not only are out of place but are distortive of social reality. I suspect that the same is true for many other urban areas as well. Prairie City is rather different from Chicago or San Francisco or Oklahoma City, for these are large metropolitan areas where the Indian population is to be counted in thousands rather than hundreds. Even in these major urban areas, however, I imagine that communities exist within the Indian population in considerably greater measure than most researchers have noted. Surely in smaller cities near reservations, like Rapid City, South Dakota (see White n.d.); Provo, Utah; Flagstaff, Arizona; Sioux City, Iowa; and many more; parallels to the situation in Prairie City could be found.

Native Americans probably have little to fear from Anglo culture. (The Indian demise is predicted and proven wrong in every generation.) Indeed, Indians frequently attest to the superiority of their own cultural orientations. What Indians have to fear is Anglo political and economic power. Perhaps scholars interested in the maintenance of Indian identity, particularly those who see that identity as valuable for Indians and non-Indians alike, will recognize this fact, and begin to turn their research sights on Anglo governmental institutions and corporate power as they are brought to bear upon Indian communities. Fieldwork with Dow Chemical, anyone? [17]

NOTES

[1] Between 1950 and 1960 the number of Indians in cities almost tripled, and in the next ten years the urban Indian population more than doubled (U. S. Bureau of the Census 1969:29; 1972:262).

[2] In the past, there has been considerable confusion involved in the usage of these concepts. Anthropologists have concentrated their attention on acculturation, and sociologists have been preoccupied with assimilation; yet to an extent both groups have been discussing the same thing (Roy 1963).

I follow Gordon's (1964) usage of these terms. Acculturation, which Gordon calls cultural or behavioral assimilation, refers to the adoption by one group of the culture traits of another. My employment of the term assimilation is parallel to Gordon's structural assimilation, which denotes the merger of the social networks of two groups, including their primary groups and social institutions.

[3] Two-thirds of the Indians are married to whites; the remainder are married to Chicanos. The extent of non-Indian acculturation/assimilation is unrelated both to these ethnic differences and to race-sex correlations. Three marriages between Indians and blacks are not included because they present a special case. See Steele (1972:113–114, 211).

[4] McFee (1972a) found that, among the Blackfeet, accommodation to white society does not destroy "Indianness" in many cases. Bicultural adaptation, in other words, is not a zero-sum game.

[5] As Hallowell (1963) has observed, a strict definition of acculturation means culture change of groups rather than of individuals. The latter phenomenon is designated "transculturalization" by Hallowell. I have chosen to use the former term because of its greater familiarity and general usage. To my knowledge, no one has yet suggested a term for (structural) assimilation on an individual rather than a group basis.

6 The criteria employed in the above discussion are adherence to Indian values and participation in the Indian community, both of which are amplified below.

7 To believe that Indians must adjust on white terms is also to ignore fundamental rights of freedom of expresssion and association. These values receive lip service, but in reality native Americans are at best merely tolerated, regarded as curiosities. Prairie City appears to be rather typical in that relatively few non-Indians recognize the potential learning to be gained from the Indian cultures of this nation. Nor do they seem to appreciate the value of the insights about American society in the late twentieth century that can be found within Indian communities (see Steele 1972:Chapter 6).

8 This list of values is closely paralleled by the findings of other researchers (cf. Gearing 1970; McFee 1972b; M. Wax et al. 1964; R. Wax and Thomas 1961).

9 Two small, contiguous reservations are located on the Kánsas-Nebraska border. These reservations, Sac and Fox and Iowa, respectively, are almost depopulated. The people from these tribes living in Prairie City are so few that they are excluded from this discussion.

10 Pottawatomis and Kickapoos are closely related in origin, have lived as neighbors in Kansas for more than a century, and maintain a high rate of intermarriage. In short, except for minor differences they share a common culture. One might expect that nonlocal Indians, arriving in Prairie City from a different cultural milieu, would be judged unfairly according to local standards of "Indianness"; however, I found that this was not the case generally. Members of the local tribes did not expect Indians from other tribes to conform to local custom, but to their own tribal ways. In other words, a person's reputation for "Indianness" was not dependent on his membership in a particular tribe. This may have meant, on the other hand, that nonlocal Indians who were culturally conservative to the point of not even associating with Indians from the local tribes might have acquired a false reputation of not being very Indian.

11 The Indian Center, where I was a regular volunteer worker, was an important base of operations during my fieldwork.

12 A widespread recognition exists in Indian communities that one of the major functions of education is socialization. Indians with a college education thus are often regarded as being "less Indian."

13 The only "campaigning" in this election was by the woman who attained the presidency. There were no "slates" and no piloting or railroading of candidates; all nominations came from the floor. Those in attendance were fairly representative of the total Indian Center constituency.

14 Some disagreements have arisen within the Indian Center over this issue but they have followed ideological contours that cut across tribal affiliations.

15 These tests, which the Indian population meets, are more important than the standard of economic independence, which it cannot meet, in specifying the existence of a community (Theodorson and Theodorson 1969:65).

16 For example, a Kickapoo man once spoke approvingly of a woman who "acted and talked Indian" even though she could pass for a full-blooded white and was married to a white.

17 The Dow Chemical Company is "developing" the Zuni Pueblo. For an excellent, in-depth analysis of governmental and corporate exploitation of one Indian tribe (Tesuque Pueblo), see Akwesasne Notes (1973). For an account of the Pottawatomis' struggle with the Bureau of Indian Affairs, see Jessepe (1972).

LITERATURE CITED

Akwesasne Notes
  1973 Pueblo Is Not for Sale. Rooseveltown, NY: Published by the Mohawk Nation. Early summer issue, pp. 38–39.

Gearing, Fred
  1970 The Face of the Fox. Chicago: Aldine.

Gordon, Milton M.
  1964 Assimilation in American Life: The Role of Race, Religion, and National Origins. New York: Oxford University Press.

Hallowell, A. Irving
  1963 American Indians, White and Black: The Phenomenon of Transculturalization. Current Anthropology 4:519–531.

Jessepe, Lester L.
  1972 Our story: The Prairie Band Pottawatomi Indians (How to survive when the government tries to steal everything you have). Mimeographed. Mayetta, Kansas.

Jorgensen, Joseph G.
  1971 Indians and the Metropolis. *In* The American Indian in Urban Society. Jack O. Waddell and O. Michael Watson, Eds. Boston: Little, Brown and Co. pp 66–113.

Kemnitzer, Luis S.
  1969 Reservation and City as Parts of a Single System: The Pine Ridge Sioux. Mimeographed. Paper presented at meeting of the Southwestern Anthropological Association, Tucson, Arizona.

McFee, Malcolm
  1972a The 150 Percent man, a Product of Blackfeet Acculturation. *In* Native Americans Today: Sociological Perspectives. Howard M. Bahr et al., Eds. New York: Harper and Row. pp. 303–312.
  1972b Modern Blackfeet: Montanans on a Reservation. New York: Holt, Rinehart and Winston.

Paredes, J. Anthony
  1971 Toward a Reconceptualization of American Indian Urbanization: A Chippewa Case. Anthropological Quarterly 44:256–271.

Price, John A.
  1968 The Migration and Adaptation of American Indians to Los Angeles. Human Organization 27:168–175.

Redfield, Robert
1947   The Folk Society. American Journal of Sociology 52:293–308.

Report of the National Advisory Commission on Civil Disorders
1968   Washington, DC: Government Printing Office.

Roy, Prodipto
1963   The Measurement of Assimilation: The Spokane Indians. American Journal of Sociology 67:541–551.

Steele, C. Hoy
1972   American Indians and Urban Life: A Community Study. University of Kansas. Lawrence, Kansas: unpublished Ph.D. dissertation.

Theodorson, George A., and Achilles G. Theodorson
1969   A Modern Dictionary of Sociology. New York: Thomas Y. Crowell Co.

U. S. Bureau of the Census
1969   Statistical Abstract of the United States. 90th ed. Washington, DC: Government Printing Office. p. 29.
1972   Census of Population: 1970. General Population Characteristics. Final Report PC(1)—B1 U.S. Summary. Washington, DC: Government Printing Office. p. 262.

Wax, Murray L., Rosalie H. Wax, and Robert V. Dumont, Jr.
1964   Formal Education in an American Indian Community. *Supplement to* Social Problems 11(4).

Wax, Rosalie H., and Robert K. Thomas
1961   American Indians and White People. Phylon 22:305–317.

White, Lynn C., and Bruce A. Chadwick
1972   Urban Residence, Assimilation and Identity of the Spokane Indian. *In* Native Americans Today: Sociological Perspectives. Howard M. Bahr, et al., Eds. New York: Harper and Row. pp. 239–249.

White, Robert A.
n.d.   The Development of Collective Decision-Making Capacity in an American Indian Community: The Politics of an Urban Indian Ethnic Community. Mimeographed. MS.

12

Mississippi Choctaw Identity: Genesis and Change[1]

BOBBY THOMPSON and **JOHN H. PETERSON, Jr.**

Choctaw Tribal Government and Mississippi State University

Most discussions of Southerners and of southern identity ignore the diversity that actually exists within the South. While the term *southeastern* Indians is well known and widely used in textbooks dealing with the native Americans, it refers to Indians in an earlier cultural area, not to a specific racial or cultural group within what is known as the South. The role of Indians within the general framework of Southern history or in relation to other inhabitants of the southeastern United States has attracted little scholarly attention (Peterson 1971). Yet, as a result of living in the rural South, the southeastern Indians have adopted many cultural traits which are often attributed to rural Southerners, both white and black. This is especially true for the Mississippi Choctaws. The Southern Baptist Church is the largest and most active religious denomination among the Choctaws. Corn bread and pork form important parts of the Choctaw diet. Choctaw women make quilts and, until recently, most Choctaw men wore bib overalls. Even the spoken English of most Choctaws bears a heavy Southern accent. A few years ago, a western Indian visitor to Mississippi asked jokingly, "Are you sure you guys aren't red-necks instead of redskins." There is little that is clearer to a Choctaw in Mississippi than that he is a Choctaw, neither white nor black, not a Mississippian or a Southerner, but a Choctaw. One's identity as a Mississippi Choctaw is not so much southern as shaped by the experience of existing for the past 140 years in the rigidly stratified society of the rural South.

Throughout their recent history, Choctaws have lived in an area where rigid social boundaries have been drawn between white and black, and discrete behavior expectations have been held for members of each group.[2] As a result, a central theme in the development of Choctaw identity has been to maintain a separate status and identity outside the prevailing social system (Peterson 1970b:274). The more rigid the social separation of white and black and the greater the differences in the role expectations for each group, the more the Choctaws have been forced to maintain complete separation from both elements of local non-Choctaw society to achieve a separate identity. The problem of achieving a separate identity was most acute following the dissolution of the Choctaw government and the loss of a territorial base in Mississippi in 1829 and 1830. Under the provisions of the Treaty of Dancing Rabbit Creek in 1830, individual Choctaws were entitled to claim the same amount of land as incoming white settlers and to have full white status as citizens of Mississippi (DeRosier 1970:174–184). The treaty provisions, however, were never fulfilled. Most Choctaws found themselves landless in a society based on the distinction between white landowners and landless black slaves. As a result, even though only 15 percent of the Choctaws left Mississippi during the first year of removal, in the following years the majority of the population felt that they had no alternative but to accept removal (Tolbert 1958:88, 106).

Only approximately one thousand Choctaws remained, avoiding both removal and contact with the local non-Choctaw society by existing as squatters on unoccupied marginal land. Here they could continue to follow in modified form their life as hunters and subsistence agriculturalists without having to own land or to accept slave status. The disruption of removal and major loss of population either destroyed or greatly weakened the traditional internal units of Choctaw society, the clan, moiety, town, and geographic district, while the importance of maintaining a strict social separation from non-Choctaws and a separate Choctaw identity became more important.

Little significant change occurred in the remaining Choctaw population from the end of the first period of removal until after the Civil War. With the freeing of the slaves, agricultural workers were no longer dichotomized as landless slaves or landowning whites. Some whites, as well as most blacks, began working for shares on agricultural land owned by whites. It was now possible for Choctaws to work as sharecroppers without totally sacrificing their separate identity as neither white nor black. As white landowners increasingly brought marginal land under cultivation during the last decades of the nineteenth century, more and more Choctaws were forced to make this adaptation. By 1900, the clearcutting of much of the remaining forest lands made this transition to sharecropping virtually complete. At the same time the Choctaws were adapting to the sharecropping system, two new institutions were reintroduced into the Choctaw population, the church (Farr 1948) and the school (Langford 1953).

There seems to be little doubt that these changes were accompanied by a change in Choctaw identity, according to the writings of H. S. Halbert. Halbert was the first teacher among the Mississippi Choctaws after removal. During the twenty years from 1883 until 1903, he lived and taught in the various Choctaw communities, learned the language, and became a serious student of Choctaw history. He was thus an active participant during this entire period of transition, and his writings are the only documentary sources on this period.

One gathers from Halbert that prior to entering sharecropping the Mississippi Choctaws remained very conservative except in those aspects of traditional culture affecting the larger kinship and governmental structures disrupted by removal. Traditional beliefs survived to the extent that, as late as 1884, a Choctaw woman was secretly executed for practicing witchcraft in one of the more traditional communities (Halbert 1896:536). But by 1898, Halbert (1898:25) records that "it is no longer fashionable to have a full belief in Bohpuli and Kishikanchak." [3] One of the most important elements in this change was the establishment of Choctaw churches and schools. Traditional leaders opposed these institutions, arguing that this would lead to forced removal as had occurred two generations earlier (Halbert 1894:576). A major factor in the acceptance of both the Choctaw church and school seemed to have been the use of the Choctaw language in both institutions, and the rapid development of local Choctaws as both teachers and preachers (Halbert 1894:575; Brown 1894:11, 21; Peterson 1970b:60–89). The church and school not only resulted in the decline in traditional beliefs, but stimulated other changes as well. Decline in the use of Choctaw names became evident, and English surnames were assumed as the names of families (Halbert 1898:25). Likewise, the final elements of the moiety division fell into disuse.

By 1900, most Choctaws were no longer living as squatters, but were working as sharecroppers in small, stable, farming communities. In most cases, these communities were located in the same area where the Choctaws had lived as squatters in the preceding decades. These communities were centered around a small church building, which also served as a school. Halbert indicates that these two institutions could only be considered simultaneously, since the church was invariably followed by a school, and both institutions not only shared the same building but also served the same group of people. In this and other respects, the Choctaw communities came to outwardly resemble white and black rural farming communities.

Some more traditional groups, secure on remaining uncultivated marginal land, refused to adapt to what they believed was a non-Choctaw way of life. It should be noted that a few traditional families continue today to refuse to send their children to school, and have little to do with other Choctaws. But the transition was virtually complete in most Choctaw communities prior to 1900. As early as 1893, Halbert (1894:574) undertook a survey of school-age Choctaw children and found that in all but one community where schools were available between one-half and two-thirds of all Choctaw children were enrolled in school. By 1896, Halbert (1896:25) stated that the "modern Choctaw" applied the derogatory term "Obalafoka" or "No Breeches" to his ancestors.

There seems little doubt that a change in identity had occurred for most Choctaws. This change affected primarily the behavior appropriate for continuing to be considered a Choctaw. Pride in the Choctaw language continued undiminished and was actually a factor in allowing change in other aspects of the Choctaw way of life. Likewise, the emphasis on maintaining a separate and distinct Choctaw identity remained as strong as ever. Halbert (1896:540) stated, "There is hope for a people having such a pride of race as the Choctaws, which they often evince by the expression 'Chahta sia hokat,' 'I am a Choctaw.' "

Thus in spite of the outward similarity between Choctaw and non-Choctaw communities, the Choctaw communities remained exclusively and distinctively Choctaw.

In 1903, the federal government made a second major attempt to remove all Mississippi Choctaws to Oklahoma as part of the allotment of Choctaw land in Oklahoma prior to statehood (Debo 1934:273–275). As with the first removal, many Choctaws refused to leave Mississippi. Fifteen years later, recognizing the failure of removal efforts, the Bureau of Indian Affairs began working with the Choctaws remaining in Mississippi. These developments, however, had little major impact on the Choctaw way of life (Jennings, Beggs, and Caldwell 1945) or on Choctaw identity. A land purchase program did result in the establishment of seven small reservations centered on the largest remaining Choctaw farming communities. Some increase in population concentration occurred in these communities, but the majority of the population continued to live as sharecroppers off reservation land.

Major changes in the Choctaw way of life and potentially in Choctaw identity did not occur until after World War II. During the 1950s, lower cotton prices and mechanization of agriculture resulted in a decline in sharecropping (Peterson 1972). At the same time, acute racial discrimination resulted in jobs in local factories being restricted to whites except for the janitorial jobs, which were restricted to blacks. The result was an increasing rate of unemployment, underemployment and out-migration of Choctaws. With the passage of the 1964 Civil Rights Act, however, the doors of local factories were opened to Choctaws. To an increasing degree, younger Choctaws have chosen factory work as an alternative to out-migration or more traditional agriculturally related occupations (Peterson 1970a: 16–21).

In many ways, the current shift in occupations by Choctaws parallels the shift in occupations by Choctaws during the 1880s and 1890s. Just as the increasing cultivation of marginal lands forced an adaptation to sharecropping, the decline in sharecropping is forcing an adaptation to newer forms of work today. As in the 1880s, a host of additional changes are accompanying this change in occupation. No longer forced to live on the lands they formerly farmed, increasing numbers of Choctaws are moving to the reservation, where a massive housing program is underway. In 1969, only 15 percent of the Choctaw population lived in modern homes with bathrooms and hot water (Harris 1970:10). By the end of 1973, 47 percent of the population will live in such homes (Martin 1972:12). Even earlier, a massive change in ownership of consumer items was evident. The percentage of Choctaw households having a gas or electric cooking stove increased from 37 in 1962 to 82 in 1968, and the percentage having an electric refrigerator increased from 26 to 82 during the same period (Peterson, 1970a:22).

This transition is occurring at a different rate in the various Choctaw communities. Modernization of housing and facilities is occurring most rapidly in the larger Choctaw communities located closest to nonagricultural employment opportunities. Particularly, the Pearl River community is coming to resemble a small modern town. Change is slower in the more remote communities distant from nonagricultural employment, and there is a definite migration from these communities to other communities such as Pearl River (Peterson 1972).

In addition to this migration from off-reservation land onto the reservation and from one community to another, there continues to be some migration away from the Choctaw communities. In the past, this out-migration was primarily to distant cities outside Mississippi, where Choctaws could find better employment opportunities. With the passage of the Civil Rights law and the resulting decline in overt discrimination against Choctaws outside the immediate Choctaw area, an increasing number of Choctaws are living outside the Choctaw area, but remaining within Mississippi. In 1960, 83 percent of all Choctaws in Mississippi lived in or adjacent to one of the seven reservation communities (Peterson 1970a:5). But by 1970, this had declined to 59 percent. While census data concerning Indian populations is always to be questioned, it is clear that within the Choctaw area, there is an increasing concentration of population on the reservation, while at the same time there is an increasing percentage of Choctaws located elsewhere in Mississippi outside Choctaw communities.

There seems little doubt that the massive changes currently underway will affect Choctaw identity, but it is too early to predict exactly what these changes might be. Choctaws in or adjacent to the reservation communities will probably continue to maintain their separate status and identity from other segments of the local population. Choctaw identity has been maintained too long and under too difficult conditions to be lost lightly. Moreover, the social dichotomization that has forced the Choctaws to emphasize their separate identity does not appear to be changing rapidly. Most local whites still perceive Choctaws to be nonwhite, and others perceive Choctaws as black citizens, especially in the areas of major Choctaw population concentration. Older local whites at times even refer to a Choctaw as "nigger," even though they are clearly aware that the individual in question is an Indian.

While the Civil Rights Act has resulted in the lessening of discrimination in local public schools and factories, discrimination by local merchants and policemen makes living in a reservation community preferable for most Choctaws. Furthermore, the tribal government has greatly increased its capacity within recent years to provide jobs and services to the Choctaw people. In 1971, the tribal council adopted self-determination as a tribal goal with the long-range aim of operating all programs and services currently operated by the Bureau of Indian Affairs (Mississippi Band of Choctaw Indians 1972). Although the concept of Choctaw self-determination is not yet completely accepted as a goal by the bulk of Choctaws, it would seem that it can offer a goal and commitment which may be central to the emerging Choctaw identity in the coming years.

The success of the tribal government in providing jobs and services to the Choctaw people will probably directly affect the need for Choctaws to move away from the reservation to seek better opportunities elsewhere. Within recent years, a return migration of those long absent from the Choctaw communities has occurred. Regardless of the success of Choctaw self-determination, it is probable that increasing numbers of Choctaws will choose to live outside the Choctaw communities in Mississippi. For these Choctaws, at least, the rigid separation of Choctaws from non-Choctaws and the emphasis on a Choctaw identity as separate from a non-Choctaw identity will probably decline in importance. This transition will occur slowly, as the children of such out-migrants grow up in non-Choctaw–speaking communities. The use of the Choctaw language seems to continue to be the key to Choctaw identity within the established Choctaw communities and this will probably remain so for some time to come. In fact, Choctaw self-determination, which includes local control of the Choctaw school system, may help prevent rapid change in certain aspects of Choctaw identity through educational programs emphasizing Choctaw language, music, and history.

Thus far, this description of origin and change in Mississippi Choctaw identity has been presented primarily from the viewpoint of an outsider. There is no alternative to this approach in dealing with the early postremoval period, since few documents exist relating to the Choctaws during this period. Even in the late nineteenth century, from which documentation is more adequate, the Choctaw point of view can only be glimpsed through material recorded by non-Choctaws. This is not to say that the description of origin and change in Mississippi Choctaw identity as thus far presented is incorrect. It is essentially accurate as an overall summary, especially as it deals with Choctaw identity in relation to non-Choctaws.

What has been lacking is insight into Choctaw identity as it functions within the Mississippi Choctaw population. Indeed, the very word *Choctaw* is alien to Choctaw identity within the Choctaw communities. *Chata hapi-a-kat, Chata il-anompoli hi-kat na-yuppa hapi-a* means "We are Choctaw and we speak Choctaw proudly." The word *Choctaw* is an English word, not a Choctaw word. As such, it is essential in communicating with non-Choctaw–speaking people, but is not used in conversations between Choctaw-speaking people.

Early travelers in what is now the state of Mississippi used a variety of spellings to attempt to indicate the word *Chata*. It would require a linguist to determine why many speakers of European languages need to end each syllable of the native word with a consonant, or why the particular form *Choctaw* became the accepted form in the English language rather than the original *Chata*. Older Choctaws simply comment, "The white man couldn't spell very well." For our purposes, however, it is sufficient to note that identity within the Mississippi Choctaw population remains Chata rather than Choctaw. For the remainder of this paper, we will continue to use the word *Choctaw* except in terms of identity. Here, we will use Chata identity to refer to identity within the Choctaw population as distinct from the Choctaw identity which has already been described.

The fact that Chata identity remains rooted in a native word points out the key significance of the use of the Choctaw language. As late as 1968, only 6.7 percent of Mississippi Choctaw households used English rather than Choctaw as the primary language at home (Peterson 1970a:23). While there are no data on language used at home for earlier periods, it is certain that even this degree of English usage is a recent phenomena. For example, in 1968, 4.7 percent of heads of Choctaw households felt that they had an excellent command of English, and this was an increase from 2.9 percent in 1962. Thus, for most of Mississippi Choctaw history, a primary requirement for being Chata was being able to speak Choctaw. When Mr. Emmett York, the long-time Choctaw tribal Chairman was asked in English if a particular individual was a Choctaw, he replied, "If he speaks Choctaw, he's Choctaw." The question would not have been asked except in English.

As a general rule, if a person speaks Choctaw, he is a Chata in the eyes of the Choctaw people. The one exception is a slight hesitation by some more traditional Choctaws to identify a person speaking Choctaw as Chata if his skin color is noticeably different. Such a person would not be identified as non-Chata, but rather the question of identity would be avoided. For example, when one older individual was asked in English if a particular person with a noticeably lighter skin was a Choctaw, the response was, "So they say." Such individuals themselves do consider their identity to be Chata, and for all practical purposes they are accepted as Chata.

Speaking Choctaw is more important than simply distinguishing between Chatas and non-Chatas. It is the key to making two important distinctions within the population of Choctaw speakers. The first of these distinctions is based on community of birth. It will be remembered that, following removal, only the local group remained the primary unit of identity within the Choctaw population. These local groups, which formed the basis for what are now called Choctaw communities, varied in size. Some were composed of only one or a few closely related extended families. Others might have had many more extended families not so closely related. Where these local groups were sufficiently large —for example, Bogue Chitto—marriage took place almost exclusively within that group. Although intercommunity migration has increased in recent years, this is still largely true. In the Bogue Chitto Choctaw community, in 1968, only 15.8 percent of all households contained a husband or wife or both who were born in another Choctaw community. Smaller local groups were forced by close kinship ties within that group to become largely exogamous, with individuals seeking mates in other nearby groups. Smaller communities may have a majority of married couples with one or both partners being born in another Choctaw community. These outsiders would be predominantly from nearby communities. For example, men and women from Standing Pine tend to marry people from the adjacent communities of Red Water, Pearl River, and Conehatta, with few if any seeking mates from the more distant communities of Tucker and Bogue Chitto. As a result, the Choctaw communities today, and to an even greater extent in the past, are not just locality groups, but to a large extent also kin groups. The vast majority of relatives of any given individual live within one community. Correspondingly, any given community is composed primarily of related individuals. The one major exception to this, the Pearl River community, has already been mentioned.

In addition to being a kinship unit, to a greater extent, the individual Choctaw community is also a speech community. While one does not often think of geographical barriers to movement in east-central Mississippi, it must be remembered that until recently this area was undeveloped in comparison to other parts of the state. The first paved road did not come through Neshoba County, where three Choctaw communities are located, until the 1920s. Even in the 1940s, the clay roads leading to the Choctaw communities were almost impassable during the wet winter months. Movement to the other communities, separated by a minimum of fifteen miles, was difficult even in the summer for people without cars. Furthermore, as late as 1962, less than one-third of all Choctaw households had a car (Peterson 1970a:22). Thus, until quite recently, the Choctaw people in Mississippi were living in separate isolated communities with very limited movement of people between communities. It is natural that under these circumstances linguistic differences in spoken Choctaw developed among the different Choctaw communities. These differences are smallest when comparing small communities located in relative close proximity. They are greatest when comparing the larger, primarily endogamous communities existing at some distance from each other. Thus, the greatest dialectical difference is found between the residents of Bogue Chitto and Conehatta Choctaw communities. While Choctaws from different communities have little difficulty understanding each other, they likewise have little difficulty determining the community of birth of an individual based on his word choice and use or failure to use certain in-fixes and suffixes.

In addition to differences in Chata as spoken in different communities, there are some differences in spoken Choctaw according to age, but intergeneration differences are minor compared with intercommunity differences. As would be expected, younger Choctaws generally have a smaller vocabulary and are more likely to make what the older people might call grammatical mistakes. Variation by age is smallest between individuals from more traditional households in more traditional communities. Choctaws can generally tell both what community another Choctaw is from as well as whether he learned to speak

Choctaw before he learned to speak English. Indeed, it is often possible to make this latter distinction based only on hearing a Choctaw speak English.

Understanding these points, it is now possible to begin to discuss Chata identity rather than Choctaw identity. Older Choctaws have probably never met any Indians other than Choctaws. For them, there is no word in Choctaw which means Indian.[4] An Indian other than a Choctaw will probably be described as *Ehata holba*, "just-like-Chata." It is not that they are viewed as being less Indian than the Choctaw, but they are viewed as being less Chata than a Choctaw. While "just-like-Chata" will suffice for describing Indians who are non-Chata speakers spoken Choctaw is also used as an important means of determining identity within the Mississippi Choctaw population. The basic point of reference is not the ability to speak Choctaw, but the ability to speak the traditional Choctaw of a given community. Because of the linguistic differences between different communities, there is no generally accepted version of Choctaw. In fact, a discussion of which version of Choctaw is more authentic or more traditional can cause some disagreement between people from different communities.

Most communities recognize that either Conehatta or Bogue Chitto are more traditional, based on the larger percentage of Choctaw speakers as well as the retention of a larger vocabulary and more traditional forms in these communities. Individuals from these communities would speak of people from other communities as being less Chata, meaning that they are less able to speak the full, traditional Choctaw of these communities. Thus, *Chata* as an identity not only separates non-Choctaw speakers from *Choctaw* speakers, but it also uses as a base point of reference the dialect of a given Choctaw community. Chata identity then, unlike Choctaw identity, has meaning in a specific community dialect. Thus far, I am speaking of Chata identity from the viewpoint of older Choctaws. Older people might feel that younger Choctaws unable to use the correct form and pronunciation are therefore less fully Chata, but this would never be stated.

While younger Choctaws maintain this community-based Chata identity, there is a greater tendency for younger persons to identify with elements larger than a given Choctaw community. For example, while an older person will be unlikely to have an identity as an Indian, increasing numbers of younger people have Indianness as part of their identity. This is not age alone, but rather exposure to and knowledge about things outside a given Choctaw community. Several factors are involved. Economic improvement in the Choctaw communities has enabled more Choctaw households to own radios and television sets. In 1962, 36 percent of Choctaw households owned a television set. By 1968, the percentage had increased to 75 (Peterson 1970a:22). Prior to the construction of a Choctaw high school in the early 1960s, few Choctaw students came in close contact with Choctaw students from other communities. Within the last three years, this breadth of exposure has expanded to include Chitimacha and Seminole students enrolled in Choctaw Central. Likewise, younger Choctaws are more likely to have traveled to Oklahoma and other areas and met other Indian students, as well as to have read about other Indians in white-oriented textbooks. As a result, younger Choctaws are interested in plains Indian dancing and beadwork, which are of little interest to older Choctaws. Thus, contact with members of other tribes and with the mass media image of Indians has resulted in younger Choctaws beginning to see their identity as *Indian*, rather than exclusively Chata. It is important to note that identity as Indian is not replacing identity as Chata, but rather is in addition to Chata identity. Younger Choctaws usually retain a strong identity as Chata in its original community sense, especially while living and working in the reservation area.

The gradual assumption of an identity as Indian in addition to an identity as Chata does not exhaust the possibilities of identity change for the Mississippi Choctaws. As was mentioned in the first section of this paper, the adoption of Choctaw self-determination as a goal by the Choctaw Tribal Council has potentially important consequences for identity change within the Choctaw population. The word *self-determination* was used by President Nixon (1970) to describe the Indian policy of his administration. It implies independence from federal control without loss of federal support. The key phrase states that the Indian "can assume control of his own life without being separated involuntarily from the tribal group." The phrase *Choctaw self-determination* has proven very meaningful in communicating to non-Choctaws the goals and objectives of the Choctaw tribal government.

Choctaw self-determination remains, however, primarily a governmental identity and goal, not an individual identity. Since Choctaw identity is different from Chata identity, Choctaw self-determination is of necessity more meaningful to non-Choctaws than to Choctaws who continue to think in terms of Chata identity. To understand the implications of this, we must briefly look at the political and legal aspects of Choctaw identity and Chata identity.

The governing body of the tribe is a sixteen-member tribal council based on somewhat proportional representation from each of the seven Choctaw communities. Each councilman is a member of a special community and represents that community's interests within the tribal council. The council itself elects one of its members to be chairman. The chairman not only officiates at council meetings, but he is the only full-time elected official responsible for the overall operation of the tribal government.

Individual Choctaw voters participate in the Choctaw tribal government by voting for councilmen from their community. But their community does not necessarily reflect a community of residence so much as a community of birth and identity. Even though a Choctaw may live in the city of Philadelphia, in Neshoba County, he may still be a voting member or even an elected representative of the Red Water community in the adjacent county. Only the largest Choctaw community, Pearl River, has a significant percentage of people who are in-migrants from other Choctaw communities. These in-migrants may well continue to vote in elections of their community of origin, which is their community of identity.

As the largest community in both acreage and population, and as the seat of tribal governmental and educational efforts, it is necessary to center many facilities and services in Pearl River. These are often looked upon by Choctaws from different communities as belonging to Pearl River, not to their own community. Facilities and services are thus identified with a particular community, just as Chata identity applies to a particular community.

The location of the tribal government and many services and facilities in the Pearl River Community has other implications. As was pointed out earlier, Pearl River is the most modern Choctaw community in appearance and contains the largest number of out-migrants from other communities. These Choctaws are more likely to live in modern homes and work in local industry or for the tribal government. Pearl River is the only large Choctaw community in which original inhabitants form a minority of the population. Members of other Choctaw communities increasingly speak of Pearl River as "not being a Choctaw community," or as not being a community at all, but rather a melting pot. These feelings are best illustrated in the words of a second-grade Choctaw student in one of the more traditional communities. The teacher was discussing a story about an Indian boy, and was trying to get across the point that all the members of the class were Indian. Being so young, they all still believed that they were Chata. When she asked do any of you know where I can see an Indian, one little boy raised his hand and said, "There's a lot of Indians up at Pearl River."

This perception of Pearl River is directly related to the perception of the tribal government centered in this community. In order to gain resources necessary to achieve Choctaw self-determination, the Choctaw tribal government has been forced to adopt many of the standard bureaucratic procedures necessary to handle governmental contracts. In recent years, the Choctaw government has changed from a tribal council acting as advisor to the Bureau of Indian Affairs to a complex governmental structure. The tribal government operates programs in all the reservation communities. In both scope of operation and method of operation, the Choctaw government is not Chata, but Choctaw. It is only indirectly based on the more traditional community-centered Chata identity. In the eyes of many Choctaws, especially older people, Choctaw self-determination can never be Chata self-determination. They may feel that self-determination carried out through bureaucratic forms defeats its own purpose. Yet, the only alternative seems to be the continued existence of a non-Choctaw bureaucracy operating all programs on the reservation.

This, then, is the problem in achieving Choctaw self-determination; a problem in developing a new identity and a form of governmental operation responsive to it. The older community-based Chata identity, being so deeply rooted in kinship relations, will probably never die as long as the Choctaw communities continue to exist. There is no question that a new Indian identity is being added to the older community-centered identity. But is there room for an additional identity that will imply a stronger commitment to the Choctaw people as a whole?

Indian identity does not provide a basis of commitment to the Choctaw people in Mississippi. Individual community identity alone does not provide the identity and commitment at the tribal level to build a sustained response in the decades ahead for the Choctaw people as a whole. But both these identities are essential. It is necessary for the Choctaws to reach out to identify with and to join in common purpose other Indian groups through such organizations as the United Southeastern Tribes. Because of the strength of community identity, it is necessary that this continue to form the basis for building a strong tribal identity. It is likewise necessary for tribal efforts to involve input from and permit self-determination in individual communities.[5] Three new programs, initiated this year, are built on such community input. If efforts in this direction are successful, it would seem that the strengthening of an intermediate level of identity between the individual community and the Indian people as a whole could play a major role in insuring the future well-being of the Choctaw people in Mississippi.

The total cultural pattern of the Choctaw people has undergone tremendous change in the past centuries. The way of life has changed from combined hunters and farmers to subsistence farmers to sharecroppers and now to industrial workers. At the same time, Chata identity has shifted from traditional kinship and geographic units to locality groups, to sharecropper farming communities, and to reservation communities. Given the total scope and degree of past changes, it will be surprising if the current Choctaw population is not able to adapt their sense of identity to meet the future, while remaining Mississippi Choctaws.

NOTES

1 While the authors of this paper are employed by the Choctaw tribal government, the opinions stated are those of individuals and do not represent the position of the tribal government or the agencies funding the specific programs on which we work. Because of the rapid changes taking place within the Choctaw communities at present, it should be acknowledged that while this paper presents two points of view on Choctaw identity, other individuals might well present other equally valid approaches. For this reason, it would seem appropriate to briefly state our own positions and experiences related to the subject of this paper and the individual responsibility for preparing it.

Mr. Thompson is a Mississippi Choctaw from the Bogue Chitto community, where his parents and grandparents were also born. He attended elementary school in the Bogue Chitto community, and high school in both Tennessee and at Choctaw Central. He completed the first two years of college in Meridian Junior College before enrolling in elementary education at Mississippi Southern University. While at Southern, he participated in the Indian Intern Program, working every other quarter in the Choctaw elementary schools. He attended one summer of graduate work at the University of Arizona. Rather than accepting a position as a teacher in a school operated by the Bureau of Indian Affairs, he chose to work for the tribal government. In 1971, he was elected as one of three tribal councilmen from the Bogue Chitto community and was elected by the tribal council as vice-chairman. From 1972 to 1973, he also served as administrative assistant to the tribal chairman and coordinated the daily operations of all tribal programs. He continues to serve as vice-chairman while directing the Choctaw New Careers Program funded by the Department of Labor.

John H. Peterson, Jr., first learned of the Choctaws while studying anthropology under Wilfrid C. Bailey, who had undertaken the first major socioeconomic study of the Choctaw population. From 1968 to 1969, he lived in the Choctaw area and directed a second tribal survey while collecting data for his dissertation. Joining the faculty at nearby Mississippi State University, he continued to be a frequent visitor to the Choctaw area, and assisted the tribal government in preparation of several grant proposals. In 1972, he secured a leave of absence to serve as chief planner of the Strategic Planning Center for Choctaw Self-Determination, funded by the Office of Economic Opportunity.

Mr. Thompson prepared the first draft of the inside point of view to Choctaw identity, while Peterson prepared the first draft of those portions of the paper giving the outside point of view. Thompson suggested needed revision on Peterson's draft based on his knowledge and experience as a Choctaw. Peterson suggested additions to Thompson's draft based on his knowledge of available statistical data. Joint revisions followed in an attempt to clarify both points of view, but no attempt was made to merge what were viewed by both authors as complementary interpretations.

Thompson is listed as senior author in recognition of the fact that his input was more essential than that of Peterson. While Thompson could provide additional insight into Peterson's analysis of historical and demographic material, Peterson's support for Thompson's analysis was primarily in terms of providing supporting data.

2 In this regard, the development of Mississippi Choctaw identity presents a major contrast with Oklahoma Choctaw identity, which has been described in terms of levels of ethnic identity by Bailey (1972).

3 These supernatural beings were an important part of Choctaw traditional beliefs (Swanton 1931:194–200).

4 Some Choctaw speakers might use the form *mashkoki* to refer to non-Choctaw Indians, although this more correctly indicates speakers of Muskogean languages.

5 It should be emphasized that the majority of tribal elected officials and employees realize the problems mentioned in this paper, although as indicated in note 1, their description of the situation might vary somewhat from that presented here. Analysis of existing situations by researchers is thus of little interest to persons participating in ongoing programs. For participants a clearer analysis of needs and the devising of creative solutions to problems is far more important than theoretical clarity in describing the situation. This does not mean that clarity in analysis is rejected at the reservation level, but clarity in analysis without an action component may well be rejected as pointless. Indeed, the authors' involvement in action programs led to this more formal analysis based on actual experience in dealing with problems at the reservation level.

LITERATURE CITED

Bailey, Garrick A.
1972   Being Choctaw: A Study in Levels of Ethnic Identity. Paper presented at the annual meeting of the American Anthropological Association, Toronto, Canada.

Brown, A. J.
1894   History of Newton County, Mississippi, from 1834–1894. Jackson: Clarion-Ledger Co.

Debo, Angie
1934   The Rise and Fall of the Choctaw Republic. Norman: University of Oklahoma Press.

DeRosier, Arthur H., Jr.
1970   The Removal of the Choctaw Indians. Knoxville: University of Tennessee Press.

Farr, Eugene
1948   Religious Assimilation: A Case Study of the Adoption of Christianity by the Choctaw Indians of Mississippi. New Orleans Baptist Theological Seminary: Ph.D. dissertation.

Halbert, Henry S.
1894   Indian Schools in Mississippi. *In* Biennial Report of the State Superintendent of Public Education to the Legislature of Mississippi for the Scholastic Years 1891–92 and 1892–93. pp. 574–576.
1896   The Indians in Mississippi and their Schools. *In* Biennial Report of the State Superintendent of Public Education to the Legislature of Mississippi for the Scholastic Years 1893–94 and 1894–95. pp. 534–545.
1898   Choctaw Schools in Mississippi. *In* Biennial Report of the State Superintendent of Public Education to the Legislature of Mississippi for the Scholastic Years 1895–96 and 1896–97. pp. 23–31.

Harris, Nick
1970   Initial Housing Element Choctaw Indian Reservation Areas. Jackson: Mississippi Research and Development Center.

Jennings, Joe, Vernon L. Beggs, and A. B. Caldwell
1945   A Study of the Social and Economic Condition of the Choctaw Indians in Mississippi. Mimeographed. Bureau of Indian Affairs document in the Department of Interior Library.

Landford, Etha
    1953 A Study of the Educational Development of the Choctaw In-
          dians of Mississippi. Mississippi Southern College: M.A. thesis.

Martin, Phillip
    1972 Immediate and Long-Range Needs for Physical Facilities at the
          Choctaw Reservation. Mimeographed statement on behalf of
          the Choctaw Tribe, Cherokee, North Carolina, December 6, 1972.

Mississippi Band of Choctaw Indians
    1972 Accelerated Progress Through Self-Determination. First An-
          nual Report of the Choctaw Self-Determination Project (July 1,
          1971–July 31, 1972.) Philadelphia, Mississippi.

Nixon, Richard
    1970 Indian Policy Statement. July 8, 1970.

Peterson, John H., Jr.
    1970a Socioeconomic Characteristics of the Mississippi Choctaw In-
          dians. Social Science Research Center Report No. 34. State
          College; Mississippi State University.
    1970b The Mississippi Band of Choctaw Indians: Their Recent His-
          tory and Current Social Relations. University of Georgia:
          Ph.D. dissertation.
    1971 The Indian in the Old South. *In* Red, White, and Black: Sym-
          posium on Indians in the Old South. Charles M. Hudson, Ed.
          Southern Anthropological Society Proceedings No. 5. Athens:
          University of Georgia Press. pp. 116–133.
    1972 Assimilation, Separation, and Out-Migration in an American
          Indian Group. American Anthropologist 74(5): 1286–1295.

Swanton, John R.
    1931 Source Material for the Social and Ceremonial Life of the Choc-
          taw Indians. Smithsonian Institution, Bureau of American Eth-
          nology, Bulletin 103. Washington, DC: Government Printing
          Office.

Tolbert, Charles
    1958 A Sociological Study of the Choctaw Indians in Mississippi.
          Louisiana State University: Ph.D. dissertation.

13

The Politics of Change: Southern Pluralism and Ethnic Identification

S. J. MAKIELSKI, Jr.

Loyola University, New Orleans, La.

That rapid political change is occurring in the American South requires little elaboration. One need only look at, for example, Virginia.
Two decades ago the stronghold of the most powerful state political
machine in the country, a rampart of Southern Democratic conservatism in the Congress, by the end of 1972 it had a Republican governor,
a Republican senator, and seven Republican representatives to only three
Democratic members of the House. The remaining senator classified
himself as an "Independent," and the lieutenant governor was the leader
of a Populist-liberal wing of the factionalized state Democratic party.
If one instance were insufficient to make the point, the roster of Southern governors who had come to office on platforms that carried appeals
to the black voter included virtually all of the traditional Deep South:

Louisiana, Mississippi, Georgia, and South Carolina. Florida, a state never considered to be a showcase of liberalism, produced a governor, Reuben Askew, who challenged the dean of liberal governors, Nelson Rockefeller, for national preeminence.

The examples could be multiplied. The more difficult problem, however, is to evaluate the nature, causes, and consequences of the changes. And, in attempting to make this evaluation, it is appropriate to focus on the intricate relationship of black politics to white politics in the South. First, however, it is necessary to offer some crucial caveats. The general schema advanced here is more in the nature of a series of hypotheses than proven conclusions. While excellent work has been done on both black politics and white politics in the South, much additional research and analysis needs to be done before any final conclusions can be drawn.[1] Furthermore, to point out the obvious, there are intrinsic dangers in treating the South as a homogeneous entity. The Louisiana Cajun, the Virginia "good old boy," the Atlanta corporate executive, the Miami Jew, the Birmingham black, and the Mississippi Delta tenant farmer are extraordinarily different people, derived from different cultural or subcultural traditions, subject to differing environments, both physical and social, and living under highly diverse political structures. Finally, the fundamental assumption of this paper is prone to challenge. There are those who could argue that the Southern leopard has not changed its spots one iota. People have been greeting a new South regularly each generation. And, or so it could be argued, one need look only at the strength of the Wallace movement, the results of the 1972 Florida school busing referendum, the events at Southern University in Louisiana, the prosecution of the members of the Republic of New Africa Movement in Mississippi, and the persistent election and reelection of racial conservatives, regardless of their party label, to Congress and state legislature to document the case.

These are serious arguments and must be treated seriously. The unproven (and perhaps unprovable) rebuttal here is that the base of Southern politics is in a period of transition. Change has occurred, and is occurring, but the change has by no means taken its final form, nor is that final form predetermined.

SOME BASIC POLITICAL STYLES

The majority of political scientists agree that, as a nation, America's politics can be described as "pluralistic," that is, involving multiple centers of power which compete with each other in a never-ending struggle to gain dominance.[2] There is sharp disagreement as to *how* pluralistic the system is.[3] There is even less agreement as to whether the national pattern prevails for the various regions, states, and localities of the country.

Some of the difficulty lies in the usefulness of *pluralism* as a descriptive structural term. It is obvious, for example, that Congress and the president are at frequent odds; that the political parties contest each other in innumerable elections; that city and state governments often are in conflict; and various pressure groups attempt to gain special advantages at the cost of other groups who fiercely fight back. As certain critics have pointed out, however, this pattern still can produce one of "stable unrepresentation," a system in which vigorous competition may occur, but in which some, or even most, elements of the population are excluded from participation.[4]

It may be appropriate, therefore, to go a step beyond pluralism to suggest that pluralistic politics can be shaped by one of three different political "styles" (see Figure 1).[5] It is necessary to amplify the illustration a bit by a brief sketch of these three styles.

FIGURE 1

THREE POLITICAL STYLES

Style	*Governmental Role*	*Characteristic Form*	*Individual Role*
Coalition	Distributor	Corporate	Beneficiary
Ideological	Promulgator	Bureaucratic	Adherent
Identification	Defender	Fraternal	Member

Coalition Politics

As its name suggests, coalition politics involves the meshing of disparate groups, interests, and aspirations in order to gain the maximum benefits that the government has to offer. The government is viewed as a distributor (or redistributor) of material resources, subsidies, opportunities, controls, and restraints. Those who win can expect to be the maximum beneficiaries, but even "losers" are not necessarily left out of any payoffs, since they may be potential allies sometime in the future.

Characteristically, coalition politics is expressed through "corporate" forms of organization. These are organizational forms which attempt to absorb and embody collective interests, usually of an economic or pragmatic type.[6] The political party, most pressure groups, and many governmental agencies conform to the corporate structure.

The individual tends to see his role in this political style as an instrumental one; he expects to be a beneficiary of victories, perhaps directly through a job or contract; more often indirectly through organizational and governmental policies that advance his interests. If he feels that the coalition or the form within the coalition to which he belongs does not serve his interests, he is free to withdraw and find another winning combination, because he plays the game not for love but to win what he wants.

Coalition politics is the most familiar style to the American, not necessarily because it is invariably our political style, but because it is the standard mode of analysis we have learned to use in describing our system. Much as with laissez faire economics—from which coalition analysis is derived—we tend to assume a politically rational man is one who bands together with others because collective effort is essential to win control of government, or some part of it.

Ideological Politics

It is an accepted political truism that Americans are not fond of ideological politics or ideologies. Generally, however, this does seem to be the case. In an ideological style of politics, the role of government is to express and advance the ideology; belief is maintained by relatively rigid bureaucratic forms, since these provide the hierarchy, record-keeping, and rule-processing methods essential to maintaining ideological purity both within and outside of government. The important role of the individual is to be an adherent to the ideology, a true "true believer."

There may actually be an element of magical thinking in ideological politics: a faith that if impurities are expunged from the body politics all other blessings will then automatically follow. Some Americans, at some times, turn to ideological politics as a preferable style to the pragmatism of coalition politics. Both left- and right-wing groups have, on occasion, managed to exist for long periods, even though they have rarely won any notable political victories.

Identification Politics

Identification politics are based on a sense of "we," especially when there is a distinctive "they." Whether the we-ness is founded on ethnicity, religion, cultural traditions, or some other criterion, the role of government is to defend and preserve the integrity of group membership. It may do so through miscegenation laws, sumptuary laws, the removal of "aliens," restrictive immigration practices, ghetto and apartheid laws, or any number of other processes and procedures. Characteristically, the basic organizational form is what can be called "fraternal," in which there may be highly egalitarian norms as long as members' "blood lines" are impeccable. The essential individual role is that of member of the identification group; deviant behavior can be tolerated, benefits will flow to the member, as long as he is a member and does not threaten group integrity.

Although Americans would be reluctant to admit it, we, perhaps, are more familiar with a politics of identification than our textbooks generally admit. Ethnic ticket-voting, suburban zoning laws, housing policies, and government personnel practices have frequently reflected strong aspects of identification politics.

As might be guessed, these brief descriptions leave more to inference than they fully explain. Further, it should be noted that each style as described is a prototype. In fact, it would be rare to find one in a pure form anywhere in the nation or in the world. Identification and ideological politics also provide instrumental benefits to members and adherents respectively, and probably could not function effectively unless they did so. Coalition politics may cheerfully use an ideological or identification element as a basis for building a winning combination, as any ward politician working the ethnic precincts of his jurisdiction well knows.

With this qualification in mind, however, the essential point must be restressed. That is, each style does represent a central tendency which can appear quite comfortably within the context of a pluralistic structure of politics. Factions within an ideology, or within an identification grouping, may dispute even violently, yet the essential style remains intact.

One further dimension needs to be added. Any of the three styles can be either exclusionist or inclusionist in approach, that is, operate to include more or fewer members of the society as active participants in the political process. Logically, one would expect coalition politics to be inclusionist, especially in the United States, where electoral majorities or pluralities are so important in winning the benefits of control of the government. As a rule, this would often be the case, but both ideological politics (especially) and identification politics can seek to enlarge their adherent-member bases. Conversely, all three styles may voluntarily accept a narrowing of the participatory base. As firmly coalitionist, for example, as many of the old-style political machines were, the bosses were not reluctant to restrict the number of active voters, since fewer voters made election victories more certain.

THE SOUTHERN VARIANT

With this general schema before us, we are now in a position to tackle the nature of Southern politics and black politics in the South.

Using the general model, we can say with a degree of confidence that white Southern politics has tended to be heavily identification in orientation, especially for the period from the end of Reconstruction until mid-twentieth century. Moreover, the identification base has been whiteness. Although the Populist Revolt saw an intense pluralistic struggle between "redneck" and Bourbon, only for a brief period did this pluralism envision the inclusion of the black Southerner as a member of a winning coalition.[7] Furthermore, what coalitions did occur tended to be in opposition to the black, rather than as inclusive of him.

Perhaps the most conclusive test of the identification base of white politics in the South is that the opportunity to draw the black into the system did, theoretically, exist. Either the Republicans or the Democrats, or some faction within one of the parties, could have chosen to become a party of the Southern underdog. Had the opportunity been taken, it is highly probable that winning coalitions could have been put together in state after state, at the local if not at the statewide level. In all fairness, it can be pointed out that the Northern states were slow to follow the black-white coalition route; yet, in a number of places, just this did happen, most notably in Chicago and New York City.

The relative exclusiveness of white pluralism in the South can be explained in a number of ways: as an historical phenomenon, as a function of deep-seated psychological fears, as a pattern of economic repression in which white stood to gain from black subservience. Any full explanation would, no doubt need to include all these factors. Probably, a full explanation would also have to include a political cultural variable. Southern politics was, and still is, in many places a "folk politics." Based on personalities, feuds, traditions of alignments, and (to non-Southerners) often confusing criteria of personal behavior as well as the more familiar class, status, and economic cleavages, the Southern politician was naturally more comfortable in fraternal political forms than corporate or bureaucratic forms.[8] And, there was simply no "logical" way the we-ness of white identification pluralism could be expanded to include blacks, given the communications and subcultural and social differences between the races. Nothing short of major changes could make Southern political behavior more expansionist in approach.

Major change is precisely what happened. The 1940s, 1950s, and 1960s brought drastic change. The role of government was reversed. Southern state and local governments served as competent defenders of white identification politics from the turn of the century to the mid-1940s and beyond. Progressively, however, the federal government dismantled that role: the white primary vanished, de jure segregation fell, the poll tax was abolished. Furthermore, however, the Voting Rights Act of 1965 went beyond a merely passive role in reducing barriers to racial integration. It undertook the registration and protection of black voters as *blacks*. The federal government haltingly moved toward a recognition of and defense of black identification.

Clearly, other factors played their part. Urbanization, the first surges of the postindustrial revolution, a steady black migration to the North and West (as well as a white migration both in and out of the South), and the growth of formal education, among other factors, have all helped erode traditional Southern pluralism in ways which are still incalculable.

What appears to have happened is that a kind of political no-man's-land was created: one in which substantial numbers of both potential black and white voters were suddenly accessible as high ground worth capturing. Coalition politics is the logical response to such a situation, and a coalitionism which is inclusionist rather than exclusionist.

As might be imagined, the process has not been so simple as a brief outline of the changes would indicate. First, a shift from identification politics to coalition politics requires not only adjustments in interpersonal relations but in the role of government. State and local governments must become benefit providers, and on a broad scale. In short, they must spend, and to do so, they must tax. The struggle is familiar enough in almost any place coalition politics is the dominant style, but where the elements of identification politics still persist, there will be those who resist strenuously taxing and spending for "them," and who are in a position to make easy alliance with those who resist spending because it is economically painful. In addition, a shift to coalition politics involves a major change in the rules of the game. Loyalty must be to a goal rather than a grouping; political forms must be built on efficiency models rather than links of kinship, friendship, ethnicity, and folkways; and the political leader is required to deliver not symbols but concrete benefits.[9]

Finally, however, a new dimension has been added. Broadened participation means a new set of demands. New initiatives appear, and as they do, both the traditional participants and the new ones are faced with terribly complex strategic choices.

SOUL AND THE SYSTEM

To this point, the discussion has concentrated on what seems to be significant changes in the stylistic base of white Southern politics. One of the most important of these changes, however, is that black Southerners have now found themselves in a political order where they are no longer necessarily passive outsiders but have the opportunity to be active participants.

From a highly general standpoint, it can be argued that not much more needs to be asked of a political system. If a citizenry has the option to participate, democratic norms have been served. From a less olympian viewpoint, however, the issues are not quite so simple, for several significant reasons.

First, the shift in Southern politics from white identification pluralism to inclusive coalitionist pluralism does not seem to be anywhere complete. Blacks have played a role in bringing the shift about, but for them to assume that changes will continue is not necessarily safe.

Second, it is in the nature of coalition politics to respond to the wheel that squeaks. And, by every index, it continues to be blacks who desperately need the education, the housing, the health care, the subsidies, the jobs, and the contracts that government can provide, that is, the "oil" that government distributes as benefits. Blacks must articulate a set of demands that expresses their needs and priorities to a leadership which does not automatically identify with those priorities or feel the same urgency.

Third, blacks are a statistical minority in the South, in the nation, in every state, and in all but a handful of local governments. In a system which emphasizes electoral politics, and where the winning coalition is the majority coalition, numerical minority status is a special handicap, and additionally so if that statistical status is also associated with some other status that runs counter to the predominant identification norms among the majority.

It is a political rule of thumb that an organized minority can always defeat an unorganized majority, but the rule works only if the minority *is* organized and agrees on its goals and strategies. The most demanding task facing the Southern black is selecting the appropriate strategy. To illustrate this point, it is valuable to examine a brief case study of a black organization which is attempting to handle just this task.

The setting is New Orleans, Louisiana, the state's largest city. New Orleans and Louisiana politics have their own unique flavor. Unlike most Southern states there is a clear-cut religious split which is reflected geographically in the Catholic southern portion of the state versus the Protestant north.[10] Since the first days of Huey P. Long, moreover, Louisianians have delighted in a free-swinging, rhetorically blood-and-thunder brand of politics that only recently has begun to moderate. In other respects, the state is very typical. At the end of Reconstruction, blacks and poor whites found themselves subjected to a poll tax and black Louisianians were handy targets for political campaigners. As in other Southern states, the *Brown vs. Board* decision created for Louisiana severe political stresses. The state became one of the six major targets of the Voting Rights Act of 1965.

New Orleans long had a reputation for greater racial and ethnic tolerance than many similarly sized Deep South cities. A relatively young port city, its predominantly Catholic population was considered to be strong on corruption but slow to race-bait in public affairs. In 1961, however, this hard-earned reputation was tested by school desegregation, and, on balance, neither the state nor the city came off well.[11]

Until the mid-1960s, communication between the races conformed closely to the pattern described by Floyd Hunter: separate "communities," each with its own leadership cadre, which dealt quietly with their counterparts but maintained a public stance of separateness and aloofness.[12] The black "establishment" was largely drawn from the clergy, especially the Protestant clergy, despite the large number of Catholics among the black population.

During the hectic period of the 1960s, however, two black attorneys who represented the Congress of Racial Equality recognized that a basic vacuum existed in New Orleans politics. Federal law and enforcement was enfranchising blacks, and a few white politicians were making hesitant efforts to reach these new voters, but there were no black vehicles broadly enough based to mobilize large numbers of black voters and convert them into a force expressive of black aspirations. The result of this perception was the creation of two major organizations: the Southern Organization for Unified Leadership (SOUL) and the Coalition of Urban Politics (COUP). Of the two, SOUL was located in that part of the city most heavily populated by blacks, especially by impoverished blacks.[13]

SOUL's first major political opportunity came in the mayoral campaign of 1969. In the Democratic primary, two racial moderates were closely matched: Moon Landrieu and James E. Fitzmorris, with the latter considered to have the advantage. Landrieu, however, dealt with SOUL and COUP directly, making concrete patronage promises in exchange for their support. Fitzmorris was, at best, vague. In the resulting vote, Landrieu carried the black precincts by overwhelming margins, while also running Fitzmorris a stiff race in all of the predominantly white areas. The result was that Landrieu defeated Fitzmorris by gaining 90 percent of the black vote and 40 percent of the white vote.

As matters developed over the next four years, SOUL and COUP, but especially the latter, became the major pipelines for appointment of blacks to the Model Cities Program, the Community Action Program, and the mayor's city hall staff. As one politically active black youth put it, "Those dudes have got a monopoly on the mayor."

As their success bore fruit, however, some of the dilemmas facing a black political organization began to appear. First, what was to be SOUL's function in relation to white politics? Was it to be merely a minor partner in coalitions with sympathetic whites, or was it to be an independent power base, which any white politician would need to deal with? The answers naturally depended in no small measure on the strength of SOUL's base. In 1971, one of SOUL's leaders, Sam Bell, entered the Democratic gubernatorial primary. His showing was well behind the registered black vote statewide and even the registered black vote in the city. It was argued that in traditional Louisiana fashion Bell's candidacy was merely a means of forcing concessions from other contenders, and it was true that the two leading contestants, Edwin Edwards and J. Bennett Johnston, vied fiercely for black support. This complex game, however, created serious internal problems. One SOUL leader, a state representative, accused the organization of selling out to white candidates for patronage. He split from the original organization and formed his own in direct competition with SOUL.

In a later series of elections for judicial offices, SOUL's endorsement and campaign efforts showed very mixed results in its presumed strongest areas. While some contenders won, others lost, raising the question whether SOUL support was sufficient to carry the day.

Late in 1972, a similar crisis brewed. At issue was a referendum vote on levee construction, a matter of some importance in hurricane-fearful, below–sea-level New Orleans. SOUL opposed the proposition, on the grounds that Governor Edwards (who favored it) had failed to deliver on patronage promises. An important member of the SOUL cadre, State Representative Theodore Marchand, accused SOUL of ignoring the threat of flooding in black areas in order to dicker for patronage. He also split from the organization.

Another dilemma facing SOUL is its relationship to the black community. Is it to be a vehicle for the personal success of its leaders, or is it to be a means for levering concessions of communitywide impact for the total black population?

The point can be clarified by a brief digression on the nature of patronage.[14] In the United States, three patronage systems have existed side by side. The most familiar is the personal patronage system. As is well known, it delivers jobs and contracts to those individuals who have supported politicians in a position to grant the patronage. Although the major purpose of personal patronage has been to build a base of support for political organizations, it has also functioned as a means of recruiting personnel for government employment, the allocation of government purchasing and contract dollars, and as a means of thereby redistributing income. While generally decried by reformers, personal patronage has been a significant means for developing leadership potential and, especially, for achieving minority representation.

The second major system is symbolic patronage. This system grants status positions to those who would not be particularly enticed by personal patronage rewards. Study commissions, advisory commissions, boards, and various recognition awards are typical kinds of symbolic patronage. In a society that has grown more affluent and more middle-class, symbolic patronage is especially useful to the politician in dealing with intellectuals, businessmen, and publishers. It has its value, also, in dealing with ethnic groups, since it is a means of granting formal recognition—at a low cost—to members of an ethnic group.

Finally, there is policy patronage, that is, "giving the people what they want." Policy decisions are slanted to appeal to and maintain the patronage dispenser's base of support, according to his understanding of the collective aspirations of his constituency.

The three systems are not mutually incompatible by any means. In fact, the astute politician will blend them to orchestrate the base he needs for continued victory. Functionally, however, personal and policy patronage are adapted to differing circumstances. The former is most useful where the politician is dealing with personalities, with tightly knit organizations whose leaders, when rewarded, can deliver their mass memberships, and with political settings where identification politics is the prevailing style. Policy patronage is best adapted to mass politics, to settings where there are clear-cut policy preferences, where governmental performance is expected to be affirmative—in short, coalition politics.

At this point in our analysis, SOUL's dilemma becomes clearer. SOUL has found itself under challenge from its own base of support because it opted for personal patronage over policy patronage, as in the case of the levee dispute. There has been a steady proliferation of black organizations to challenge SOUL's leadership in its own precincts.

Furthermore, SOUL has begun to discover one of the hidden costs of personal patronage. As one black said, with some passion, "Every time SOUL keeps a job for themselves, they are leaving some other fellow out. And every time they sell themselves to the Man for a job instead of something that helps all the brothers, they are deserting the community."

The complexities of SOUL's position were underscored by two events late in 1972. During the autumn, the New Orleans Police Department, with the public approval of Mayor Landrieu, established the Felony

Action Squad, a special strike force to operate in high crime areas and with controversial instructions to use the maximum appropriate force, including "shoot to kill" orders. A number of black leaders protested the F.A.S. vigorously before the city council on the grounds that the F.A.S. was, consciously or not, providing the police force with a license to kill black citizens. Although individual members of the organization spoke before the council, SOUL as an organization was quiet. Then, Southern University in Baton Rouge and Southern University in New Orleans, both predominantly black schools, exploded in student dissent. Although once again individual members of SOUL sought access to the governor in an effort to moderate an approach toward the student revolt, the organization was itself silent.

Some observers sympathetic to SOUL argue that in the case of the F.A.S., it was clear that blacks would be primary beneficiaries of the strike force's efforts; and, in the case of Southern University, the issues were tangential to SOUL's areas of competence and concern. Less sympathetic observers argued, however, that both instances indicated SOUL's increasing inability to keep in touch with the issues and policies affecting the lives of New Orleans blacks, and moreover, SOUL's leaders had become too bound to mayor and governor by personal patronage agreements to act in any interest but the white politicians' and their own.

SOUL and other black organizations like it are thus confronted by some painful political choices. The pursuit of personal patronage has been an accepted American practice, one which is useful not only to the individual beneficiaries, but the organization from which they come and the political system itself. Yet, personal patronage obviously is not enough. For one thing, it is one of the cheapest concessions which can be granted by the political order. For another, it does omit from its benefits far more people than it includes, and exclusion has been the burden that black Americans need to shed.

There is, however, another side to the story. Certainly, blacks need to develop a cadre of trained and experienced leaders. Governmental positions are one place where such leadership can develop. Furthermore, the South has not yet moved to "pure" coalition politics in which policy dominates the personal. Given the incompleteness of the shift, is it not desirable for blacks to gain a toehold in government where they can help to further the shift towards a politics of inclusiveness. Moreover, as long as the transition in Southern politics remains incomplete, perhaps the most any black organization can hope for is the kind of patronage which fits the style of politics in operation.

What has happened is that perfectly intelligent rationales exist for two separate strategies. Black political organizations function in a political system that is partly coalitionist and inclusionist in impulse and partly exclusionist and white identification-based. In such a system, any black political organization can expect to be battered by political leaders, both black and white, and expect to lose some support, white, black, or both.

The difficulties are by no means insuperable, nor are they unique to black political organizations. They do, however, point up some of the extraordinary complexities which exist in a politics of change where black-white relations are involved.

Black Southerners face the problem of whether to act themselves on a coalitionist base or on an identification base. If it is to be the former, does the black Southerner have the political clout to be a full partner in black-white coalitions? Any answer must be speculative, and, for that reason, a political gamble. In addition, coalition politics *does* require corporate forms which assert cohesive demands on the system. What precisely are to be the demands of blacks? Personal patronage or policy patronage? Who among blacks are to receive these benefits? There is, without doubt, a "black interest," but general formulations begin to fragment when confronted with precise political requirements.

If the choice is to be identification politics, how is it to be expressed and executed? A good case can be made for the need for a period of identification politics for black Americans, if for no other reason than this would permit the formulation of a clear black interest and program.[15] One important consideration must be kept in mind, however. Whites were able to pursue identification politics under the sheltering arms of government. As Figure 2 indicates, black Southerners are far from having that protective role available, unless the federal government intends to undertake it.

Figure 2 shows three sets of data. First, it lists the number of black officials, as of March 1972, in relation to the total number of officials in each of the eleven Southern states. Second, the table shows the "hypothetical" number of black officials one might expect to see holding office were elective offices crudely reflective of "one man, one vote." Third, the table shows the actual as a percentage of the hypothetical. The table thus provides a rough index of both black success in organized electoral politics and an indicator of the degree to which blacks can expect a commitment to their identification aspirations from state and local governments.

FIGURE 2

BLACK ELECTED OFFICIALS IN SOUTHERN
STATE AND LOCAL GOVERNMENTS

State	Total No. of Elected Officials	Total No. of Black Officials	Percent of Black Population	Hypothetical No. of Black Officials	Col. 2 as Percent of Col. 4
	(1)	(2)	(3)	(4)	
Alabama	4,060	83	26.4	1,072	7.7
Arkansas	10,289	97	18.6	1,914	5.1
Florida	5,070	51	15.5	786	6.5
Georgia	7,226	65	25.9	1,872	3.5
Louisiana	4,761	119	29.9	1,424	8.3
Mississippi	4,761	129	36.8	1,752	7.4
N. Carolina	5,504	103	22.4	1,233	8.4
S. Carolina	3,078	66	30.4	936	7.1
Tennessee	7,877	48	16.1	1,268	3.8
Texas	23,038	61	12.7	2,926	2.1
Virginia	3,587	54	18.6	667	8.1

Sources: U.S. Bureau of the Census, *Census of Governments, Popularly Elected Officials of State and Local Governments*, 1967, p. 8. Joint Center for Political Studies, *Supplement to the National Roster of Black Elected Officials*, March, 1972, p. 1.

Obviously, any such tabulation ignores highly significant variables. White elective officials can be and, on occasion, are as sympathetic to black aspirations as some black politicians. Voting strength is not the same as the percentage of population: the proportion of legal minors within a subpopulation, the distribution of the subpopulation geographically, and various institutional barriers all have important impacts on voting effectiveness.

Even with these important qualifications in mind, however, the essential point is still that, after six years of intensive effort by both federal and nongovernmental organizations to strengthen black representation in Southern state and local governments, only moderate inroads have been made. The result, from the black standpoint, is ominous. If the federal government chooses to slacken its efforts, white Southerners are still in a position to play a politics of ethnic identification. Control of state and local governments, and the huge array of protective and distributive benefits that governments possess, means white Southern political leadership can either move towards a coalitionism that includes blacks or fight an ethnic defensive action that excludes them. Because the situation is still fairly fluid, black political organizations possess strategic advantages that twenty years ago did not exist; but the strategic advantage requires careful analysis and action to be brought to fruition.

THE POLITICS OF CHANGE

The discussion in this paper has centered around an hypothesis that Southern politics has been undergoing a significant change in its stylistic base. With this change—a shift from a politics of white ethnic identification to one of coalition politics—have emerged new opportunities for the black Southerner. It has also been argued, however, that the change is less than complete. Identification politics are rooted in cultural rather than purely political or economic variables, and cultural norms change slowly.

It has been further argued that in a politics of coalition, winning combinations respond to concrete demands. It is necessary for those who wish to break into the system to articulate what it is they want and how they expect their demands to be met. The struggle over two differing kinds of patronage symbolizes, first, two different types of responses the system can make to demands, and, second, the degree to which black Southerners are still uncertain of their role or their goals in relation to a coalition politics. It would, of course, be foolish to expect a solid front of unanimity within the black population of the South on any issue, but another of the burdens placed on the shoulders of minorities is that in a system poorly adapted to meeting minority demands they must maximize the use of their resources and opportunities.

It is worth repeating that there is nothing in the logic of coalitions that *demands* inclusiveness of all segments of a population. The South, like large parts of the North, could choose to work out its political struggles with blacks and other minorities as, at best, only incidental participants in the process. This means, as Harold Cruse has pointed out, that blacks must be clearer about who they are and what they need than white Americans ever had to be.[16]

NOTES

[1] See especially V. O. Key, Jr., *Southern Politics in State and Nation* (New York: Alfred A. Knopf, 1950) and Harry Holloway, *The Politics of the Southern Negro* (New York: Random House, 1969).

[2] Good examples of the pluralist position are David B. Truman, *The Governmental Process* (New York: Alfred A. Knopf, 1950) and Robert A. Dahl, *Who Governs?* (New Haven: Yale University Press, 1963).

[3] C. Wright Mills, *The Power Elite* (New York: Oxford University Press, 1956) is the most famous criticism of the pluralist position at the national level. See also Theodore Lowi, "The Public Philosophy," *American Political Science Review*, 61 (March 1967), pp. 5–24.

[4] William Gamson, "Stable Unrepresentation in American Society," *American Behavioral Scientist*, 12 (November–December 1968), pp. 15–21.

[5] Much of what follows is an enlargement and amplification of materials which appear in S. J. Makielski, Jr., *The Beleaguered Minority* (San Francisco. W. H. Freeman, forthcoming).

[6] The term *corporate* received unfortunate connotations from its association with fascist ideology. Its roots go back to syndicalism and British pluralism, however. It is a useful phrase to describe the organizational form based on an aggregating of "rational" interests into a coherent demand-expressing entity.

[7] C. Vann Woodward, *Tom Watson: Agrarian Rebel* (New York: Oxford University Press, 1963).

[8] Perhaps most typical of the Southern fraternal organizational form is the "courthouse gang." Unfortunately, too little research has been done on the courthouse gang, but both David G. Temple, *Merger Politics* (Charlottesville: University Press of Virginia, 1972), pp. 34–36, and Herman S. Horn, "The Growth and Development of the Democratic Party in Virginia," Duke University, unpublished Ph.D. dissertation, 1949, Chapter 6, have valuable examinations of the internal sociometry of these forms. S. J. Makielski, Jr., "The Virginia Town, Part 2," The University of Virginia News Letter, 48 (September 1971), pp. 1–4, suggests a similar pattern occurs in the governing of small units of government.

[9] Governor Edwin Edwards of Louisiana is perhaps a classic example of the transition stage political leader. Elected in 1972 on a highly coalitionist platform, he has vacillated between rewarding his own south Louisiana cronies

and seeking highly "businesslike" approaches to state government. Some critics view him as simply a not very artful manipulator, but it seems more likely that he is caught between two stages of political development.

10 There are, of course, less overt religious splits in other Southern states which often appear in the form of class conflict.

11 Robert L. Crain, *The Politics of School Desegregation* (Garden City, NY: Doubleday, 1969), pp. 250–345.

12 Floyd Hunter, *Community Power Structure* (New York: Doubleday, 1953).

13 Most of what follows is based on interviews with knowledgeable black observers. In addition, the following written sources are valuable. James Chubbuck, Edwin Renwick, and Joe E. Walker, "The Emergence of Coalition Politics in New Orleans," *New South*, 26 (Winter, 1971), pp. 16–25; Charlotte Hays, "Black Power for Sale," The Vieux Carre Courier, 9 (August 25–31), pp. 1, 4; and Allan Katz, "SOUL-Marchand Rift," The States-Item (November 7, 1972), p. 2.

14 The only systematic effort to analyze patronage in the United States is Martin and Susan Tolchin, *To the Victor* (New York: Random House, 1971). Unfortunately, the Tolchins treat all patronage as being the same in purpose, function, and effect, and thus provide no useful analytical framework.

15 Stokely Carmichael and Charles V. Hamilton, *Black Power* (New York: Random House, 1967).

16 Harold Cruse, *The Crisis of the Negro Intellectual* (New York: William Morrow, 1967). Compare with Carmichael and Hamilton, *op. cit.* "Most of the black politicians around the country are not examples of Black Power. The power must be that of a community. . . . The black politicians must stop being representatives of 'downtown' machines, whatever the cost might be in terms of lost patronage. . . ." (p. 46).

ETHNICITY AS
CULTURAL CHARACTER

(The "Old Ethnicity"?)

*

14

Some Depictions of German Cultural Character

ETHEL NURGE
University of Kansas Medical Center

GERMAN NATIONAL CHARACTER STUDIES

The systematic study of national character did not begin until the outbreak of the Second World War. Yet, an assumption of the existence of personalities marked by "national" characteristics is found as far back as ancient times when historians and travelers wrote about the strange behavior of alien people. Good examples can be found in the writings of the Greek historian Herodotus; and the work entitled *Dialogus, Agricola, and Germania,* by the Roman author, Tacitus, is in good part general ethnography (1925:257–301). These early accounts were subjective; their authors did not attempt to compensate for their own biases, nor to seek the logical origins and the inner rationale of the behavior which they were recording. Early writers and, in fact, some contemporaries are apt to extend the knowledge they have from some few individuals to statements about the characteristics of

217

the whole group. Early writers had no concept of culture to guide them, and differences in other tribes and nations were often ascribed to assumed biological differences and, what is worse, their imputed inferiority.

At the outbreak of World War II, government and military officials no longer looked only to traditional sources for information. Those in the social sciences had begun to make descriptions and generalizations of such penetration and power that they were increasingly called on for help. Social scientists were asked to give whatever help they could in interpreting the actions of the people of Japan and Germany and, in some cases, to advise military and civilian personnel. Germany was an enigma in the sense that so much of her past history had been that of European nations in general. There had been the same slow development out of the feudal society, the searing conflicts of the Protestant Reformation, the attempts at unification of small political units, industrialization, and periods of expansion and colonialism. All these were shared by most European nations (with regional, minor variation, of course), so that the real problem for the national character studies was to discover what was distinctive about German national culture within the European historical experience and what effects this might have had on the people who carried and perpetuated German culture.

A national character study utilizes the premises and techniques of the personality and culture studies but has a distinguishing feature: the persons studied are chosen because they are "nationals," the citizens of a sovereign political state. During wartime, it was impossible to visit the group studied and the technique called participant observation could not be employed; that is, the target group had to be studied at a distance (Mead 1953:642). Reconstructions of national character at a distance were made from the study of documents, and also by interviews with, and observations on, people who were nationals but who were not then resident in the society being studied. National character studies continued after the war's end, but then included investigation of nationals in their own country.

What national character studies and the more general kinds of studies known as culture and personality studies have in common is a focus on the way human beings embody the culture in which they have been reared. Embodying the culture or learning the techniques for living is almost always studied in one or another psychological framework, for instance, learning theory, perception theory, or psychoanalytic personality formation theory (Mead 1953:643); thus child rearing practices and family form are central to any kind of personality study.

In the studies that follow we draw not only from national character studies, either carried out at a distance or those carried on after the war and in Germany, but also from the perceptive characterizations of other writers who have been fascinated by the Germans and by things Germanic. The technique for each study will be given as it is considered.

Let us begin with a disclaimer. Any large mass, and most certainly a nation, is not homogeneous throughout its parts. Size as a factor and complexity as an inevitable component mean heterogeneity, *but* large size and complexity do not mean lack of pattern. The challenge then becomes: describe the pattern, including, as much as possible, the variability of the parts. Put another way: habits of the wider cultural pattern may be systematically shared by members of any subgroups in that culture but knowledge of the pattern of any particular subgroup will not give us predictive ability to speak about other subgroups (Mead 1953:647f.). For example, we expect to find a belief in the freedom of the individual and the need for separation of the church and state among Kentucky mountaineers, New Jersey busdrivers, New England millworkers, and second generation Italians, but each shows distinctive eating and drinking habits.

In all of the studies that follow, I have attempted to state the population or sample the writer is concerned with. This was not always possible, however. The reader is reminded that these statements are about different parts of Germany and by different investigators, and even in different time periods. Whether or not any particular set of descriptions or conclusions is intended to convey, or can well-describe the character of the whole of Germany is a problem of magnitude and, perhaps, the central challenge for the formation and use of material gathered in national character studies. Some of the descriptions are very persuasive, but the problem of the reliability and validity of the description remains just that—a problem. Much more study is needed before we can speak with confidence of the generalizability of specific characteristics. Therefore, it is necessary to proceed with caution.

I believe that the applicability of the findings of national character studies are considerably limited but, nonetheless, the concept has such potential and interest that we are going to continue to make national character studies for some time. One possible development that would increase the applicability of national character studies is that investigators may find that there are several characteristics whose distribution throughout the mass can be queried and counted. Statements can then be made in terms of the frequency of the appearance of such a trait—say bellicosity, industriousness, preoccupation with cleanliness, and so forth—and graphs prepared showing the frequency and clustering of traits. It is not likely that a similar clustering of six or more traits will appear in all portions of the population, but it may very well be possible to say trait *a* appears in 70 percent of the population, trait *b* in 75, and traits *a* and *b* together in 50 percent, and so on.

There are other ways that the limitations and legitimate application of the findings may be made explicit. In a study made to advance the hypothesis that there is a Nazi variant of German culture which approximates "or falls under the 'compulsive character' of psychoanalytic theory," (Kecskemeti and Leites 1945:1) the authors limit the universe of applicability of their hypothesis by denying that the character structive was equally prevalent among all categories of members of what they designate as the Nazi variant of German culture. They feel that it might safely be said that it is more widely diffused among the lower middle class than among persons higher or lower; among males than among females; and among those who were adolescents before or around 1933 than among those who were adolescents afterwards. It is more prevalent in northern Germany than in southern Germany; among Protestants than among Catholics; among city people than among country people; and among political followers than among political leaders (Kecskemeti and Leites 1945:3). Such painstaking attention to detail, such patient continuing attempts at deriving verisimilitude, is a necessary endeavor and needed component if any core value of the concept of national character is to be realized. We turn now to some studies. The problem at hand is the relationship between national culture and national character. What are the significant features in the German experience that have influenced the creation of a national culture distinctive to the country, and, therefore, the cultural context within which the national character develops? How did the human beings who embody the culture, learn it and live it? How have various writers depicted German personality traits? To answer these questions, we begin with some description; we direct our attention, in part at least, to the history of Europe and Germany's place within this historical framework. The following is a "character description."

> In 1789, Immanuel Kant surveyed his fellow Germans from his ivory tower in the little East Prussian city of Königsberg. His analysis was surprisingly felicitous, especially, be it remembered, since he was speaking of the behavior characteristics of citizens of a congeries of states—some major, some petty, but each an ostensible nation—and not of a single nationality. The German, he said, is honest and home loving, traits that make for phlegm instead of brilliance; he is industrious, saving and cleanly; he possesses few of those qualities of alertness that make for genius; and he is persistent in both his reasoning and endurance. Able and intelligent, he lacks, nevertheless, sharpness of wit and refinement of taste. Among all civilized peoples, Kant noted, it is the German who becomes most docile under government. He fashions an elaborate hierarchy of rank, according more worth to these factors that promote a class structuring of society and a total absence of egalitarianism, than to natural ability. Further lacking confidence in his own abilities, he becomes imitative and methodical, fears to take an original step, and becomes pedantic (Spencer paraphrasing Kant 1965:160).

The anthropologist Robert F. Spencer writes in "The German Paradox: A Problem in National Character" that Kant's description, indeed, his adjectives are still applicable and that the actions and patterns described are German and cannot be applied to other Europeans (Spencer 1965:160). Kant's observation and method were, of course, not objective to the degree that we have been able to attain today; and therefore, it is all the more remarkable that what he intuitively saw and so incisively wrote are essentially the same conclusions as are reached by other students traveling different paths 180 years later. Spencer did no fieldwork (personal communication), but he has a knowledge of German, a German background, and an interest in things Germanic. It is clear that he has read extensively and prefers a cultural framework for exploration and investigation.

Spencer is interested in the origin of the paradox of the German character, which he finds in the marginal position Germany had in relation to the rest of Europe—in particular England and France. Building on Kroeber's concept of a cultural center with outward eddying circles of influence, Spencer distinguishes a marginal culture as one which, always peripheral, develops in isolation from cultural centers, away from the movement, the inspiration, the stimulus, and the action; a marginal culture is, it is generally assumed, one which is less inclined to invent and more prone to borrow ideas and inventions. One consequence is that a marginal culture is therefore characterized by the lack of any well-integrated unity (Spencer 1963:166). Spencer goes on to sketch briefly some highlights in the development of German science and art and argues that each of these areas of intellectual pursuit developed many years after the period when they first originated in Europe. The Germans are refined, polished, and improved, he says, but they are largely lacking in originality and creativity. Their reaction is one of insecurity and a necessary tightening against the intrusion of unwelcome outside cultural influences.

In Spencer's view, Germany's historical experience and geographical setting is largely responsible for the development of traits which many researchers have found to characterize Germans: for example, a highly stratified society and authoritarianism in interpersonal relationships. Marginal culture is "by nature conservative, it is indifferent to innovation, rigid in its social structure, and indeed, often puritanical in defense of its own institutions (Spencer 1965:166)." Spencer also sees a connection between marginality and the structure of the family. On the surface, the German family seems no different from the family in other areas of Europe. It is monogamous; the marital tie is essentially permanent; the parents are engaged, primarily, in the care and management of the young; but there is a difference, and it is one of shading—a difference in degree and not of kind; there is a strong patriarchal tone already present in the Germanic tribes of Tacitus' time. German family pattern began to differ from those of the rest of Europe when Germans were forced to a more conservative retention of patterns while the rest of the continent could permit change more freely.

> They have invested the institution (family) with a preciseness of definition of social role. . . . This is the marginal consequence repeated. Insecurity and uncertainty lead to precision of form and adherence to fixed pattern (Spencer 1965:181).

Yes, the German family is an authoritarian institution; and it seems the Germans have chosen to stress this feature "somewhat longer and to accord it, a greater pattern and institutionalized emphasis than has been true of other western national cultures" (Spencer 1965:181). Spencer also points to the ideal and idealized German families in which the patriarchal, authoritarian father functions well and justly, and because it is possible and sometimes occurs there is a paradox.

One final insight for which we can be grateful to Spencer is about the nature of submission among the Germans not only in the family, but among contemporaries, at work, at play, and in other socially structured situations. Submission to the German is not a docile nor passive behavior; it is a willing giving of oneself to the properly constituted authority. There is no lack of self-respect or honor in such submission. It is a conscious subduing of one's will to a higher authority. One who is submissive in this sense is not being meek but instead is resolute and may indeed have a positive inspired feeling brought about by the sense of doing what is fitting, proper, and honorable (Spencer 1965:181). The obedient German is not a robot, he is an honorable being.

An interesting question follows from Spencer's formulation: will a native-born German find in his own culture those same characteristics which were discerned by Spencer? In 1929, a German author wrote a book which was later published in English entitled *Germany and the Germans* (Diesel 1931). Described by the author as a philosophical or artistic geography, the book is a popular account, part of which would be excellent to stimulate tourist trade, the theme of which is the relationships between geography and history and how these two factors influenced the development of German culture within the European tradition. The book is, in fact, human geography for the layman, but it is also filled with shrewd observations not only about Germans but also about the French, English, Swedes, and Americans. The author is an educated, sensible, and intuitive man and much that he writes strikes a responsive assenting chord: "Ah yes, that is how it is." Despite the differences in training of the two men and the intent of their writing, both Spencer and Diesel find many similarities in German national culture and its effects on the character of the people, even though Diesel concentrates his observation on people in their daily lives and seems more intimately and at firsthand aware of regional differences, while Spencer writes from a wider and more distant perspective.

Diesel writes that when particular eras of German history have run their course, Germans have always felt themselves confronted with chaos. This is in contrast to the English, who are characteristically stable, are able to weather the storms and revolutions and resume operations on an even keel (Diesel 1931:9). From this he infers that the inability of the Germans to establish a stable historical focus has led to the development of a national character characterized by a lack of inner poise. This perception is parallel to that of Spencer, who sees the German personality as being insecure and uncertain. Diesel's reflections on the psychological effects of German history is such that he writes of an ever impending "atmosphere of stifling gloom, the lack of any firm stability and cohesion. The tragic epic of life is played against a chaotic, incoherent background, lacking all unity and compactness" Diesel 1931:149). Furthermore:

> Everything has conspired to deny them a personal and national focal point; the short duration of their national unity, which has not yet become a part of their inmost being; their genius for the particular, for the family, the community, the club; and finally a certain lack of balance, a certain wilfulness and restlessness (Diesel 1931:149).

He also emphasizes how important work is, being the rationale for life and living. "To the German work is what gives meaning to his life and destiny and to the life and destiny of the state" (Diesel 1931:175); "Germans show great patience in their work and in submitting to rules and regulations, but they show little patience in dealing with their fellow-men and the trials of circumstance" (Diesel 1931:150). The lack of inner stability is a theme throughout the book.

> We were tossed to and fro. . . . Everything was done by halves: the colonization of the east, the defense of the west, our maritime exploration, our aristocracy, democracy, and revolution. Thirty years long German fought with German on German soil, and the only result was to make confusion worse confounded (Diesel 1931:8).

Unlike Spencer, however, he thinks of Germany as being the focus to European events, the center on which they clash and jar; not as a nation which is outside the main development, but, nonetheless, he feels that the influence of Europe on Germany is greater than is the influence of Germany on Europe (Diesel 1931:137), an observation which, perhaps obliquely, corroborates Spencer's ideas of marginality, late flowering, and lack of inventiveness. At least, Diesel agrees with Spencer that "one finds . . . thorough and industrious, rather than creative work" (Diesel 1931:152). Although this idea is not a main or developed theme in his book, he does touch on it now and again. "German culture, especially in the fields of philosophy, science and literature, seems to have developed extraordinarily late in the day compared with the other West European countries" (Diesel 1931:181).

PSYCHIATRIC ANALYSIS

In the literature which has been specifically written in an attempt to describe German national character as objectively as possible several research methods have been used. These include: (1) direct or indirect observation of child rearing practices; (2) clinical analysis of adults; (3) questionnaires and interviews; and (4) the analysis of symbolic cultural materials such as books and movies. Both the concept of national character and the techniques of study used in research have been frequently, although not always justifiably, criticized. (For a good discussion of the arguments, see Mead 1953.642f.) Clinical case studies of adult personality, interpreted in the light of familial experiences, frequently follow hypotheses suggested by Freud's studies; symbolic cultural material is also interpreted in psychoanalytic terms. In such studies, the focus is on the family and how it transmits systematic patterns of behavior from one generation to another. The object is to determine whether there is any significant relationship between the character of a particular population, its child training techniques, and the patterning of its culture as a whole.

Henry V. Dicks, an Englishman, made several studies in a psychoanalytical framework while he was a psychiatrist in the British army (1950a; 1950d). Dicks, who is bilingual in German and English, took some academic training in Germany. His case studies of prisoners captured during the Second World War throw light on the connection of character structure to political organization. Using a random sample and a prolonged interview with a schedule, Dicks feels that he has produced a broad picture of the general recurring regularities of German mental behavior. He finds the source of adult male personality in a boy's relationship with his family, and in particular with his father. Submission, repression, aggression, and projection (psychological mechanisms important to personality formation) are illustrative of the emphasis on status in German social structure, most frequently expressed through dominance and submission. Submission

> was a strong factor in the love of military life and discipline, that perfect expression of a hierarchical pattern for wielding collective power, for being respected, and for strutting. To make submission palatable, it was idealized. To curb one's self-will, to subordinate oneself in blind obedience became the hall-mark of a fine soldierly character (Dicks 1950b:201, 202).

Perhaps Dicks emphasizes too much "blind" obedience and does not recognize that unquestioningly following constituted authority is an ideal, and a difficult one to realize. As Spencer has pointed out, it may be a virtue difficult of attainment. The American emphasis (which has its roots in Luther and other Protestant reformers) that the individual is personally responsible for interpretation and reaction to authority and to "rules" is likewise very difficult for many people.

Be that as it may, the German ideal is to rely greatly on authorities, and such an ideal embedded in a social structure is not without detrimental effects on the personality of the individual. Converging with Diesel and Spencer in their interpretation of the German personality, Dicks concludes that the emphasis on submission and dominance in an authoritarian system historically derived from and buttressed by Prussian sources does grave injury to the individual: the adult males, at least, are left with a resultant residue of unexpressed, frustrated rage, which, deflected by custom and taboo from its primary object, the father and all his symbols in the nation, manifests itself in other ways. (Some bully all who are weaker; and some repress rage, in which case it is evident nonetheless in a sense of inferiority, of inability to control oneself, a dread of the unknown, and of inner anarchy.) (Dicks 1950b:202)

The question is raised as to the presence throughout the population of personality types so described. Dicks says:

> In any culture there will be some more and some less complete representatives or active carriers of the pattern. Once the Prussian authoritarian pattern . . . had become the dominant trend in Germany, those who were most efficiently displaying its characteristics were likely sooner or later to "reap the social advantages of going furthest along the approved path of behavior. . . ." And so he accounts for the excesses of World War II. On the other hand, the ideals which the Nazis claimed to incarnate were however so widely and pervasively preached in German institutions that even persons of "non-authoritarian" personality accepted them. Only the small group who might be called compulsively anti-Authoritarian . . . could bring themselves to real rejection of the Nazi pattern, and then usually because they had cathected some other systems—e.g., Catholicism or Marxism (Dicks 1950a:152).

If I may rephrase, the author says, even individuals with personalities a little different from the norm, even with individuals who were not carriers of the common or characteristic German personality type, even *they* shared the ideals, the life experiences, and the end result in personality and behavior. A final sum in the psychoanalytic jargon of two decades ago:

> The picture is thus mainly one of an ambivalent, compulsive character structure with the emphasis on submissive/dominant conformity, a strong countercathexis of the virtues of duty, of "control" by the self, especially buttressed by re-projected "external" superego symbols (Dicks 1950a:139).

Apart from the validity of, and the meaning contained within, psychoanalytic terminology, we note that Dicks based his analysis on a sample of 138 German prisoners of war, men who were living in a period of great psychological as well as physical stress (1950a:121). There is no information about the personality of women and the feminine depiction of German character. Will a similar interpretation be found in a much broader sample of the German population including both sexes? This is the question to which we turn next.

In the *Father Land*, psychiatrist Bertram Schaffner poses the question, "How does a German become German?" In search of an answer, he looks at the different roles in the family, and taking the hypothesis that early family life may be used as a key to the understanding of culturally regular behavior, he explores the theme of authoritarianism in the German character. He writes that "what makes the study of the German family so crucial is the remarkable parallel between the rules that govern it and the credos of national, political life" (Schaffner 1948:4). He sees a relationship between the patterns of behavior which characterize the men who exercise the power of the government in the name of the country, and those values and behaviors which are instilled into the child during socialization.

Schaffner was born in the U.S.A. in a German-American community, but his mother and all four grandparents were born in Germany. He had had some public schooling in Germany, studied the adjustment of Germans in America to the American way of life, and was concerned with the changes the Third Reich brought to Germany. The information on which the *Father Land* is based was gathered while Schaffner was chief psychiatrist for eight months for the Screening Center of the Information Control Division, a center established by the American military government for the purpose of selecting German professionals to work in communications and other influential media. Through the use of various psychological devices, the Screening Center personnel attempted to learn something of political beliefs and the then-current political sympathies toward the Nazi regime among the candidates who were seeking licenses to work in the sensitive and influential field of communications. In addition to the psychological techniques used to gather information to make judgments, a questionnaire was administered to people outside of the Center to a sample of 2,000. Considering the population touched by the two techniques together, the study was more broadly based than was Dicks's in that included in the sample were Germans of all ages, both sexes, and all social levels. The Center respondents were primarily from the American zone of occupation and the American sector of Berlin but some had come from elsewhere, and the same to whom the questionnaire was administered included people from central, northern, and southern Germany, from small and large communities.

The people whom Schaffner and his colleagues studied, then, represented a wide range of Germans. Since the respondents ranged from nineteen to seventy years of age, they included people who had lived through every aspect of German history since unification in 1870. It is an illustration of the stability of culture that to all intents and purposes and, insofar as we are able to reconstruct after the fact, the basic premises of German family life did not change significantly during those many decades. Indeed, only a thoroughgoing social revolution can bring such change about and it takes a very long time. In the German case, stability over time is aided by the tendency in parental training to encourage the repetition of existing patterns. Thus, there is little room for the evolution of newer, freer customs. Even Hitler's attempt to lessen parental influence did not constitute the attack upon the structure of the German family which it was sometimes believed to be. Rather,

> it was an extension of the principles of the home to the state, merely shifting parental authority from the actual parents of the children to Hitler himself as the supreme parent of all Germans, children and their parents alike (Schaffner 1948:14).

The question we now ask is: How does the authoritarian pattern influence the forms of behavior which the child learns? We will consider Schaffner's description of how the child is trained to the traditional patterns of German behavior, as well as what forms of behavior are defined as virtues in German culture. Discipline characterizes every aspect of the child's world and only if he does what he is told does his world become simple and rewarding. From infancy on, he learns that he is part of a system in which he is of inferior rank; a world in which he must be obedient to superiors whose exacting assignments he strains continuously to meet (Schaffner 1948:41f.). "Parents desire their children to be constructively busy at all times, *fleissig* or industrious. Laziness and idleness are almost synonymous vices, not to be tolerated" (Schaffner 1948:42). The child is expected to develop the ability to work hard and for long periods of time, even though the work be strenuous and repetitive.

Under the considerable social pressure to conform to the rules and the discipline set by the family and other educative institutions in the society, Germans eventually develop an

> obsessive character trait in their involuntary tendency to repeat or to hold on to certain patterns, physical as well as emotional. They show this trait over and over in everyday life; they enjoy following established formulas (Schaffner 1948:43).

Schaffner hypothesizes that the Germans' inability to adjust easily to changing circumstances derives from the fear of authority which was established in childhood and from anxiety brought on by any deviation from the established or traditional forms of behavior. Fear and anxiety, however, can be reduced by conforming to the established rules, and, therefore, German behavior is both conforming and repetitive. Compulsive tendencies are probably best exemplified in the concept of *Pflicht* or duty. One must perform one's duty no matter what the hardship and self-sacrifice. Parents can assure obedience by reminding the child, "This is your *Pflicht*." Disobedience, then, is not only a violation of one's respect for parents but also a violation of duty (Schaffner 1948:44).

The emphasis placed upon duty and discipline tends to restrict the forms and varieties of behavior which children are permitted, and this also has a constricting influence upon the development of the personality:

> At few points, if any, does the typical German child come to know the meaning of freedom . . . fantasy is discouraged. . . . He is not taught to express himself as an individual but to make himself like the German ideal. He becomes purpose-minded and goal-minded. He learns to concentrate all his energies on the task at hand, disregarding related problems which might interest him but for which no solution is demanded by his parents (Schaffner 1948:46).

He is not only denied freedom; he is induced not to want it. The child is therefore not rewarded for initiative and, indeed, any type of freedom is apt to be defined as lawlessness and lack of discipline. The ideal in German culture is a strict obedience to the existing structure of authority. Here we have a nice convergence of two psychiatrists on the same idea. Dicks said these things too. The ideal of strict obedience, says Schaffner, imposes demands and restrictions which lead to frustration and aggression. Aggression is often expressed in brutality, especially in punishing one who misuses authority and in retaliating against those who cause the frustrations. Functionally, then, the authoritarian system exacts passivity and submissiveness from those on lower levels, but provides little emotional outlet for aggression against authority; inded only when that authority is seen as clearly and decidedly unacceptable (Schaffner 1948:48), a rare occurrence, can the subordinate react assertively if not aggressively.

Many German virtues are, of course, related to the emphasis on obedience. One such is orderliness. Orderliness "includes punctuality, meticulosity, propriety, and is epitomized in tidiness. It is essentially respect for the arrangement of things as opposed to people" (Schaffner 1948:52). I noted, too, that from a very early age, the child is made aware that order must be maintained in his world; that there is only one proper way to do things and that this way must always be followed. The following maxim, already well learned in childhood, aptly describes this German notion: A place for everything and everything in its place. Everything must be named, labeled, classified, and arranged —and kept that way. Dislike of disorder remains with Germans throughout life and helps to explain resistance to change, evolution, or revolution.

Closely related to orderliness is cleanliness. It usually applies to the physical surrounding of the child: his house, his clothes, himself. The phrase "Cleanliness is next to godliness" well expresses the emphasis, but the German concept of cleanliness is extended. According to Schaffner, the German

> identifies cleanliness with purity (The German word *rein* is applied to both). He begins to judge people and things in these terms. He hears his father dismiss individuals as *schmutzig* (dirty). He hears that other children, other families, other nations are inferior because they are not clean. He comes to learn that cleanliness is a standard of measurement to be applied to cultures and nations (Schaffner 1948:54).

Order and cleanliness are two virtues; a third, the cardinal virtue for the German male, is manliness. Manliness implies a strong massive body; powerful muscles; athletic prowess; and endurance of illness, fatigue or privation. More importantly, and from the point of view of the young child, the boy must develop a bearing which implies authority and a manner to inspire fear and compel obedience (Schaffner 1948:54). Many different types of behavior are taboo for anyone aspiring to manliness: reading fiction, helping a woman in the kitchen, or pushing a baby's carriage. A manly man does not waver in a decision nor alter the decision once made. The training in manliness leads to a rigid, militaristic style of behavior:

> The small boy enjoys imitating the marching and drilling, likes the prospects of donning the uniform one day himself, and attempts to acquire a military ring in his voice. He looks forward to a continuation of the *Disziplin* he learned at home and in school, to the security that comes from knowing the limitations of freedom, and the orderly, ritualistic, repetitive activities of the soldier's life. He derives satisfaction from performing his *Pflicht* to his country, and has a permitted outlet for his aggressive tendencies; in soldiering he finds the embodiment of the manly ideal (Schaffner 1948:56f).

The head of the German family is the father. "He is omnipotent, omniscient, and omnipresent, as far as this is possible for a human being" (Schaffner 1948:15). In contrast, his wife occupies a secondary position in the family. She has the same status as her children and exercises authority only in the name of the father. Because she cannot always expect her decisions to be supported by her husband, she occupies an unstable position with her children, who may sympathize with her against the wrath of the father, or may pay little heed to her commands. The house in which she lives is a male sanctuary. Only the kitchen and the nursery are her own domain. In these areas of the house she is her own mistress. Here she can exercise authority over the servants who occupy a status lower than she. She exercises her greatest influence over the children, especially up to the age of five, after which discipline falls principally into the hands of the father (Schaffner 1948:34–35).

"The German word expressing the traditional attitude toward one's father is *Ehrfurcht;* it is usually translated as 'respect,' but means, literally, 'honor-fear' " (Schaffner 1948:16). The German father lives aloof from his family. In him is vested sole authority; he sets the standards on which the children are to model themselves. If the German father provides for his children food, shelter, clothing, and an education, then he is considered by the community to be a good father. No consideration is given to whether he may be extremely difficult to live with, or have an intolerable personality. The father may never become close to his children (he prefers them to feel awe, admiration, confidence, and fear), for then his position of authority within the family may be weakened. To maintain his authority, the father uses frequent punishment. "To withhold punishment, or to delay it, is a sign of weakness, inconsistent with the ideals of fatherhood and manliness. . . ." (Schaffner 1948:21) He exercises the same authority over his wife as he does over his children, believing that it is within "his right to scold or to punish her when she is at fault. . . ." (Schaffner 1948:31) He will not tolerate any argument from her. The marriage is not commonly based on romantic love but is apt to be based on socioeconomic considerations and contracted in accord with the parents' wishes (Schaffner 1948:27). Father's authoritarian attitude is never relaxed within the nuclear family. Only with his grandchildren can the German father be freer and more emotionally responsive in his relationships (Schaffner 1948:33).

Moving from this consideration of family factors, Schaffner scrutinizes political organization. The rise of Nazism in Germany had complex causes. From a psychological point of view alone, the National Socialist Party was most successful for several reasons, the first of which is that it appealed to a wide variety of people who were more heterogeneous than at first seemed plausible. The party appealed to certain particular interests of each so that the end result was they seemed more homogeneous than they were (Schaffner 1948:72f.). Secondly, the Nazi program showed to the Germans a model of the state, based upon the same principles as the authoritarian family; a form that was familiar and congenial to the great majority. Hitler promised them protection, security, work, food, and clothing if they would grant him authority. He asked them to make themselves his children; in turn he became a kind of superfather (Schaffner 1948:73):

> He asked for confidence in his plans with complete authority for himself and implicit obedience from the German people. To a large percentage of Germans, this was neither absurd nor dangerous but a natural arrangement between a leader and his subjects. . . . (Schaffner 1948:73f.)

Thirdly by describing the disabilities and frustrations the country was in as due to dirty elements in the population and also to foreign enemies, Hitler appealed to two fundamental German psychological values—the love of cleanliness, "with its corollary compulsion to cleanse and purify," and to anxiety about one's own status with dislike of the outsider (Schaffner 1948:74). Fourthly, Hitler's bearing, his personal behavior, and his policies met the requirements of the German ideals of manliness. Strong and aggressive in policy, he promised to avenge German honor

> not by the soft, suspect methods of diplomacy, but with powerful, irresistible tactics. Hitler did not ask permission, he made demands. Hitler did not consult others for advice but relied on his own judgment and wisdom. He did not hesitate or waiver; he knew what was to be done and ordered it that way. His bearing and his speeches were belligerent. The tone was positive, the voice loud, the language strong (Schaffner 1948:75).

An event which Schaffner describes aptly illuminates the authoritarian pattern which runs through German culture. In the summer of 1946, the American military government began to permit Germans to assemble for the purposes of political discussion and education. These discussion groups were observed by Americans. Schaffner attended such a meeting and heard a high school youth give a report on American attitudes in which he described "the American esteem for the value of the individual, for freedom of restraint in the presence of elders or superiors, and for the right to question authority" (Schaffner 1948:83). The adult reaction to this report was quick and vigorous. A teacher asked how one could conduct a class when the students were free to raise questions; it would be embarrassing. A school superintendent "did his best to undermine the youths' confidence in their own ability to reach decisions without help, and asked them to continue to come to the authorities for the answers" (Schaffner 1948:83). Parents supported them with feeling, asking for a return of "decent" family life and respect for one's parents and authority. This effectively ended any debate. As Schaffner writes:

> the democratic point of view had held the floor barely fifteen minutes, only to be choked out by the same adults who had organized the discussion group, in the name of German re-education, to stamp out Nazism and prepare the youth for a different world (1948:83–84).

Contemporary developments in Germany (student protests and labor strikes) indicate that perhaps Schaffner was too pessimistic about the inculcation of democracy. We turn now to some other earlier delineations of German personality. The emphasis is still on the family, but the technique of investigation changes.

ANALYSIS OF DOCUMENTS

In a sense, most readers are analyzing a document. One reads a book and makes judgments on what is said and on what is not said. One makes, it is to be hoped, systematic perusal and use of a document. In a sense, what this essay has been about is analysis of documents: the culture-at-a-distance study of Spencer, the lyric apostrophe of Diesel to his fellow countrymen, and the two psychiatric analyses of Dicks and Schaffner, were each, in turn, treated as documents and studied, and their findings abstracted for presentation. I want now to turn to another form of document analysis: three studies in which the author looked at the printed or handwritten record and abstracted therefrom repeated actions, recurring events, congruent continuities, coherent wholes, themes; in a word—patterns. The three studies are an analysis of child-care literature, another of juvenile fiction, and a report on story completions by German children. They are all by the same author: Rhoda Metraux.

Rhoda Metraux, in 1953, wrote "Parents and Children: An Analysis of Contemporary Child-Care and Youth Guidance Literature," (in Mead and Wolfenstein 1963) in which she discusses the German conception of the unsocialized child and the direction which socialization should take in order to train the child in the traditional forms of German behavior. Metraux bases her discussion on the information contained in child-guidance books published in Germany between the First and Second World Wars. One finding, which corroborates what Schaffner said about unchanging child-raising patterns, is that there has been little change in child-care literature since the 1920s.

The question may be raised immediately as to the relevance of studying child-care literature. Is there a relationship between the material in child-training manuals and the actual attitudes and behavior of parents toward their children? The procedures presented by the experts are ideals, ideals which, perhaps, neither they nor any mother can wholly achieve, so that we are led to a larger question of the relationship between the real and ideal patterns of culture. There is always some congruence between real and ideal; there is always some achievement; but there is also always some failure, some inability, and even some patterned evasion of the behavior demanded and the frustrations raised by trying to live up to the ideals. But it would be foolish to presume that there is a wide gap between what is advised and what is practiced :

> In every area of moral utterance there is a tendency to reiterate commonly held values, as an ever renewed avowal of faith. It seems likely . . . that the precepts in child-training litera- ture in part coincide with widely held beliefs in culture and in part urge reform (Metraux 1963:149).

Another possibility is that perhaps the literature more nearly approxi- mates older and changing behavior than it does the practices of the readers it is designed for, and this is, undoubtedly, a consideration and a limitation, but it is also one which limits all studies. The thing studied is no longer the thing it was before being studied. An inevitable limi- tation aside, the point is that child-care manuals are needed, are sought and read, and to an unestimable degree have their influence on moth- ers. Whatever the limitations of the use of child-training manuals, it is clear that they provide a valuable source of data on mothers and children.

In the child-care literature that Metraux surveyed there are several themes all couched in the imperative. (1) The child must learn to obey so that he or she can master the tasks set by life. Obedience must be exact, automatic, natural, and unthinking. (2) The child must become autonomous so that he can face life independently of others but also enter into relationships with others. (3) The child must develop a sense of self but not strive to be nor become the center of attention. (4) The child must be loved and protected from danger, but not spoiled or weakened by tenderness or overprotection. Demands must be carefully graded to its growing powers. (5) Education must take place in an atmosphere of impersonally expressed, self-disciplined, insightful love, since this fosters the child's trust in the adult (Metraux 1963:214).

Behind the strictures of the child-guidance writers is an idea of an ordered world in which one may define steps and stages. The adult is adjured to be orderly, consistent, quiet, and patient, and to repeat the same sequence over and over until the child can perform it alone. It is assumed that the babe has an inborn need for order; it is thus pre- pared to accommodate itself to orderliness and regularity; and it will, and does, trust and enjoy the adult from whom these behaviors are learn- ed. The child also, of course, is rewarded by the pleasures of orderli- ness and regularity. Thus, in careful, predictable stages, which can be scheduled, a child learns and enjoys that which is proper to its stage and its station (Metraux 1963:215f.).

This notion of orderliness and progression appears in several popular images: one is that the parent is a gardener and works with the earth in which the seed of selection falls, and the child may be likened to a blade of grass; another image is that of steps which must be ascended to reach adulthood; still another is of unrolling, unfolding, or developing externally: For example:

> We are . . . given . . . a kind of metaphoric mosiac—
> of the child who is born with certain predispositions and innate
> qualities *(Keim,* 'sprout,' is sometimes used to refer to these),
> who goes through stages *(Stufen)* of predetermined growth, in
> the course of which there is a process of opening up, of revealing
> *(Entwicklung)* and during which the parents work on the child—
> preparing the ground, fostering some qualities, implanting some
> qualities, removing and uprooting others (innate or implanted),
> even creating ground (i. e., the ground of common personal rela-
> tionships) in which roots can take hold and grow—so that the
> child will reach a kind of ripeness at each state and, finally, the
> ripeness of adulthood (Metraux 1963:213).

There are, of course, both physiological and psychological stages of childhood which have been well investigated, although such postulated stages have not yet been thoroughly tested cross-culturally. Investigation into many diverse cultures is needed for corroboration and verification of the existence and nature of the stages. For instance, a look at one of the postulated stages will illuminate a German preference. Children, in their second and third years, have a tendency to pedantry. They are ready and eager for exacting obedience and other kinds of precision and routine in their life. In fact, during this period they pettishly dislike change and very much want exact routine. The point is that, in the U. S., this is considered a stage that is difficult to get through, whereas in Germany it is a welcome period and one whose characteristics, it is be-lieved, should be seized upon in order that they may be perpetuated for the rest of life (Metraux 1963:217).

Aside from stages, the authors of child-guidance literature emphasize training to fulfill life's tasks and the development of firmness of char-acter, defined as the ability to overcome obstacles or, failing that, to ac-cept circumstances (Metraux 1963:205). Another emphasis which may be contrasted with the United States is that in German culture, the school and the home are categorically separated in the task of raising the young. In the German manuals, the feeling expressed is that children get instruction in the school but are formed at home. Indeed, if the parents and the teacher each do their job properly, there is no need for them to meet (Metraux 1963 :205f.).

A child is not considered an adult until his character (his will, his feelings, and judgment) have fully developed, and the process of raising a child in a German family can be very lengthy, extending into the years of young adulthood.

> Thus the German child is prepared in the home to become an independent individual, who, through the practice of willing obedience to parental rules, has learned to obey all rules of his own accord and who, through painful experience, has trained his will to master the problems of life. . . . The intention of this education is not to prepare the individual to make choices but rather to know what is right and to have the strength and fortitude to do it (Metraux 1963 :224).

The path set by the expert is not a simple one to follow. There are hazards:

> Although a child will be stunted in its development if it lacks attentive love, and will be endangered and dangerous if it is neglected, and will become a rebel or a sycophant or a will-less slave if too great demands are made and too great pressures are put upon it, and will come to grief if it fails to learn self-discipline through obedience, and be unable to face and master life if it has not achieved autonomy, the greatest anxiety expressed by experts is connected with the idea that the child may be weakened and spoiled, may become unsocial and prematurely sexually aware (*frühreif*) through parental overattentiveness, overcarefulness, and overfeeding with foolish affection (Metraux 1963 :222).

Finally, a look at the basic justification for the total parental authority over the child, the instruction of the educator to the parents, and the self-education of the educator: the child at birth is neither good nor bad, but has unformed potentialities. Misguided or left to its own devices at any point, the child is incapable of developing its own good potentialities. On the other hand, if the parent looks to the educator, if the educator continues his self-education, and both apply the principles to the child, that child can be guided, molded, and formed into a proper German (Metraux 1963:224).

In 1966, another commentary on child-training manuals showed that the situation has not changed much from that found by Metraux in 1953 (which is when she prepared material cited here in a 1963 publication). "German children are obedient (even docile), helpful, mild tempered, good eaters, and uncomplaining long-distance walkers" while in contrast American children seem "boisterous, undisciplined, volatile, and lazy, but they are also more natural, and inclined to be more . . . independent than their German contemporaries" (Shabecoff 1966:179). These words are written not by a trained observer but by an intelligent, interested observer, an American mother with two children of her own growing up while the family is in residence in Germany for a few years. She makes broad generalizations, of course, but they illuminate some pervading differences in child-training practices in the two countries. The author goes on to say that one reason for the differences between American and German children is that discipline and authority have a long and respected tradition in Germany, which gives assurance to parents; in contrast in America, the parents often spend long soul-searching periods wondering whether they are doing the right thing. Shabecoff makes her observations not only from personal experience but also draws upon a child-rearing textbook and a child-guidance book, both of which emphasize obedience on the part of the child and quiet dominance on the part of the mother; however, in dominance a mother avoids violence and displays of anger (Shabecoff 1966:179). One hundred ten mothers were asked in a study, "What traits would you especially value in the six year old?" The 15 percent top of the list said obedience; the bottom 1 percent said friendliness. The summary finding for the 110 mothers is that they do not see a six year old as an individual requiring respect but rather as an object to rear, form, and impress; indeed, it is incumbent upon them to form and impress the child. Molding begins in infancy during which, we should not be surprised to note, demand feeding is not very popular. Some of the textbooks advocate demand feeding, but more advocate a schedule and regimen to which the child should be subjected and made familiar as soon as possible. Mothers are exhorted to be consistent in training their young, and this consistency should extend beyond always handling problem situations the same way (an impossibility to begin with). One textbook advocates that the child be fed always at the same time and in the same place and that playing, prattling, and dawdling not be permitted. We need not think that this results in a cold mother—it does not—all exhortations to mother to handle her child firmly or consistently are followed with qualifying phrases about patience, serenity, and affection (Shabecoff 1966:180), which attitudes, if not actual behaviors, there is every reason to believe mothers develop.

Asking about the range of choice the child has points up one of the differences between child training experts in the U.S. and Germany. Dr. Spock says, "Offer the child spinach," whereas Dr. Haarer (a German counterpart) says, "Give the child spinach."

Shabecoff reports that most German parents believe that children should be seen but not heard. I expected to hear this admonition and to see children constantly drilled in silence, but I never did. I think in public or with visitors for a short period children may be quieter than their American counterparts, but in any prolonged stay, as I had, in the domestic situation the children may very well be very noisy. However, Shabecoff has as her authority a Munich textbook (Shabecoff 1966:182).

Also, from her observations, note the emphasis on cleanliness and orderliness:

> In this kindergarten, the children played with neat little toys taken from neat little shelves. When they had arts and crafts period, the articles they produced were cut out on indicated lines and pasted together in pre-arranged patterns. The last three quarters of an hour each day was spent sitting in a neat circle singing folk or religious songs. No child was ever dirtier at the end of the day than when delivered in the morning (Shabecoff 1966:182).

Finally, Shabecoff ends on a note of optimism based on a talk with a German pediatrician. He, at least, advocates a much less Prussian cadet tradition of authority, but he also realistically feels that it will be some time until most German mothers have changed their techniques of raising children.

Another exercise in analysis of documents is Rhoda Metraux's "A Portrait of the Family in German Juvenile Fiction." In this study, samples of the books read by a generation of German children were collected and studied "to throw light on the writers who prepared them, the parents who selected them, and the adults, part of whose childhood experience they formed" (Mead in Mead and Wolfenstein 1963:16f.). The novels chosen concern only family life as portrayed for adolescents and present highly idealized and moral versions of family life, which, predicably enough, revolve around the problems of the young heroes and heroines. The stories were written between 1880 and 1939 and were still being read when the study was done in 1953. Again, we note conservatism and marked stability over time in that there has been little

change in the ideals that the novels portray (Metraux in Mead and Wolfenstein 1963:254). All examples cited were from city families and I suspect no rural families were apotheosized in the novels chosen for analysis. The authors are concerned with the problems of character building
and fulfillment. The heroes and heroines live in a family which is an
integral unit, with practically no affinity to a larger social system or
with events beyond the garden wall (Metraux 1963:257). In fact,
"Germany exists as an idea—as a beloved way of doing things, as a
series of landscapes, as the summation of a kind of character—but
hardly as a political entity" (Metraux 1963:258). "References to officials and governments are rare—, incidental, and limited to a locale.
In contrast, the family is lovingly drawn in detail. They tend to
be big but not close knit families. While the novels suggest repeatedly
that deep attachment to home (*die Heimat* and, more narrowly, *das El-
terhaus*) is necessary and good, residence too close to home may be a
sign of dependence" (Metraux 1963:260).

The table is a symbol of the unity of the family (Mead and Wolfenstein 1963:260), in the dining room, used for coffee elsewhere in the
house, or picnicking in the woods. Around the table are celebrated
birthdays, anniversaries, and other special occasions; and in the winter
evenings the family sits there together. They may have separate activities (mother sewing, children doing homework, father reading), but they
sit together. Away from the table, each member of the family has his
appointed place—study for father, sewing corner for mother, room for
grandmother, and children have a locale too. Mother runs the house
and father provides for it. She exhibits responsibility by having a per-
fect household always ready for father and arranged for the care and
control of children. Although parents have separate responsibilities, they
are one in decisions and the expression of opinions about family decisions. The children do not see the preparatory steps. Mother, as a matter of course, adapts herself to a father's personality and needs. When
she cannot, or will not make such an adjustment, the marriage runs into
difficulties. Yet, in the stories, neither father nor mother is a domi-
neering or dominated person (Metraux 1963:261f.).

A central theme is that the harmony and happiness of the family and,
indeed, the well-being of the children grow out of complete natural obedience (Mead and Wolfenstein 1963:267). Willing obedience means
emotionally knowing that overcoming one's passions in accordance with
the customs and dictates of the group is the only sure path to harmony

and happiness. The child must learn to do what is right and not to do what is wrong as a part of his own will, his own character.

The family world of the story-book is not altogether a happy one. People age and die and are mourned. Children sicken or die in fatal accidents. Families have to struggle and learn to do without. Dreams have to be revised and hopes postponed or sacrificed. Friends and lovers sometimes disappoint, are not what they seem. Nevertheless for the person who controls his own will, so that he can give up what he desires and do what he dislikes, who (as a child) can obey willingly or (as a parent) can lead unfalteringly, who has learned by and accepts suffering, who is what he is entirely and without concealment (except for the sake of others), this family world offers security and warmth and completeness, irrespective of the troubles in the world outside. Then parents can be fond and children can be happy, and the German family can live in harmony—and Germany is well off. (Metraux 1963:273).

A final example of content analysis as it reflects themes in German culture is "The Consequence of Wrongdoing: An Analysis of Story Completions by German Children" by Rhoda Metraux. If we analyze the answers of a series of problems presented to one child, we get some insight into the imaginative reworking of experience by that child; however, if the same series of problems are given to a group of children and those answers analyzed, we derive a pattern of expectation about a type of experience. From this we can infer with a fair degree of reliability and accuracy the organization of attitudes towards such experiences in a given culture (Mead and Wolfenstein 1963:306). Following is an analysis of the attitudes of German children toward wrongdoing expressed in a series of story completions. The tests were administered to children in a West German city school in the summer of 1952. Analysis is presented in terms of children's handling of the plot and identifies the dominant themes that emerge (Mead and Wolfenstein 1963:306f.). One hundred fifty ten- and eleven-year-old children were given the stories, and the analysis is based on a sample of the total material (we are not told how that sample was derived).

Each of the situations presented to the children involves a child who commits, or is supposed to have committed, a misdeed. In each, there is a limited cast of characters, a restriction which limits the outcome. The theme-writing children are predominantly preoccupied with punishment and their major expectation is that punishment will follow wrongdoing. Interestingly enough, they do not differentiate sharply between

an accident, an accident that follows on a misdeed, or a deliberate misdeed (Mead and Wolfenstein (1963:316) but they agree that punishment is inescapable if the culprit is discovered. (In fact, adults have
said that for children there is an eleventh commandment, Don't let your-
self get caught.) In the story completions that the children write, the
culprit blushes, is red-faced, stammers, or cannot meet his mother's eye
in expectation of punishment. In other words, the child signals the
wrongdoing to the parent (signaling is a theme which also occurs in
juvenile fiction).

Punishment does not seem tailored to fit the cime, that is, shouting,
scolding, threatening, slapping, boxing ears, immobilization in the house
or school, making the child use his own money to make good a loss, and
so forth, are standard results of the various misdeeds the children hy-
pothetically engage in (Mead and Wolfenstein 1963:317). It is interesting to note that in the child-care manuals, parents are repeatedly ad-
monished that punishment must follow a misdeed and that the punishment should be appropriate to the misdeed. Children seem to be subject
to, and have internalized, the first part of this teaching, but either the
children or the parents, or both, have not learned or the parents have
not applied the second part (Mead and Wolfenstein (1963:317).

There is another interesting dimension. In some of the stories, punishment sets in motion a process that has no necessary end. It is not
enough that one person punish the child. Mother tells father; in school,
teacher tells the principal and also mother, and so forth. Each then
begins to punish the culprit and an ever-widening circle presses in on
the young wrongdoer. A contrary interpretation, where the wrongdoer is pictured as a victim, may result in the child asking for help or
being aided by a bigger or stronger person and the child may protect himself to a limited extent by confessing, asking for forgiveness, apologiz-
ing, or promising restitution.

> Thus the complementary relationship of child and parents and
> the endless hierarchy of the weak, the slightly stronger, and those
> still stronger are invoked in the punishment of wrong, the restora-
> tion of goodness to the wrongdoer, and the protection of the vic-
> tim. From the viewpoint of the child writers, the only escapes
> from this system for the comparatively weak are in the mainte-
> nance of exact equality with equals . . . or in the secrecy
> and solitude of the wrongdoer, who, undiscovered, resolves to do
> right and be good. . . . From the viewpoint of the child,

only the strong adult . . . gets away with impunity (Mead and Wolfenstein 1963:320).

So appears the world to the ten and eleven year olds as they struggle with a hypothetical situation and as they project their understanding and cultural interpretation into minimally structured situations. The results are interesting and not incongruent with the analyses previously presented. We pass on to some other depictions of Germans.

LOWIE

As I prepared for fieldwork in 1964 and 1965, I read Lowie's *The German People* twice. Written from lectures given to men who were going into Germany in wartime, Lowie describes his book as an inquiry into social psychology, or the attitude of Germans of different classes and at different times, ending in 1914. In 1954, he published another book extending the coverage to 1950. In *The German People,* Lowie writes from the point of view of the anthropologist, "the orientation that comes from trying to see any particular manifestation of culture comparatively, to determine its place among the cultures of humanity as a whole" (Lowie 1945: preface).

Taking first the problem of deciding what is German, Lowie, like Spencer, decides that it is not language, for the Germans have many dialects and only a slight difference is enough to be marked. And it is not race. Diesel, using a layman's conception, had spoken as if subraces existed within Germany, but Lowie reviews the scientific evidence which, in his day, was anthropometric measurements and hair and skin color judgments and finds the conclusions for the existence of definable and delimitable subraces inadequate and unconvincing (Lowie 1945:20). Nonetheless, Lowie once believed in the existence of a distinctive German culture:

> Notwithstanding their linguistic and physical diversity, the Germans, partly through natural diffusion, especially after the adoption of a common literary medium, partly through the deliberate efforts of various prophets, partly through governmental action, developed certain similarities of attitude and social behavior. In consequence we may speak of a distinctive German culture. . . . (Lowie 1945:20).

This is important because later, in his 1954 book, he changed his mind about the existence of a distinctive German culture. Even in his earlier book, he did not define it clearly. He spoke once of "ethos" (Lowie

1945:21) but he never made explicit what ethos included. While believing that there was a distinctive German culture, Lowie also noted the great diversity and differentiation within the national whole: deep and abiding provincial differences (sometime characterized as "church steeple politics"), a parochialism that "recognizes no kinship or solidarity beyond the range of the village church bell" (Lowie 1954:21).

A salient factor in understanding Germans is, for Lowie, social class. He talks about classes in terms of the aristocracy, the middle class, the working class, the peasant (he did not cavil at calling a peasant a peasant), artisans and tradesmen—a categorization derived from the Middle Ages. The aristocrats were sometimes poor, almost always boorish, and very late in history (with residue still extant today) treated with great servility. They had no economic interests except deriving benefit from their landed estates, or recouping losses through political advantage. An interesting insight into German manners is given by Lowie, who tells us that the aristocracy failed to produce gentlemen and a tradition of gentlemanly behavior thereby, of course, depriving the middle and lower classes of models of gentility to imitate. The middle class evolved with characteristics noted by Schaffner and to be further commented on by me. These are orderliness, the limiting of goals, and the setting of boundaries. Lowie chooses this example from the life of Goethe:

> Let foreign countries take care of themselves and do you consider the political heavens at most of a Sunday or holiday. Let each man begin on himself and he will find much to do. Let him use such undisturbed periods of time as are granted us in working for his own and his dependents' legitimate profit; thus he will bring profit to everybody (Lowie 1945:65).

The above, a speech of a nobleman in one of Goethe's farces is cited to indicate a restriction of self—a restriction of time, energy, and commitment which marked the middle class. Lowie brilliantly expounds that what Goethe and his thousands of imitators did was to deny and leave out of their lives the study of and the involvement in social and political life. Politics were not something the scholar should sully himself with, something he should give his creative time to; his obligations on this earth were to demand and do anything necessary to keep a stable environment in which he could continue to develop (allow to unroll) his character. Thus would he support a Bismarck or a Hitler, national leaders who promised stability—regardless of what their other characteristics might be.

Lowie warns that there is great variability within the peasant stratum : the main causes being differences in the fertility of the soil, the location of the land in reference to urban or industrial centers, and the size of the holdings. He also says the peasant has come to be looked down upon by other social classes and so is not the social or psychological equivalent of the American farmer. Given these variables as a baseline, the peasant has then developed unevenly. In the Ruhr, anomalously, he had become a business farmer (beginning between 1840 and 1870), but elsewhere he had remained a peasant.

His treatment of family life is brief. From two biographies he sketches the life of a middle-class family of moderate means and that of a factory worker, with a few additional words on the peasant. Unlike Spencer, Lowie sees the differences in family types as being a matter of economics and ideology (Lowie 1945 :84–86). In fact, what Spencer called the impressive authoritarian family becomes for Lowie the economically secure, though not much more than adequately endowed household; and what Spencer saw as the repressive authoritarian family may actually be the family in a subculture of poverty, a family deprived of material necessities and suffering the social and psychological deprivations which trail in poverty's wake.

I turn now to Lowie's second book, titled *Toward Understanding Germany* (1954). Although Lowie's first book was written from his memories and in his armchair, for his second book he spent a week in Vienna, two and one-half months in Switzerland, and four months in West Germany; this was in 1950. His subject is again social psychology with special attention to family life, the position of women and the class system (Lowie 1954: preface). Much of the material he presents is taken from his 1945 book, some of it verbatim, but augmented. His definition of a German is this time different :

> "German" shall denote anyone who uses standard German as his primary medium of communication in so far as he does not employ his local Germanic dialect. The social psychology of Germans thus circumscribed, as exhibited during the last two centuries forms our theme (Lowie 1954:15).

I might point out that although Lowie circumscribes his population to those using standard German, he devotes time and space to those who do not—rural populations, for instance. All of Chapter 14 is on rural families who undoubtedly use dialect.

Still interested in the comparative method, Lowie included Switzerland in his study so that he might have a Germanic people in another nation for contrast and comparison. His use of written materials includes what travelers said about Germany, what traveling Germans said about other nations, scientific and literary writings, and newspapers (even the classified advertisements and obituaries); these are all sources which most anthropologists studying a literate society find useful. He was aided in his content analysis and participant observation by his wife and sister. In addition, of course, he traveled, lectured, chatted, picked up hitchhikers, and talked to people from all walks of life.

Lowie's main argument is introduced early and repeated often, that much of what we think of as purely German is really a historical circumstance or, "much of what is popularly conceived as German is in reality either generically human or occidental or Continental European" (Lowie 1954:30). A similar argument was advanced in 1957 by Theodor Heuss while he was president of the Federal Republic of Germany. He does not refer to Lowie's work and does not believe that language is a key factor, but argues for a temporal perception of history, pointing out that the period of time at which one views a country can significantly influence the judgment about the character of the people.

> Those same Germans who were once epitomized as "poets and thinkers" (the phrase dates from 1837) were noted a few decades later as chemists and physicists whose scientific achievements quickly brought practical benefits (Liebig, Bunsen, Siemens, Röntgen, etc.). In 1864, 1866 and 1870-71 the same people won several wars with speed and éclat, and promptly became fascinated with military glory as nations are so apt to do. In the minds of the rest of the world the Germans became *the* bellicose nation—a reputation formerly in the ages of Louis XIV and Napoleon I, accorded to the French (Heuss 1957:104).

Heuss's interpretation of the historical experience of Germany is in direct contrast to Spencer's. Heuss does not consider Germany as a marginal culture (he may not have had this concept in his lexicon) but, rather, he looks to the divisive autonomy (early established and unconscionably late maintained) of the petty states which became Germany and the great diversity of the several political structures. He feels that history denied the Germans sufficient opportunity to shape their political destiny democratically (Heuss 1957:105). Returning to the theme that the opprobrium Germany suffered had earlier been the fate of other European nations, he says:

> It is permissible to recall that world-wide condemnation such as the Germans have now brought upon themselves, was applied 150 years ago to the French people. They were then charged with being eternal troublemakers. And historically, the "imperialism" of the Spaniards, the British, the French, the Russians, and even the Swedes was actually of greater order of magnitude in terms of territory. Here again, then, we are not dealing with a peculiar feature of the German constitution (Heuss 1957:107).

Finally, President Heuss also delineates other characteristics or traits which are supposedly German: overreliance on theory with resultant doctrinairism (which he finds in other nations too), rational efficiency, a faculty for abstract thought, ideological susceptibility, active curiosity about the world, a desire for intellectual enrichment, and that strain which is so seldom investigated because it is so difficult to define— romanticism—and he suggests that time or history be the arbiter in the value accorded these traits and what their meaning may be to the nation (Heuss 1957:106–109).

We contrast this with what Lowie has picked out of the historical stream to compare and contrast with other European nations. History shows us, Lowie says, that Germans oscillate between urges to nationalism and particularism—but Germany is not peculiar in this respect; so, too, do other nations. One difference may be noted: in Germany the integrating forces have been weaker than the separatist trends. (So also said Heuss.) Lowie discusses change in class structure within Germany and gives much space to treatment of Jews in many nations. The Jews have been separate in all nations, but individuals have entered the social structure at the higher levels, and there have been many exceptions to the rules of exclusion and the practice of discrimination. In German society as a whole, class lines have softened and the structure has come to be a continuum rather than a series of levels. Still, distinctions are important to the Germans, and neither class consciousness nor distinctions have disappeared, although there is much less arrogance than formerly. (Lowie 1954:191).

As to family life, Lowie gives scores of cases, each of which is interesting, of course, and accomplishes what he set out to do: showing diversity and differentiation, but this also makes it very difficult to arrive at generalizations. Lowie notes two extreme types of families.

One is the idyllic family situation rapturously described as the ultimate in human warmth and love, and the other is the strongly authoritarian family, ugly and distasteful to the outsider, in which the tyrannical father is master, arbitrarily bending wife and children to his will. Of course, neither the romantic idealization of a family nor the depiction of a wholly vicious tyrant father can be held as a true conception. Lowie has pointed out and Spencer concurs (Spencer 1965:180) that both of these extremes are rare and that the family structure in Germany falls somewhere in between. But whether it is panegyric or indictment, there is still agreement that the family is authoritarian (Lowie 1954:197–266), although Lowie argues that the degree to which it is authoritarian is overstated and also that it is changing.

He, of course, gives us a great deal of detailed data—some of it fascinating indeed! And one must agree with his main arguments that much of what he picks to talk about is not Germanic—it is European. I guess that all we can say is that it is unfortunate that he did not choose to continue the search for that which was particularly German to expound upon it. I think he knew what it was: German thoroughness "whether in research or in the household, in the love for work as an end in itself. In one of its noblest forms, it appears as the proletarian's craving for intellectual and asthetic culture" (Lowie 1954:355). But Lowie could not develop these positive aspects since his native land was at that time so widely hated and condemned. He was defensive. He had, perforce, to take much of his time and energy in defending Germany and Germans against the condemnation and the calumny in which they existed at the end of World War II.

What is one to say of Lowie? He puts those who come after him in a most difficult position. And indeed that is because he was in a difficult position. A self-proclaimed spokesman for the Germans, he spoke first about them from a distance and then, after the war, had an opportunity to visit his *Landsmann*. While in the first book, he was not on the defensive, in the second he definitely was. Let us consider his position. He was born in Austria and had his academic career in the U.S. Any fieldworker knows the combination of sadness, relief, and pain on returning to one's own culture after having been steeped in another. One has a new perspective on one's homeland, not always complimentary. Lowie was going home. I say this even though he came to the United States at the age of ten. His family brought German culture with them; it was in German culture that he was reared. Although he may have visited Germany earlier, he was sixty-seven years old when he visited with the intent of writing the second book. In a certain sense, his long sojourn in America was fieldwork during which he learned new ideals and values.

We can look at this from another perspective; when he visited Germany at the age of sixty-seven he was an acculturated American and appears to have felt compelled to explain his birth culture to his adopted land. In his capacity an an anthropologist and with his heritage in two cultures, he had taken it upon himself to explain what made the Germans German. It was no enviable position to be in. He has, on the whole, done the best he could with a very difficult chore. He need not have set for himself this task; he took it on voluntarily; yet we should be unhappy to have Lowie's reputation based on this book. Given the difficulty of his task, the dilemma of his bicultural identification, and the point of his study, one is, nonetheless, disappointed that at first he thought there was delimitable German culture, but in his last work denied that it was so. "The concept of a German culture sphere with which we have been tentatively operating thus turns out to be an ill-defined, if not indefinable, entity" (Lowie 1954:354). And there is another factor. Lowie was one of the last holdouts to psychoanalytic theory and to the validity and value of studies of child rearing. In his 1954 book, he devotes much space to chiding and refuting one psychoanalyst (certainly not the one who made the best case for national character) and he (Lowie) seems totally unaware of other psychiatric interpretations. Indeed the whole aspect of culture learned at mother's knee seems to be unimportant or nonexistent to him (consider the low esteem women are accorded in Germany). At best, he failed to give child training any emphasis.

I will paraphrase the conclusions in Lowie's *Toward Understanding Germany*. The racial constitution of Germans does not differ from other western Europeans. Hence, if there are any innate tendencies among Germans, they must also be found among Danes and Swedes. Differences in social behavior are due to historical causes, which bring individual tendencies to the fore in some areas but not in others. No findings about purported German traits are valid until we know the distribution of such traits in time and space. No trait, he says, is *the* German trait or attitude unless it is pan-German and pan-diachronically so (across time), and such a trait is *not* German unless it is found only among Germans (Lowie 1954:354). These terms are very restrictive ones, and if we were to stick to them, we probably could not talk about national culture anywhere on the earth. Subcultural differences within Germany are marked and important. There have been swings between a trend for particularism and centralism; these polarities never disappear. Family life remained authoritarian in Germany later than elsewhere because Germany became industrialized later. The status of women legally and practically was not inferior to that of Spain, Italy, or France (Lowie 1954:355).

He reiterates, then, that we cannot treat Germany as a unit marked off from the rest of western civilization and adjures us to study social classes across national lines. This is probably a good lead. He finally says that making studies on linguistic or national boundaries are the inexpensive type, and that we must actually study Europe in terms of large culture areas where neither the language nor the boundary will be the diagnostic criteria (Lowie 1954:355f). I am inclined to think he is right, although how we study a thing always depends on what it is we want to find out. And if we study a culture area we will get culture area characteristics, not national ones.

MY DEPICTION OF GERMANS

Previously, I undertook fieldwork in Germany to learn about German culture, to learn if there was indeed something peculiarly Germanic. Five years and many thoughtful hours of analysis later, I still struggle with the question. Yes, yes, of course, there is something that is Germanic, but have I or any of the other investigators succeeded in isolating it? Have we pushed aside traits or characteristics which are European, or peasant, or modern rural, and been able to show clearly as on a slide something which is purely German? I just do not know.

Difficult as is this consideration, it is only the first part of the question. If any of us has succeeded in depicting some "Germanness," to what extent does this Germanness appear in individual Germans? Is it, indeed, possible to make statements about the appearance of national characteristics in individuals in large masses as heterogeneous as a nation? Is it helpful if we can? One saving thought is that it may be possible to deal with "national character" data in the framework of and within the limitations of probability theory. That is, study of the data may enable us to make statements on the order of, "The German people have a propensity to be clean and orderly, and to search for absolutes." If we can accept this and similar depictions as statements of probability, we can increase understanding, sharpen and economize description, and have a probability basis for further action and study—even if we do not know whether or not each and every individual has all three propensities. Even when there are portions of the population who have characteristics not listed in the statement, or contrary to the statement, there is still utility in a depiction cast as a probability. Let me draw an analogy from health care. When we say that the age at which a mother is most likely to bear a child easily and free of defect are the years from eighteen to forty, this does not mean that a seventeen-year-old girl or a forty-three-year-old woman could not bear a whole and healthy child (nor indeed, heaven forbid, that we should attempt to deny them the opportunity to do so), but rather that there are limiting optimal conditions which apply to the greater proportion of the population. The optimal characteristics can be stated quite clearly. Then we can be very careful with pregnant women over and under the optimal ages and not in optimal health. Another example: when we make statements that a three-day weekend holiday death rate is 600 people (U.S.) we cannot identify in advance the 600 victims (nor do we need to), but we can plan, and implement plans, to lower that figure. In other words, identifying cases or individuals may be unimportant and unnecessary for many kinds of action. Herein lies the practical value of derived economical descriptions of mass and heterogeneous populations.

My own observations in a village of 500 in central Germany and in Frankfurt are such that I am in essential agreement with the various depictions presented in this chapter. Nothing I observed or heard was widely variant from the descriptions given. The authors have given descriptions which, while they represent different approaches and are cased in different frameworks, are congruent and compatible; they are well drawn and highly convincing, and they illustrate anew what we know from other studies of the nature and force of culture—that there are societal expectations, pressures, and rewards that mold and form individuals. The expectation and the pressure to meet it that impressed me most both during my stay in Frankfurt and in the village were the tendency, nay the compulsion, to orderliness. Drawing on an ancient heritage, with roots at least as old as Greece, the German believes in an orderly universe, a bound universe with categorizable parts, and he is not peculiar in this. If we did not presume, if we did not have faith, if there were not, indeed, a good deal of order in the universe, we could not endure. But an individual or a people may have a greater or a lesser belief in and drive to orderliness. With the Germans, the propensity to put things in order was a theme that arose again and again. Most individuals that I met—almost all— exhibited a need to straighten things out, to place into categories, to pigeonhole, to strive for precision, to map the territory, to state the boundaries, or to fill in the blanks. Here, it seemed, was a driving force that pervaded much of life and was illustrated in widely divergent manifestations. Some examples follow.

Any of the professions within a country, of course, will focus on fields and subjects of interest to everyone in that country. For example, in the United States, the interest of members of the medical profession in capitalism and economic growth has led to the development of a structure in which each physician is cast as a small businessman seeking to maximize profits. This compelling interest in "business" informs every aspect of medicine and is part of the widely held belief that any group medical practice and most forms of governmental supervision are anti-capitalistic (if not socialistic). In surgery, in Germany, members of the medical profession have developed an operation which is in keeping with the general proclivity to make things neat and orderly; they have perfected surgery to shorten the legs of girls who are too tall. Tall girls are pitied because they obviously do not have a place in the neat scheme of things in which men are taller. Those tall girls who are also pretty, intelligent, and educated are among the rare ones who are given opportunities to rise in the professions; opportunities are very few. I do not know enough about Japanese culture to know why their medicine has developed the way it has, but the fascinating fact is that it is the Japanese who have developed the techniques for inflating breasts.

German advertisements for lipsticks included a feature I had never seen elsewhere and one which is an illumination of the German proclivity for precision as well as order. A colored full-page advertisement advised that at a certain temperature (and the temperature was given) lipstick would begin to cake. The point is that somebody had made this measurement (presumably; I do not know if German advertising copywriters are any more addicted to inaccuracy of detail or misstatement than ours are) and published it knowing that the public would be interested in a measurement, that they would derive satisfaction from having a measurement, and from knowing precisely what the caking temperature of lipstick was.

One time, a small whale from the North Sea got trapped in the Main River. Naturally, this was a subject of interest to the news media, both the radio and the newspapers. What made the news coverage Germanic and what illustrates a Germanic need for precision and specificity is that every sighting of the whale reported located the mammal precisely and told how many times the animal blew within a specified number of minutes.

I once discussed with a German colleague, a curator in a museum, the problems involved in compiling an inventory of ethnological collections. We were discussing how museum ethnological collections are used and how they might most profitably be inventoried and indexed. My colleague liked the problem and the project very much: it involved getting things organized and categorized, putting things in "boxes," and naming the boxes. He emphasized the necessity for having the inventory complete and up-to-date, arguing that after all, the task is not rightly and properly performed if it is not complete, if the inventory is not clear and unambiguous. But here we have a dilemma. Complete, up to the minute records are an ideal impossible of achievement. The inevitable delays in data collection, in ordering and delivering, in analysis and recording, are such that we must always live in an imperfect world of inventory. Yet, if ever there is a group who have more culturally derived propensities to keep an as up-to-date as possible inventory, it is the Germans, for they, with their striving to neatness and their never-flagging industry in the pursuit of order, are the ones who will keep inventories as complete and correct as possible. Lowie himself may furnish an example:

> Obviously, it is a counsel of perfection that one should systematically scan the remarks of various foreigners on German life and to supplement them with a similarly exhaustive survey of what Germans have said about English, American, French, Italian, and Spanish ways and manners. But it is equally clear that for a definitive study of Germany such studies would be one prerequisite; and though they must remain an ideal, the ideal remains one to strive for (Lowie 1954:27).

Here is a final example from a professional. One time, I interviewed a social worker about the referral and treatment of disturbed children. She said that if the child has a clearly defined problem, they treat him; otherwise they send him home again. His symptoms have to be classical, specific, and traditional, or he would not be treated. In other words, the social worker would not struggle with uncategorizable complexity; she

lacked both the orientation and the habits to tolerate ambiguity or lack
of structure. With an extraordinarily low tolerance for ambiguity, "Box
me in," begs the German. He needs boundaries; he must know the limits; all must be clearly stated, delineated and known.

Other observers have commented on German orderliness, of course,
Diesel noted the need for, and propensity toward, order in his countrymen. He thought that the neatness and tidiness so often admired were
due more to the passion for order than they were to the love of cleanliness. And he also, in prepsychoanalytic days, thought of the passion for
order as based on deep-rooted insecurity. The need for order is diffused
throughout all of life: the family, the club, work, the bureau, and borders and is projected on to other countries.

> The German feels that there is something undecided and unjustified, something lacking in clarity and definition about the eastern frontiers. Where Slav and German meet, the frontier cannot
> be considered satisfactory from either the geographical or racial
> point of view (Diesel 1931:14f.).

> No country is outwardly more orderly . . . than Germany.
> The concept of order is a sacred one, but it is not so much an
> organic order that is meant as an ordering and regulating of the
> conditions under which people live. During the war one often
> heard the remark: "We'll soon put things in order in such and
> such a country!" The German will not realize that the whole
> world does not necessarily want his particular type of order, a type
> which he considers to be "order" in the absolute sense (Diesel
> 1931:153).

Finally, here are three examples of the drive to order from German
migrants to the New World.

A chaplain recounts that German war brides delivered of their children in a midwestern medical center were urgently concerned to have
their babies baptized very quickly. The urgency had nothing to do with
religion; they were not thinking that the child should be cleansed of
original sin, but they wanted to have the baptism performed because it is
the fitting and proper thing to do, because "it is what we do, because it
is right." A woman told me a tale of her great-grandmother's immigration to the United States from Germany with her new husband. Greatgrandmother brought with her a handmade trousseau, prepared before
her marriage by friends and neighbors gathered to help sew the clothes
and linens she would need. There were many items ranging from long
white stockings to beautiful linen napkins and tablecloths, all numbered

in red; the socks were numbered at the heel and the napkins in the corner. Migrant to a new country, a German community in Kansas perpetuates this church seating arrangement: the unmarrieds sit in the balcony, females separated from males and age group separated from age group as follows. The balcony curves around the church like a horseshoe, and at the end nearest the pulpit sit the first graders. As they advance in school, they move over and around the circle. Each grade has a supervisor, who keeps an eye on them, frowning coldly when they talk (if they become really unseemly in their conduct, they might also be "noticed" by the minister). Through promotions, the children advance along the balcony until they are in the eighth grade, at which time they become eligible for confirmation instruction. When they begin to undergo confirmation instruction their seating in the church is dramatically changed. They go downstairs and sit on two sides of the apse in direct view of the congregation and under the eye of the minister. After confirmation, they again go upstairs to a higher prestige section of the balcony. When they marry they come downstairs again to seats which again are age-graded—the less prestigious ones are off to the side under the balcony and the males and the females are still separated. The seats in the center aisles, the core of the church, are for the mature married couples and the respected elders.

I hope these examples have served to communicate to the reader the informing force found behind many actions, beliefs, and phenomena exhibited by the Germans I studied. There are, of course, many other examples; and, equally important, a norm of orderliness is only one of the multiple norms that structure German society. Still, it is an overriding, a pervasive and an important force.

We have in this essay been concerned with various depictions of Germans; we have looked at national character studies, psychiatric interpretations, content analysis of written materials, Lowie's analysis and, finally, my impressions. The concept of national character is not dead. It will be renamed and will rise again.

LITERATURE CITED

Dicks, Henry V.
    1950a Personality Traits and National Socialist Ideology. Human
    Relations 3:111–154.

1950b Some Psychological Studies of the German Character. *In* Psychological Factors of Peace and War. T. H. Pear, Ed. London: Hutchinson and Company. pp. 195–218.

Diesel, Eugen
1931 Germany and the Germans. W. D. Robson-Scott, Trans. New York: Macmillan.

Heuss, Theodor
1957 German Character and History. R. and C. Winston, Trans. Atlantic 199(3):103–109.

Kecskemeti, P., and N. Leites
1945 Some Psychological Hypotheses on Nazi Germany. Experimental Division for the Study of War Time Communications. Document No. 60. Washington, DC: The Library of Congress.

Lowie, Robert H.
1945 The German People. New York and Toronto: Farrar and Rinehart.
1954 Toward Understanding Germany. Chicago: University of Chicago Press.

Mead, Margaret
1953 National Character. In Anthropology Today: An Encyclopedic Inventory. A. L. Kroeber, Ed. Chicago: University of Chicago Press.

Mead, Margaret, and M. Wolfenstein, Eds.
1955 Childhood in Contemporary Cultures. Chicago: University of Chicago Press.

Metraux, Rhoda
1955a The Consequences of Wrongdoing: An Analysis of Story Completions by German Children. *In* Childhood in Contemporary Cultures. M. Mead and M. Wolfenstein, Eds. Chicago: University of Chicago Press. Phoenix edition, 1963. pp. 306–323.
1955b Parents and Children: An Analysis of Contemporary German Child-Care and Youth Guidance Literature. *In* Childhood in Contemporary Cultures. M. Mead and M. Wolfenstein, Eds. Chicago: University of Chicago Press. Phoenix edition, 1963. pp. 204–228.
1955c A Portrait of the Family in German Juvenile Fiction. *In* Childhood in Contemporary Cultures. M. Mead and M. Wolfenstein, Eds. Chicago: University of Chicago Press. Phoenix edition, 1963. pp. 253–276.

Schaffner, Bertram
   1948   Father Land. New York: Columbia University Press.

Shabecoff, Alice
   1966   Bringing Up Hans und Gretel. *In* New York Times, November 13.

Spencer, Robert F.
   1965   The German Paradox. *In* Journal of the Minnesota Academy of Science 32(3) :160–182.

Tacitus
   1925   Dialogus, Agricola, and Germania. London: William Heinemann.

15

Kinfolks and the Covenant: Ethnic Community among Southern Presbyterians

GWEN KENNEDY NEVILLE

University of Florida

In recent years, social scientists have turned from the search for the melting pot to a search for the dynamics of cultural persistence among subgroups within the American national culture. Early studies concentrated on the most easily visible among these segments—the blacks, Jewish, Puerto Ricans, and Irish. (Glazer and Moynihan 1963). It has recently come to light that in addition to these obviously "ethnic" elements within our society there exist numerous other identifiable groups within what has been considered mainline American Culture. These include white subgroups that have remained separate from all others over a very long time period and which appear to be bounded by the same type of cultural, religious, and racial identity that is used to delineate ethnicity. Pursuing this line of inquiry, Killian (1970) treats white Southerners as an ethnic subsegment based on regional identity and associational patterns. Charles Anderson (1970) lumps together *all* white Protestant Americans nationwide, based on their overriding identification with the Protestant community against the threat of encroachment by other enclaves.

It is also possible to look more specifically at internal segments within white Protestantism as having a separate cultural, or ethnic, identity. The research on which this paper is based was designed as an inquiry into the dynamics of group-life preservation (the maintenance of ethnicity) among one such Protestant denomination in the American South—the Southern Presbyterians. While a case can be made for treating all white Anglo-Saxon Southerners together, sharing a world view and value system, or for lumping Southerners with other white Protestants, there are flaws in this approach. The greatest weakness in the treatment of ethnic identity in its aggregate form is that this approach looks at *categories* of people and of culture traits rather than at the groups and net-works of actual observable communal life. Milton Gordon calls for this communal life approach (1964) as a key to increasing our knowledge not only of the phenomenon of individual ethnic identity, but also of the nature of group life itself and the dynamics of group preservation. Gordon concentrates on the twin concepts of the ethnic group and ethnicity in explaining and describing subsegments of American social structure. He invents the term *ethclass* to define the intersection of ethnic and class variables which determine the network of participation within which an individual acts out his or her life.

Building on Gordon's work, this paper attempts to formulate a process model for viewing ethnic groups within the framework of community theory. As a transgenerational, structured cultural system consisting of three generations and two sexes interacting over an annual cycle, an ethnic group fulfills Arensberg's basic criteria for a community (1965). Alternately, this represents a labyrinth of subcommunities tied together into a larger web of interwoven units.

As a macrocommunity system, the ethnic group provides for its participants a reference population and a core of socializing agents who operate through ritual gatherings and ceremonial life to both preserve and transmit their shared world view.

In order to explicate this process model, it will be necessary to first put forth a working definition of the words *ethnic* and *ethnicity*, then to examine the "community" aspects of these new definitions and the way in which ritual gatherings may be a productive locus for analysis of cultural maintenance and transmission.

IDENTIFYING AND DEFINING THE ETHNIC COMMUNITY

Gordon defines an ethnic group as a group who shares "race, religion, national origins, and 'a sense of peoplehood' " (Gordon 1964:28). Two aspects of a national culture must be preserved in order to continue such a consciousness, or *ethnos,* which makes a people distinct from surrounding or intermingled populations. One of these features is structural isolation over time through endogamous marriage patterns. This structural separation provides the separate racial-cultural matrix of population necessary to pass on not only a gene pool but also a "culture pool" of traits to the following generations.

The second feature necessary is a shared meaning system, or world view, that unites a people into an ideological entity and provides values for the shared sense of peoplehood mentioned above. This meaning system might be expressed through shared language, or the common codification of reality through linguistic symbols. More often within Protestant America the meaning systems are symbolically codified through ritual language and the formalized language of religious creeds and beliefs. The sense of being set apart from other groups and having an identity as a people is ritually reinforced every time this symoblic language of ritual interaction is spoken (Hall 1966). It is partly spoken and written in confessions and doctrines but it is more powerfully expressed in behavioral enactments through recurrent rituals and ceremonies.

If a group possesses these two features, Gordon suggests that a person belonging to such a group is encapsulated from birth to death in a protective covering of relationships based on his group membership. Previous studies have assumed that this encapsulation must encompass all types and ranges of activities in order to classify the group as "ethnic." This assumption quickly spotlights the slum, the Indian reservation or urban enclave, the Jewish or black ghetto, or the suburban gilded ghetto as loci within which totally separate cultural worlds obviously exist. Among white Protestant middle-class Americans we find the impression of assimilation or nonethnic associational and occupational patterns. However, if one closely looks at the personal, kinship, and religious areas of these seemingly assimilated individuals, new data emerge on encapsulation. Individuals who work together side by side in factories and in bureaucracies may during leisure hours live in totally separate cultural worlds from one another in terms of meanings and values as well as in interactions with ceremonial communities of other Methodists, Baptists, and Presbyterians. A form of encapsulation does in fact exist in these white Anglo-Saxon groups, but it is a symbolic and ritual encapsulation that is expressed around significant individual and group transitions and events. Work on the significance of these events for the individual and the group by Turner (1969), following the pioneer theories of van Gennep (1960), suggests that within the rites of passage and other rituals are found an intensely powerful mode for enculturation of the individual and the continuity of his or her cultural loyalties.

The social structural separateness and the cultural separateness both reinforced by gatherings and rituals over a transgenerational time period lead now to an examination of this type of group as a form of human community. This form of cultural interaction will be called the ethnic community. Among white Protestant Americans each group, or web of subgroups, will have separate culturally defined patterns of behavior. The residence pattern for all of these, however, appears to be that of the scattered nuclear family household with only two generations present. On Sunday or other weekly church gathering days a wider network of families emerges at the congregational level, with a three-generational depth but not necessarily kin-based. At yearly kin-based gatherings which often are connected with religious holidays and events an even wider net appears.

If viewed in this model, as a form of community, the ethnic group then might be identified and better understood by focusing on its significant gathered ceremonials as a locus within which cultural traditions and classic community-cultural forms will reappear. These will be in fact the only place where a significant kin-religious-cultural assemblage appears within which these otherwise invisible community and cultural forms are visibly, observably expressed.

Ceremonials centering around the life crises are one point of ritual regathering—when a new baby is born, absent kin appear to pay homage or to attend a baptism; at weddings all the kin within reasonable range congregate at the core of the ceremonial; and a funeral draws the largest attendance of all. Another point of ritual assemblage might be centered on group values and group solidarity, such as Passover, Christmas, Carnival, and in the rural South, the family reunion or church homecoming. In the postindustrial South the church homecoming has been replaced in many denominations by a more institutionalized inter-congregational grouping, the summer conference center.

This paper will argue that group life—ethnic community life—within white Protestant America is preserved and transmitted through the recurrent ritual gatherings and ceremonial events celebrated by a people. Descriptive material from one of these groups will be introduced in support of the contention that gatherings perform several important functions in the cultural maintenance process. These functions might be stated as follows:

1. Gatherings provide a locus for reenactment of shared meanings and values and for rehabituation of the participants into culturally defined behaviors.

2. These events provide a mechanism for preserving structural isolation over time by perpetuating in-group marriage.

3. Ritual and ceremonial celebrations serve as kin-religious encapsulators providing a protective covering for the individual throughout the important life cycle transitions.

Data in support of the above argument are based on three years of ethnographic study of the ritual and ceremonial gatherings among the Southern Presbyterians. This group is a regional denomination covering fourteen states. Its organizational structure is that of federated local congregations under the republican form of church government embodied in districts (Presbytery) and statewide (Synod) councils. It is peopled by individuals of Scottish descent who brought the original Presbyterian government and doctrines and in addition by those whom they have married and those who have in the present mobile society simply decided to join the Presbyterian church nearest their suburban home. The core membership of Scottish-descent Presbyterians are the focus of this study.

Three phases of the study were carried out over a three-year period. The first was a summer-long community study of the denominational summer conference center at Montreat, North Carolina (Neville 1971). This was followed by visiting and interviewing during the winter season within local Southern Presbyterian congregations in Atlanta, Georgia. Finally, during the summer of 1972, comparative study was done over a six-week period of visiting and interviewing among the Presbyterians of Scotland and the north of England in an attempt to isolate the cultural antecedents of the Piedmont church patterns.

The summer community will be described first as a background for discussions of kinship and world view.

THE ANNUAL GATHERING AT MONTREAT

The basic component in this particular research was a community study in 1970 of the annual ceremonial gathering of Presbyterians at Montreat, North Carolina. This assemblage was studied intensively as an example of a group *rite of intensification* (Chapple and Coon 1942) during which the core symbols and community forms of early Scottish Presbyterian tradition were found to express themselves in the religious and family activities. These activities have continued over a seventy-year period in the same locale, a college and conference center built in a cove of the Blue Ridge Mountains twenty miles from Asheville, North Carolina. Montreat was established by the denomination at the turn of the century in response to the growing industrialization of Piedmont towns and the move of many rural communicants into urban areas. As the functional equivalent of the church homecoming, Montreat provides a locale for families to gather for reunions and for the alliances of families to share in worship and Bible study. In addition, during the summer-long interaction with a homogenous cultural group, children have an opportunity to learn the ways of their primary people and to meet and court marriage partners from the acceptable marriage pool.

While only a few thousand of the 945,000 members of the regional denomination attend Montreat every year, its influence is felt in every congregation as a node of coordinating activities and of reestablishing ties among an otherwise widely scattered interurban network of people. Those who attend Montreat, whom I call the "core Presbyterians," are the families who own a cottage. There are 418 cottages in all. The cottage owners are largely upper-middle-class, professional families, owners of businesses and mills, and Presbyterian ministers. They are proud of their ancestry of devout churchmen, all Scotch-Irish and Scottish Presbyterian. The women of the cottage families come in June with the children and spend the entire summer, with visits from the husband on weekends and on his vacation. Daughters come to spend long periods of time with their mothers, bringing along their own children to play with and get acquainted with cousins.

Among the cottage families deep ties exist that have grown out of many successive summers of play and visiting. A supervised program for children, known as "the clubs," provides structured activities and games for ages five to fifteen, with college students from the long-term Montreat families serving as paid club leaders. These young adults are hand-picked from the large number of applicants to insure that they are the best possible counselors and teachers for the task of passing on the culture to the young. Within the club groups fast and long-lasting friendships are formed. These friendships are reported to be the closest the participants have through life. This can be understood with the help of Turner's idea of *communitas* and the sacredness of associations formed during transitional periods in the ritual process.

A second circle of participants at Montreat surrounds the inner core of cottage people. These are the conference attendants, active church persons who are not descendants of older families and whose cultural identity may be less centrally fixed to the Presbyterian way of life. These participants stay in transient conference hotels and rarely mix with the core families of cottage people.

The cottage people are of particular interest in terms of defining and delineating the dynamics of the scattered ethnic community. It is this central core of 418 extended families—an estimated 4,000 to 5,000 individuals in all—who are at the center of denominational life throughout the South. It is this inner circle of interrelated families who claim descent from Scotland and the early Covenanters, who control access to the important Southern "First Church" pulpits, who teach at the seminaries and church colleges, who serve as elders, ministers, and as denominational level church board executives, and who have provided the social network of marriage ties that preserve structural isolation of the Southern Presbyterians from other Protestant groups.

The core community of Presbyterians qualify for definition as ethnic through their shared emphasis on their common racial and national origins and their intense feeling of "peoplehood." In addition, their common participation together in weekly worship services and congregational activities and their annual shared community life at Montreat over a transgenerational period serve to encapsulate them in a kinship-based ceremonial cocoon which lasts from birth to death. The two central cultural themes uniting this group into a community with a sense of peoplehood are the twin emphases on the family and on the church. Kinship and the tradition of the Covenant have been fused into a world view which perceives the universe as orderly and well-planned, with humankind as a great extended family under the fatherhood of God. Kinship and the Covenant are treated here as ideology and also as behavior. The preservation of community form and of patterns of grouping over time has direct connection to these two parts of Presbyterian world view.

KINFOLKS AND ANCESTORS

The first strong unifying theme in the shared world view of the Montreat cottage people is their emphasis on descent from a group of ancestors who entered this continent from Scotland and the North of Ireland in the eighteenth and early nineteenth centuries. These immigrants were essentially Scottish Presbyterians of the dissenting, or "Covenanting," tradition in the southwest of Scotland and throughout the lowlands. Many had first emigrated into Ulster Plantation between 1610 and 1710 before leaving for the American colonies. In this country they were branded Scotch-Irish because of this 100-year stopover, but there is no evidence to suggest widespread intermarriage with the Celtic Irish, who were Catholic and remained bitter enemies of the transplanted lowland Scots (Leyburn 1962; Thompson 1963).

The migration stream of early settlers leads from Philadelphia and the Susquehanna Valley downward into the Shenandoah Valley and outward onto the Carolina Piedmont. By 1790, the Carolina upcountry was heavily populated with Scottish Presbyterians, about 100,000 according to Leyburn (1965).

The Presbyterians had moved as family clusters and as whole congregations, bringing along their minister—or in many cases coming with him as the organizer. Each congregation, then, consisted of a minister of the Church of Scotland and his small flock of three to four extended family groups of small farmers and in some cases merchants and townsmen. The settlement pattern was predominantly that of scattered farms with the church building at the center of a rural neighborhood. Here at the worship service on Sunday morning the mainstay of interfamily communication took place.

Because of the small size of local congregations and their kin-based nature, there were not enough marriage partners to go around at the time young people were ready to be matched. It was during times of joint meetings between congregations that matches were made, especially at the large joint services held in fall and spring for preaching, communion, and "dinner on the grounds."

In the contemporary rural Piedmont, two types of joint meetings continue to be held. One is a meeting of two or more congregations for preaching services and joint communion. The second, for all the children of one congregation, is known variously as church homecoming, the May Meeting, the October Meeting. These are seasonal gatherings at which time all the kinfolks return to their home church (congregation of birth) to visit family for several days and renew extended kin ties.

A strong emphasis on descent from hallowed ancestors is evidenced in these meetings. All people who have ancestors buried in the graveyard are expected to return for the occasion, and one of the preliminary activities on a Saturday before the meeting Sunday is to clean the graveyard and put fresh flowers on the ancestors' graves. In northern Appalachia this custom is still followed under the label of "Graveyard Reunion," and has recently been studied by Simpkins (1973) as an example of Scottish cultural persistency in America.

In the Piedmont South this custom of joint meetings between Presbyterian congregations has become the integrating key to the retention of a tight kin network over time. Other family gathering patterns lend themselves to endogamous marriage. These include the customs of "visiting," of life crisis ceremonies, and of the "family reunion."

Visiting is the practice of a young mother returning to her girlhood home in summer with her children to visit her own mother for several weeks or longer. During this period, mother-daughter ties are reinforced and strengthened, sisters retain contact and strengthen ties to each other, and the young cousins grow up playing together each summer at grandmother's house. Cousins in earlier days married each other. More recently, the children marry those to whom they have been introduced over long periods—children of the mother's girlhood friends who are visiting their own grandmother.

A second form of family gatherings were once held for celebration of the life crisis events—baptism, marriage, and funerals. At these occasions kin and family solidarity were reinforced by cooperation in planning and carrying out the religious service, by the custom of staying over for several days to visit, and by bringing in food and gifts, which of course had to be reciprocated later when the giver was involved in a similar transition. Many informants report courting individuals whom they had met while being wedding attendants for a kinsman or friend.

A special annual gathering of the greater family provided the epitomy of family ceremonial life. This gathering, still held today among Southern Presbyterian families, is known as "the family picnic" or "the family reunion." The custom is also shared by Southern Methodists and Baptists in rural areas, but the Presbyterians seem to emphasize to a far greater degree the descent aspect from one common ancestor, rather than just the laterality of kinship relations. The large family picnics are attended by from 100 to 400 individuals. The meeting is often held outdoors at a church, church camp, or at Montreat. After the visiting and eating, a master of ceremonies introduces the "head" of each family segment. The head of each family, the oldest person in the nearest generation to the ancestor, then introduces his or her children and grandchildren. More distant relatives are mentioned in passing, but they are definitely not included in the descent chain.

It is the ancestor focus which has led me to classify the family form of the group as a "cognatic descent group" (Fox 1967) All relatedness is traced through descent from one common ancestor, who stands at the apex of a great cone under which his children are each one head of subsidiary cones. The diagrammatic representation resembles a segmentary lineage system. It appears to be closely related to the Scottish system of *clann*, which is itself a Gaelic word meaning "children of." All the children of an individual by blood descent (both male and female equally) are members of the cognatic lineage. While they carry the surname of the father's descent group, each child is also a member of the mother's descent group and often carries that surname as a first, or given name, and is addressed by that name as a way of keeping the mother's lineage as visible and significant.

The world of kinfolks and of Presbyterian ties places a premium on the role of the mother in handing down the traditions and bringing up children in a pattern known formally as "the nurture and admonition of the Lord." Males hold respected public world positions in the church, the mills, industries, and businesses dominating the economic and religious interests of the South. The females are meanwhile taught to devote themselves to the arts of the home, of child rearing, the improvement of school and community welfare. The males inhabit the outside world, the females the protected inner world of family and kin.

Close examination of the customs of inheritance and of mother-daughter visiting ties indicates that there is a very strong subverted matrilineal principle within the cognatic lineage. The closest relatives after siblings are the children of sisters, and summers spent at "grandmother's house" appear to refer predominantly to the mother's mother. Meanwhile, the mother's brother's children are off with their own mother's sister's children at their mother's mother's house. This particular aspect of the kinship system of the Presbyterians has not been fully explicated and needs more research in order to show conclusively that such a primacy of the mother's line does exist. Preliminary tests of this idea on Presbyterian informants, however, have indicated that it is sound.

In any case, it is the mother who teaches and cares for the young, who introduces them to the proper marriage mates by bringing them each summer to Montreat, who arranges and supervises the wedding and the homecoming of the newborn infants, who sits on the porch at her daughter's Montreat house in her waning years, and who wills to her daughters all of her own sacred home objects of silver, table china, and personal jewelry. At the death of the aged mother the sorrow is great, and her gravestone carries glowing epitaphs of having been a "virtuous woman, whose children shall rise up and call her blessed."

The importance of ancestors and of family ties over time are spotlighted in the second dominant idea of Presbyterianism—that of the Covenant People. In order to fully appreciate the contemporary communal life, it is necessary to get a historical perspective from early Scottish days.

COVENANT AND COVENANT PEOPLE

The original Presbyterians were children of the Scottish Reformation, the sixteenth century and seventeenth century struggles in Scotland to establish the Reformed church over against the Episcopacy. In the southwest farming regions of Scotland the resistance took a form of meeting secretly in the forest to sign *banns,* or treaties, in which participants promised to fight together until they established their True Religion. These signers and their followers became known as Covenanters and their cause as Covenanting. The Covenant idea is based on the Old Testament notion that an all-powerful God has offered to save his chosen people from the wicked world. Their agreement to serve God in return for His mercy and Grace is known as the Covenant. The Covenant of Works often refers to the Old Testament and the Covenant of Grace refers to the coming of Jesus. In his *History of the Scottish People,* T. C. Smout describes the Covenanters as being perfectly convinced that they represented "the New Israel" and that their reformed church was the only true "bride of Christ." (Smout 1969:62)

The Covenant tradition in southwest Scotland took several forms in terms of gatherings and ideology. It was in this region where the famous "field preachings" of the 1700s originated and grew. These local intercongregational meetings were held outdoors in the old Celtic tradition of a sacred grove. They included all the elements of kinship and religious feasting, praying and matchmaking that persisted in the later days of Piedmont Presbyterianism. Robert Burns has captured the essence of the outdoor meeting in his poem "The Holy Fair."

Burns writes with tongue in cheek of the questionable motives of the pious folk of Mauchline, whose tent was pitched so that the back entrance gave access to Nanse Tinnock's tavern, where the supplementary activities of visiting and drinking took place while the services were in progress. In the tavern and in the adjoining meadows he notes the "lads an' lasses, blythely bent To mind baith saul an' body . . ." (Burns 1797). The event Burns describes was held in conjunction with the Sacrament, or the Communion, which at this time was observed on the second Sunday in August, when the weather is clear and the "crops are laid by." Other popular annual Communion times are in May, "after the roads are passable" and in October "before the winter sets in."

The tradition of the field preaching in connection with Communion gained power throughout lowland Scotland, into Yorkshire and Northumbria, and over into Ulster. It is not surprising that early frontier camp meetings of the Methodists and tent revivals of the Baptists were fostered and peopled by the great hordes of Scotch-Irish and North English descendants who poured into America in the following century.

In the present day Church of Scotland the main kin-based local congregational event continues to be the annual gathering for the Communion, during which time all the sons and daughters of the congregation return home to take part in visiting, eating, and religious celebration. Annual communion is rooted historically in the need for each church to keep records of all communicants to turn in to the General Assembly of the Church of Scotland. Every person is considered a member who takes communion once a year, regardless of his or her weekly round of participation. In order to partake of the communion elements, each communicant member must be examined by the Kirk Session on his or her doctrinal and behavioral piety. Those who "pass" (generally all members) are given a communion token which is presented at the service as an entrance ticket. Anyone not having such a ticket is not allowed to partake the elements but may sit as a visitor.

The in-group formed by all communicants of one congregation is a nuclear expression of the larger in-group of all those united together by having received the Covenant of Grace. In fact, the Covenanters themselves took communion in the sacred groves to cement their commitment to the cause.

The Southern Presbyterians of today have brought with them from their Scottish past these same practices and loyalties to their in-group of related congregations. The Covenant idea expresses the feeling of solidarity and of community in which the whole congregation received the Grace of God together—not individually. Individual conversion experiences are played down, and the emphasis is instead on the "children of" the Covenant, and the "children of" Grace, born into a long line of holy and pious people who have been primary recipients of God's love.

This fusion of family, ancestors, and the handing down of the Covenant is evident in the titles of Sunday School curriculum materials and in the formal rhetoric used at ceremonies. The overall label for materials is "The Covenant Life Curriculum," which includes books entitled *The Family of Faith, Claiming the Inheritance, The Book of God's People,* and for young couples, one called *Families Within the Family.*

The local congregation is the embodiment of the Covenant people, and the events of an individual life are also congregational events. When an infant is baptized, he is called by name and then by "child of the Covenant. . . ." Those who are born to Presbyterian families are said to be recipients of the Covenant of Grace, and the baptismal ceremony is held within the Sunday morning worship service so that all the members can publicly agree to assist the parents in rearing this child in the ways of the church. In this way the entire congregation stand as godparents and are responsible for the child's religious growth. At a wedding, the whole congregation is viewed as a corporate witness and as a corporate support. A common prayer for newlyweds calls them "heirs to the Grace of life" and asks for their protection from the temptations of the world outside the church. Funerals are also congregational events, and the proper burial begins with a service in the church where hymns and psalms eulogize both the dead person and his or her connections to the life of the greater past and future church. The highest compliment is that a person lived "a Godly life" and "walked in the footsteps of the saints who have gone before."

The saints are also known as the priesthood of believers, part of the living Body of Christ, alive and well in the Church. The saints who have gone before and the living members of the community are all joined together in a long line through which "the water of life flows, with each link in the pipeline being a Christian." The old are revered in this ethnic community because of their long association with the church on earth and because of their closeness to the church in heaven.

In relation to the rest of the world, the Covenant community stands together as passengers in a lifeboat afloat on the seas of a sinful world. Sermon imagery from Montreat and from separate congregations is placed with allusions to the sinfulness and depravity of the "World" and the all-powerful redemptive actions of the Sovereign God, who has reached down to His people and offered a rescue.

In his history of an early Presbyterian congregation, that of Rocky River Presbyterian Church in North Carolina, Thomas H. Spence describes a May Meeting and dinner-on-the-grounds as the embodiment of the covenant and kin so dear to this tradition. The description could apply equally well to a family picnic, a graveyard reunion, a Scottish communion in the Southwest of the seventeenth century, or to the summer-long gathering at Montreat.

> The May Meeting not only reflects the joy of the treasured feast of Israel, but stands as an earnest of that uninterrupted gathering around the Father's table, when the saints of all ages shall drink anew of the fruit of the vine in the blessed Kingdom of their Redeemer. It is not only a backward look to the days of Alexander Craighead, John Makemie Wilson and Daniel Lindley . . . but a prospect of the time when they, and those who follow them across the intervening years, shall assemble in the house not made with hands, at the end of the age, beside the waters of another River, which flow forever by the throne of God. (Spence 1954:168)

SUMMARY AND CONCLUSION

This paper has attempted to illustrate the manner in which gathering patterns and important ceremonial events over time have served to forge a continuity of tradition and of social structural isolation among the Southern Presbyterians. By providing a locus of value and belief reinforcement the kin, family, and congregational regroupings have served as rites of intensification to rehabituate the participants and enable the persistence of culture among a scattered people.

Rituals and group ceremonials have been shown in the anthropological literature to be efficient symbolic communicators of culture (Leach 1966). It is within the core symbolic enactments of a cultural group that the most essential features are preserved, enacted over and over again, and transmitted to consecutive generations. The work of Turner (1969) has made us keenly aware of the cohesion and continuous force of the sacred friendships forged within the liminality of *communitas*. This model might be fruitfully utilized to understand the dynamics of cultural transmission and ethnic maintenance within other ethnic subsegments of American Protestantism. By coparticipation in group rituals and group ceremonial life, the kin and ethnic identities of individuals can thusly be created and preserved. These ceremonials then in fact serve as encapsulators, even though participations happen infrequently. The impact of the occasion and its meaning in the life cycle of both the person and the group appear in these cases to outweigh the other types of public, bureaucratic relationships the individual experiences in the courses of his or her daily urban routines.

Some of the theoretical implications of this research might be summarized as follows:

1. Ethnic as a label should not be reserved only for categories of the population who define themselves as "ethnic" or for segments who are forced into cultural separation by economic or social deprivation. Instead, the label must be reapplied to all *groups* (within white America as well as other segments) as interacting networks which retain a shared sense of cultural past, shared meanings, and a sense of peoplehood.

2. A new label of "ethnic community" might be useful in delineating that biosocial group of individuals who interact over time and space with shared understandings and transmit these to their children.

3. The ritual gatherings of a group may provide the significant key to finding and studying the true expressions of cultural identity, if in fact it is within the seasonal assemblages that the core values and basic kin and religious loyalties are restated symbolically.

With these redefinitions and these constraints in mind, it is important that anthropologists proceed in describing further the various subgroups in American life that have previously been classed as "assimilated." A new understanding of the dynamics of group separateness and cultural persistency will hopefully lead to a clearer understanding in general of the dynamics of American urban society.

LITERATURE CITED

Anderson, Charles
1970   White Protestant Americans. Englewood Cliffs, NJ: Prentice-Hall.

Arensberg, Conrad M., and Solon Kimball
1965   Culture and Community. New York: Harcourt, Brace and Co.

Burns, Robert
1897   The Holy Fair. *In* The Complete Poetical Works of Robert Burns. Cambridge Edition. Boston: Houghton Mifflin.

Chapple, Eliot D., and Charleton Coon
1942   Principles of Anthropology. New York: Holt, Rhinehart and Winston.

Fox, Robin
1967   Kinship and Marriage. Baltimore, MD: Penguin Books.

Gennep, Arnold Van
1960   The Rites of Passage. Chicago: University of Chicago Press (originally published 1909).

Glazer, Nathan, and Daniel P. Moynihan
1965   Beyond the Melting Pot. Cambridge: MIT Press.

Gordon, Milton
1964   Assimilation in American Life. The Role of Race, Religion, and National Origins. New York: Oxford University Press.

Hall, E. T.
1966   The Silent Language. Garden City, NY: Doubleday.

Killian, Lewis
1970   White Southerners. New York: Random House.

Leach, E. R.
1966   Ritualization in Man in Relation to Conceptual and Social Development. *In* Reader in Comparative Religion. William Lessa and Evon S. Vogt, Eds. New York: Harper and Row.

Leyburn, Janes
1962   The Scotch-Irish, A Social History. Chapel Hill: University of North Carolina Press.

Neville, Gwen K.
1971   Annual Assemblages as Related to Culture Patterns, an Arthropological Study of a Summer Community. University of Florida, Gainesville: unpublished Ph.D. dissertation.

Simpkins, K. L.
    1973   Folk fra Amerikas "13 kolonier" Sydens hjlandsboer. Jordens-
        folk. 1972 8 ARG NR 3.

Smout, T. C.
    1969   A History of the Scottish People 1560–1830. London: William
        Collins and Sons Ltd.

Spence, Thomas H.
    1954   The Presbyterian Congregation on Rocky River. Kingsport,
        TN: Kingsport Press.

Thompson, E. T.
    1963   Presbyterians in the South. Richmond: John Knox Press.

Turner, Victor
    1969   The Ritual Process. Chicago: Aldine.

Warner, W. Lloyd
    1964   A Black Civilization. New York: Harper Torchbooks.

16

Ethnicity and Collective
Identification: The Old West*

STANLEY G. WALENS

Northwestern University

The definition of ethnicity generally accepted in America has been severely limited. For scholar and nonscholar alike, ethnicity is an abstruse quality which is possessed by members of certain "ethnic groups," a special attribute whose ownership seems strategically restricted only to people with certain specific historical backgrounds. A place on the list of recognized ethnic groups often seems to be a matter of arbitrary assignment rather than the ownership of empirical characteristics.

Ethnicity, the search for a collective identity based on a special historical ancestry, is not limited to members of certain politically recognized minority groups, yet typically "ethnic studies" have dealt with only these peoples. It is difficult not to see such groups as more

* The ethnographic research for this paper was conducted in the Summer of 1969 under the auspices of the National Science Foundation Field School in Urban Anthropology, directed by W. D'Azvedo, J. Price and R. Provencher at the University of Nevada, Reno.

or less tiny enclaves struggling for independent identity in the midst of America's vast population, and we often fail to see the struggles for collective identity that also characterize that vast population itself. Actually, the only major difference one can see between minorities and the majority population with respect to their search for identity is that one of them turns to the history of this country for its inspiration and heritage and the others turn to the history and heritage of other nations. Yet is this a scientifically meaningful distinction? Are those people who turn to American history any less "ethnic" than members of recognized "ethnic groups" merely because the focus of their historical interests lies in a less exotic geographical area?

Anthropologists have difficulty transcending this limited idea of ethnicity as a peculiar heritage of special segments of society. They seem only too ready to romanticize the non-Western culture and to criticize the Western culture, a process which Dalton terms "reverse ethnocentrism." Is it not ethnocentric for us to mock as pretentious those people written about on the social pages of the *New York Times* who trace their ancestry to pre-Revolutionary America and yet admire the assertiveness of those people who maintain that their ancestors were big chiefs back in Africa or brave warriors on the American Plains?

The concept of ethnicity cannot be limited only to those groups who have a nonnative American background. Instead, we must broaden our conception of the processes and strategies by which the search for a collective identity is carried on in all societies. The striving for cultural and historic identity is a common feature of all ethnic groups—but only because it is a common feature of all cultures. We can see the search for collective identity as a universal process, a necessary part of culture, a process in which all men must participate to some degree. The process of ethnic identification, through which the individual relates himself to a group with a distinctive and often admirable historical heritage. is a common feature of socialization.

Nor can we expect to find concrete evidence that indisputably defines some peoples' identity as ethnic and others' as nonethnic. Ethnicity is not an empirically testable fact, it is a set of symbols, attitudes and values. As Schneider points out, those qualities that define the ethnic identification of a person need not have an objective existence. Instead they need exist only in the set of attitudes and values held by the members of that culture. Ethnicity and ethnic identification are qualities that are ascribed, adduced or attributed, but not necessarily possessed.

High in the hills east of Reno and Carson City, Nevada, stands all that remains of what was once the cultural center of the West, the greatest city west of Chicago, and the site of the most famous and richest gold and silver lodes in the United States—Virginia City. When, at the beginning of World War II, the mine whistles blew for the last time, the once prosperous town had dwindled until all but 75 of its former 75,000 inhabitants had left. C Street, the main street, where miners and millionaires had squandered their money on wine, women, and more wine, where great carriages had rumbled, and fancy women had shown off their jewels, stood deserted, a dead street in a dying town. In the last fifteen years, however, a number of factors have combined to make Virginia City into a major tourist attraction, with an estimated 5,000 visitors per day, and a resident population of over 500. The first factor is the great influx of people into Nevada, both as tourists and residents. The second major factor is the writings of Lucius Beebe, a renowned, wealthy journalist. Beebe portrayed Virginia City as a wild western town, full of the passion and violence that is so stereotypically part of the American conception of what the West was like. But he also emphasized an important aspect of this image— Virginia City as a scene of immense wealth. He wrote of the millionaires Virginia City had spawned, and of how the miners had tossed their high wages to the wind in countless extravagant ways. In his writings, Virginia City's image becomes more than that of just another typical western town—it is a pipe dream for a materialistic culture.

The greatest impetus to the tourist trade and consequent growth of Virginia City was the beginning of the television series "Bonanza," which supposedly takes place on a nearby ranch. While the town which it portrays bears little relation to the historical Virginia City, nevertheless this show, based as it must be on literary stereotypes of the West, lends immense weight to the image of Virginia City as Beebe portrayed it. Through the medium of this program, Virginia City has become a household word, an archetypal representation of the Old West. Many of the tourists that come ask about the Cartwright family, and the townspeople, realizing the advantages of association with the program, play up the image of Virginia City presented in the show, even to the exclusion of its true history. For example, the Roos Brothers store, the first department store in the West, has been renamed the Cartwright Emporium; a new restaurant has been named Kitty's Long-branch; and pictures of famous western outlaws, none of whom were ever in Virginia City, can be bought in almost every tourist store, along with Indian tomahawks, toy six-shooters, and rubber snakes.

It is here that the residents of Virginia City are first constrained to present an image of Virginia City congruent with myth rather than history. The success of their businesses is based on their ability to convey to the tourist an unblemished image of Virginia City as a true representative of America's glorious past. But as the only image of the Old West which the average American has is its literary image, it is this image that they will accept as authentic, and this image alone. People won't pay to see merely the oldest department store in the West, but they will pay to see the store where their favorite TV heroes buy their groceries. Indeed, most people who come to Virginia City have also been to the set where "Bonanza" is filmed, which is also maintained as a tourist attraction, and feel it to be much more authentic, for of course the movie set is a far better approximation of their ideal western town.

Like the tourists, the residents have come to Virginia City in order to identify with the past. Yet this identification has a different purpose for them. The residents feel their personal aura, their status, to be higher the more closely they commune with the past, and this forms the core of the image they try to maintain. As a result, they interact with each other in a way which is subtended within the same mythos as the one they must portray to tourists. Thus, they may consciously do such things as dress in a cowboy-type style, or speak with a fake western drawl, or walk bowlegged. Unconsciously, the effect of the mythos on their lives is even more pernicious. For example, their moral system is derived from the moral code of fictional shoot-em-outs. Their system of greeting behaviors and interactions are exact reproductions of those found in TV westerns. And their most frequent type of interaction is that seen amongst the townspeople of the TV cattle town—aggressive and destructive conflict, sometimes physical but usually in the verbal guise of vicious, backbiting gossip. It is this gossiping, the mutual exchange of information essential to creating and maintaining social relationships, that forms the chief mechanism of ethnic identification in Virginia City.

A thorough understanding of Virginia City's image as created by Beebe and "Bonanza" is possible only if one examines some of the underlying beliefs Americans have about the Old West. The lure of the West is great, and for a wide variety of reasons. In general however, stories about the American West function in ways which are typical of all folklore—they present a story of a mythical time with which the listener can identify and thus vicariously satisfy some of his fantasies and desires. A brief discussion as to what some of these desires are, and how the image of Virginia City acts to fulfill them, will add insight to our examination of the residents' ethnic identification with America's past.

One need not look far in American society for instances of a desire to escape from civilization and return to nature. It is one of the most widely expressed American values and is manifested in ways such as the emphasis on camping, hiking, and buying a little cottage in the country or on a lonely stretch of beach. In the myth of the West, the country is more than just a setting, it is the crux of people's lives.

But the return to nature is valued not only as a "religious" experience; it is also an escape from the constraints of society. Returning to nature insures one's personal freedom and autonomy: under the stars, a man is answerable only to himself and to God. The removal of the constraints of society and the need to stand up for oneself engender egotism. The individual becomes important and his wishes are constantly being thwarted by the encroachment of "the baddies." The twilight shoot-out of ego against ego is the climax for many of the conflicts in westerns. Whether the fight is about women, homesteaders, sheep ranchers, or Indians, the frequency of ego-confrontation in the western mythos emphasizes the importance of personal autonomy and freedom in the image which people can create for themselves through the myth of the West.

The right to portray this image becomes the third crucial aspect of the western myth. To portray an image, there must be a boundary between the public and the private, the front regions and the back. The right to privacy in the back region becomes an inalienable right of all western people. The archtypical western hero rides into town one day. No one knows where he is from or why he has come to town. Some deep, dark secret is hidden from the townspeople and it is inaccessible to all but the hero's closest friend, to whom he *may* divulge it. Entire stories may hinge on little more than the protagonist's attempt to keep his hidden stigma from being brought to light, in order that he can build a new, better life on the ashes of the old one. Sometimes this secret is even represented physically as a mask or a disguise, as in the case of the Lone Ranger. Divulging a friend's secret is the worst sin the western man can commit. Indeed, the most nefarious varmint in the pantheon of western baddies is the double-crosser.

The three themes which I have just outlined—escape from urban society with a return to an arcadian life, personal autonomy, and the right to maintain unchallenged an artificial public image—are important parts of the myth of the West, and as such they form a crucial part of the image and heritage which Virginia City represents to the towns-people and the tourists. (We should note that these three particular themes comprise the foundation for ethnic identification in many American minority groups also.) In Virginia City, each of them is crucial to the ways in which people define their behavioral setting and in how they represent themselves within that setting. Despite the fact that the real Virginia City was a mining town and not a cattle town, that most of its residents lived in squalor and not in extravagance, and that it was not overrun by Billy the Kid and the James Brothers, the myth of the West is powerfully present there. The mere trappings of the historical West—the wooden sidewalks, the pictures of bandits, the costumes of the store operators—reaffirm the place of Virginia City in the American heritage. In some ways, the Virginia City that really existed in 1870 is irrelevant to the Virginia City of today. The people today are living in a world of television and newspaper origin, but the fact that it is a bastard of the media does not make it any less their town. The image is no less real because it is untrue, and it is no less viable a cultural heritage merely because it is historically inaccurate. The image of Virginia City is important in that it is the context in which people in the town define their personal ties to the West; the image defines a set of roles and expectations, a set of goals, a set of ideals. In short, the television-created image of Virginia City provides a firm basis for a collective, *ethnic* heritage.

Nevada as a whole accommodates the image of escape in many forms: quick marriages and divorces and legalized prostitution; gambling; and dude ranches. It is small wonder then that many of the people who have settled in Virginia City in the last two decades have done so in a conscious attempt to escape from a stigmatized past life—lives marred by divorce, homosexuality, prison convictions, mental illness or alcoholism—and to build a new life in the land of opportunity. There are few people in Virginia City who do not have some major secret stigma in their past from which they are trying to escape.

Virginia City's ties with the past give both residents and tourists a chance to escape the pressures of an urban existence and enter a reconstructed place which represents the magical past of America's cultural heritage. Indeed, most residents earn a living from the tourist trade. Consequently, fierce competition and hostility have become the dominant motivating forces in Virginia City and are the bases for nearly all interpersonal relationships there. This hostility is channeled by the residents in such a way as to severely limit the number of people whom they consider to have, as they themselves do, rightful claims to identification with Virginia City's past. Almost all interactions between residents are composed entirely of the denigration of someone who is an outsider to the interaction. In Virginia City, people are friends not because they like each other or have common interests, but because they hate the same things. Through the mechanism of gossip, residents try to discredit the performances of their co-residents, before those people can threaten theirs. The resident, by restricting the number of people whom he considers co-residents, is able to severely limit the number of people whom he feels have, as he does, a justifiable, meaningful link to the American past.

Through the study of myth, symbols, and values in Virginia City we gain a better perspective on the nature of the search for collective identity. We can see that many of those characteristics we have observed in Virginia City can be found in other ethnic groups as well. These similarities include such features as financial insecurity; rejection by the greater society; antipathy towards out-groups as a primary cohesive force within the in-group; the use of a reconstructed, romanticized mythic history as the focus of the group's heritage; the adoption of specific traits that serve a priori as markers of ethnic identification, traits that may or may not have objective existence; and the tendency for individual identity to be seen as a metaphorical extension of the group's collective identity.

We can also see that, in these terms, ethnicity is a universal of culture, not the province of only certain cultures. As such, we can study it not as an aberration but as one of the ways of mankind.

The dust of the mines has long been settled and the ghosts of miners, millionaires, and madams have long since stopped haunting the skeletal ruins which they once frequented. The Virginia City of today is not so much a part of history as a three-dimensional rendition of a modern mythology, the child of dime novels, Wild West shows and shoot-em-outs. The ghosts who silently walk the streets now and swagger into candystores and hamburger stands are a new breed, a breed of Cart-wrights, Matt Dillons, and Jesse Jameses. Virginia City is a dime novel brought to life with just enough of the *real* West beneath the reconstructed saloons, fake costumes and museums of memories to successfully create the illusion with which the residents have come to identify. The stereotype of life in the Old West has become the foundation for life in the new West.

The place of Virginia City in the American heritage enables the people who go there to search for, and often find, an ethnic, collective identity based on American history. An individual's association and identification with that heritage are the result of his personal identification with attributes of the Western mythos, the obtaining of certain characteristics which other members of the culture consider to be indicative of his identification with that past, and the ascription to him of certain nonempirical characteristics which are an inherent part of the symbolic heritage of that culture. As such, the identification of the Virginia City resident exhibits the same processes and features as does that of those groups who look overseas for the source of their heritage.

LITERATURE CITED

Schneider, David

 1968   American Kinship: A Cultural Account.   Englewood Cliffs, NJ: Prentice-Hall.

Walens, Stanley

 1970a   Social Structure and Impression Management in Virginia City. *In* Twelve Doors to Reno. John A. Price, Ed. San Diego: N.S.F. Field School Report.

 1970b   Meaning and Form: Interaction Ritual and Impression Management in a Western Tourist Town. Northwestern University: Masters thesis.

 1972   Life in the World of Illusion: Image Management in a Western Tourist Town. Paper presented at the Annual Meeting of the American Anthropological Association, Toronto.

ETHNICITY AND CLASS

*

17

Ethnicity or Class?
Social Relations
in a Small Canadian
Industrial Community

EDWARD ROBBINS

Washington University, St. Louis

I.

There has been a growing debate in anthropological circles about the problems of ethnicity and class. Anthropologists have changed their views on the concept of ethnicity, typified by a shift from ethnicity as group to ethnicity as identity. However, in either case, ethnicity becomes a cultural or ideological category. Moreover, these new definitions of "ethnicity" have rarely included consideration of the concept of "class". For the most part, anthropologists seem to have accepted traditional sociological notions about class which limit the utility of the concept to traditional capitalist society. Or, said differently, anthropologists have accepted the notion that the concept of class is not particularly useful when analysing what have been called "plural societies." This, I would argue, is the result of both a traditional anthropological emphasis on cultural groupings and the acceptance of a concept of class which does not elucidate the basic structure of industrial society.

Ethnicity

Traditionally, the definition and description of ethnic groups as social categories has been, in anthropology, an elusive task. Questions have arisen as to whether ethnic groups should be categorized on the basis of cultural, organizational, political or social factors, or some synthesis of these various factors (cf. Barth 1969, Cohen 1969). Intellectually elusive as the concept of ethnic group may be, its persistence in the literature bears witness to its importance as a concrete and empirically valid entity. Ethnic groups are, in complex societies, a social reality. Differences about the categorization of ethnic groups therefore have not revolved around the identity of particular ethnic groups in specific local areas. Rather, these differences have been the outcome of fundamental disagreements about the nature and importance of ethnic groups once they have been identified and disagreements over the nature of ethnicity.

Is it true that the persistence of ethnic status is due to an accorded superordinate status in society, as Barth (1969) holds, or do they constitute cultural expressions of political or economic variables (Cohen 1969)? Can ethnic group categories be utilized to explain social process, or are they empirical entities produced by the social process?

A barrier to clarifying the discussion has been the tendency of some analysts to define ethnicity in terms of its social "being," or ontologically. Judgments as to its social relevance have been included in delineations of its diacritica (cf. Barth 1969). While not questioning the validity of these conclusions, the inclusion of the analysis in the definition has limited discussion. By focusing on the ontology of ethnic groups, a general category has been derived which loads any discussion. Disagreement as to the role and relevance of ethnicity is defined away, and ethnic groups are what they are and do what they do by intellectual fiat.

To avoid loading the discussion of ethnic groups it is necessary to define groups in the context of a definition of the whole structure of the society. Only in that way can one validly discover whether ethnic groups are superordinate, derivative, or, perhaps, irrelevant. Moreover, as ethnicity and ethnic groups are usually identified empirically, the particular ethnic groups denotated are usually limited to a particular social domain. Said another way, the particular ethnic groups defined or identified are usually unique to particular societies and are not usually found elsewhere, even within societies of similar structure. The particular ethnic groups found in France, for instance, are not found in Canada. Unlike concepts such as class, role, and occupation, which are defined largely by reference to noncultural and nonideological factors, ethnicity is, to a great extent, dependent on self-conscious cultural definitions (cf. Barth 1969, Cohen 1969, Naroll 1964). In all cases, ethnic groups are identified by discovery of their clear cultural delineations. In one instance, religion may be the defining parameter, in others it may be culture, language, ideology, or some synthesis of these. While classes, roles, occupations do exist whether people choose to recognize them or not, ethnic groups do not so exist. Ethnicity is effectively a cultural or ideological value, or a set of perceptions by a group about itself.

The definition of ethnicity should, therefore, rest primarily on the identification of shared cultural norms which are realized in overt forms and which are self-consciously recognized by the "ethnic groups" and by other groups as well. In this way, we are directed by commonsense understandings of a particular community in describing and identifying ethnic groups. Its role and place in the social fabric remain to be analyzed.

As ethnicity, in all its definitions, refers to a cultural ideology, it cannot suffice analytically. To reduce society to its own categories and to explain divisions by these categories simply affirms the consequent of its premises. Moreover, it results in an idealist explanation and confuses social reality with its cognition. While social ideology is important, it must be rooted in a larger structural framework of society. What is needed is a conceptual analysis which recognizes the importance of social ideology and roots such ideologies in the determinant structures of society. Such a concept is *class*. The analysis of class is rooted in the social relations of production. It assumes that production is critical because, as Lucien Goldmann (1969) has so aptly pointed out, so long as man must labor to survive, production will be the *sine qua non* of existence and society.

The Concept of Class

Recent anthropological work on ethnicity has recognized the importance of an analysis that does not result in a tautological explanation for the importance of ethnicity. Nonetheless, the emphasis has been on the cultural and idiomatic expressions of ethnicity and the importance of those factors in militating social division and conflict which may be rooted in other causes, such as power or competition for resources. It may be argued, though, that this emphasis has a tendency to reify the superficial aspects of social relations while avoiding a discussion of more critical underlying problems, one of which is class.

Partly, the problem emanates from confusion between class as a category, and class as a relationship. Traditionally, *class* in American sociology has been defined largely as a social and economic status grouping (Gordon 1958, Warner 1957, Ossowski 1963). Class as a *social* category replaced class as a *relational* concept emphasizing production. Although Weber conceived of class as a situation or position vis-à-vis property, economic power, and the market, social class came to be defined by sociologists as "earning power" or income and the social attributes this could buy. Thus the classical parsimony of proletariat and bourgeoisie proliferated into a series of socioeconomic status gradations, as in Lloyd Warner's six-class scheme (Warner 1957).

For American sociologists, class came to refer to a series of quantifiable and measurable behaviors and attributes. As a result, there could be no clear structural position as such, only specific nodes in a social continuum, each derivative of more general social phenomena. Social categories, including class, were defined as statistical categories based on stipulated criteria (Warner 1957). Class, although based on income, was a social node only insofar as it allowed for a different style of life, a different education and other socially "valued" properties of life. Class and status became essentiallly one and the same.

However, in this definition, confusion arises between social aggregates and social structures. If society is simply the sum of the actions of a set of statistical categories, then society has no structure. Relations in society are only enduring as mass actions are enduring, and society has no internal structural logic or force. Social actions are then the result of the mass dispositions and tendencies of individuals. We are left with either trivial explanations such as "people act because they value such actions," or simple tautologies of the sort, "people act because that is *the way they act.*" With such reasoning and models of society there can be no determination of what makes people act the way they do and why.

Furthermore, the definition of class as a social phenomenon establishes a system of dependencies without recognizing them. Those of lower social classes are subordinate in the social hierarchy, not so much for structural reasons, but as a result of a unitary definition of "social value" and "worth," that is, social value as defined by those with economic power. Economic power, itself, is not the basis of the social hierarchy. If social value is a unitary entity—and there is reason to doubt it—then the question must be raised as to how social value is defined and by whom. Once this is raised, the question of dominance must necessarily refer to structure, or why certain forces come to define and dominate the formulation of social value. Class then is not the result of social value *per se*; rather the hierarchy of social values must be explained by reference to the social structure.

It may reasonably be assumed that all societies have a "structure." If, as Ossowski points out, structure is a metaphor for the relations of "space" and "place" (1963: 9, 20), then class as part of a social hierarchy must be a concept which refers to a particular position in a vertical space. Status, on the other hand, usually refers, beginning with Weber (Mills and Gerth 1946) to a social estimation of honor. Status is not a social position; it is an estimation of the "worth" of that position. As an ideological component of society, status is derivative. While power as income may be critical, it is not necessarily so.

The definitions of class discussed above confused social position with its potential social honor. While a social position may be imbued with social honor, and while social values may be predominantly associated with aspects of a given social group, this is not an inherent association. One class may subscribe, to a certain degree, to the values of another, but it does not do so necessarily, nor at all times. At issue is why a given group does or does not ascribe to a particular set of values. As Tawney points out, it is a confusion of "the fact of class with the consciousness of class, which is a different phenomenon. The fact creates the consciousness; not the consciousness the fact. The former may exist without the latter, and a group may be marked by common characteristics and occupy a distinctive position vis-à-vis other groups, without, except at moments of exceptional tension, being aware that it does so" (Lockwood 1958: 7).

In order to correct the problems of the definitions stated above, class has been, by some, reduced to categorization by income alone. Problems remain nonetheless. Most obviously, how does one accurately delineate classes in a meaningful way? Is a man earning $30,000 in a different class from a man earning $20,000 a year?

More importantly, such a definition avoids a central issue, to wit: what is the basis of the income earned? Income does not necessarily define social hierarchy because income is not simply a thing in itself. It is derived from other sources, and it is the source which may be of critical importance. The problem of income as the basis of class and the objections to it may be central in the debate about class.

Yet this equation remains questionable. What is not provided for in this equation of class and income is that social structures are not purely economic and economy is not solely income. Social structures also have political, ideological, and social aspects as well. So, might we add, does economics itself. Therefore, income may be just as much a result of structural position as structural position may be a result of income. While income is one critical factor in defining social position in modern society, it is only one factor and often a dependent one. What has often been forgotten is that hierarchies are defined in terms of power, that is, a political-economic relationship. Differential income alone does not necessarily yield qualifiably different bases of power. Indeed, ownership and control of resources and the power and influence which is attached to such ownership and control, is extremely important in the economies of class.

Structural position cannot be defined by reference to a single factor any more than it can be defined by its ideological associations. It is as Marx pointed out a *relation*; one that is concrete and complex. It is a mix of social, political, and economic factors. Those who define class by reference to income have recognized a critical factor of modern society; the dominance of the market and economics. Differentiation in such a society is not along a continuum of income but between those who control the market or the organization of production and those who do not. From this perspective "there are only two classes; the working class, disposing of its labor power and the capitalist class, which has a monopoly of the social means of production" (Marx 1967: 421).

For our purposes such a definition is too general. It does not specify the various intermediate positions in the social structure, especially those in the distributive sector, although it lays the groundwork for isolating such positions. Modern political economy offers a range of roles neither clearly worker or clearly owner. Nevertheless, these intermediate positions have not obscured the general divisions noted by Marx but have been defined by them. The various occupational positions and roles available in modern industrial society are not neutral as regards the two polar class groups, especially those positions embedded in the industrial economy. As such, they form a part of one class or the other, if only as its representatives. More importantly, these various intermediate positions have related differently to the organization of production, and to each other; which, following Marx, allows and necessitates differentiating them. Intermediate positions evince the same or similar internal differences as the more general classes do.

Under "class" would be included the following criteria: (1) the source, size, and type of income, the degree of job security, the opportunity for mobility; and (2) the role on the job, the position within the work situation and its relationship to the organization process and administration of production (cf. Lockwood 1958). It might be noted that status remains outside our definition; whether it is reflected in a class position is to be discovered not assumed.

The definition of class proposed here emphasizes two important things that traditional sociological definitions ignore. First, it argues that class is a relationship; and second, that class is rooted in the social relations of production. As such, it does not aim at replacing notions of ethnicity. Rather, it attempts to place a baseline for ethnic research, that is, the productive base of any society and the structural constraints that it may impose on that society.

II.

Wabush

Wabush, Labrador-Newfoundland, is what may be called an inorganic community; it has no history and was created all at once, so to speak, for a given purpose. Wabush, built for the purpose of extracting iron ore, is a uni-industrial community. As such, it provides an excellent opportunity to examine the various hypotheses about the utility of concepts of class and ethnicity in modern industrial society.

Wabush is, in terms of family settlement, about eight years old. It is located in the relatively isolated hinterland of Labrador. The total population is 3,387 (D.B.S.1972) of which about 1,000 are adult males. Of these, about 75 percent are from Newfoundland. Emigrants from Quebec, the British Isles and Ireland, mainland Canada, continental Europe, India, and the West Indies comprise most of the other 25 percent. About 90 percent of the adult male population work for Wabush Mines. The remainder are employed by the various service industries and range from auto mechanics to school teachers. There is practically no unemployment except for the summer months of June, July, and August when migrant workers from Newfoundland come seeking employment on construction gangs. If jobs are not available, these workers generally return immediately to the island of Newfoundland.

Wabush is a relatively affluent community. In a 62 percent random sample of adult males, all earned above $6,500. Of these, 87 percent earned more than $9,000 per year (see Table 1).

TABLE 1

ANNUAL EARNINGS FULL TIME (in thousands)

	6–7	7–8	8–9	9–10	10–11	11–12	12–13	13–14	Above 14	No Response
Total no.	3	4	7	9	9	11	10	2	6	2
Percentage	4.8	6.5	11.3	12.9	14.5	17.7	16.1	3.2	9.7	3.2

This compares favorably with Canada as a whole where only 32 percent of the non-farm adult male population earned $8,000 per year or above and only 57 percent earned $6,000 or above (D.B.S. 1970, p. 77). For most who came to Wabush, emigration has also meant a marked rise in income (see Table 2).

TABLE 2

EARNINGS FULL TIME WABUSH AS COMPARED TO TOTAL EARNINGS
YEAR BEFORE COMING TO WABUSH (in thousands)

	Below 4	4–5	5–6	6–7	7–8	8–9	9–10	Above 10	No Response
Before coming to Wabush	22	8	11	1	3	3	0	3	11 [1]
Wabush	0	0	0	3	4	7	8	38	2

[1] Includes nine who had never held a job previous to Wabush.

All occupational groups—supervisory, hourly workers, teachers— earn generally between $10,000 and $20,000. Many hourly workers earn more than supervisory personnel.

Not only is Wabush a new town, it is also a relatively youthful community. Of a total of 1,827 adults over the age of twenty, 72 percent, or 1,374, are between the ages of twenty-five to thirty-four. This compares with a total of 20 percent for the whole of Canada. In the random sample of adult males, 63 percent were between the ages of twenty-five to thirty-four, while for Canada the total was 21 per- cent (D.B.S. 1972). Although the figures for Canada as a whole are from 1967 and those for Wabush from 1971, the age distribution in Wabush since 1967 has tended, if anything, to increase.

Being a relatively new, affluent, and young community primarily involved with a highly capitalized, industrial economy, Wabush fits the conditions set forth by those who argue that class structure is declining. It is in just such a community where one would expect that factors other than class—such as ethnicity—would be of primary im- portance in shaping the social interactions outside of work. Wabush has a relatively small population—Labrador City, which is three miles away by road, has a population of 7,622 (D.B.S. 1972)—and Wabush is de- signed so that for the most part the various class and ethnic groups live side by side.

Furthermore, people in Wabush have migrated to a community with no particular history or tradition. The majority, Newfoundlanders, come from a fiercely egalitarian tradition and have escaped the limits of class and ethnic prejudice in their areas of origin. Others are seeking occupational and status mobility. For example, the British are moving in to take supervisory positions. Given the opportunity to build a community from scratch, what factors are most important in the con- struction of social relations in Wabush? What concepts are most useful in describing and explaining the nature of social patterns in such a community?

Since many analysts have suggested that plural factors such as ethnic- ity are more critical than class in advanced industrial societies, it was necessary to examine the nature of ethnicity in Wabush. Residents of Wabush were cognizant of ethnic divisions and identities. In inter- views, respondents identified the following ethnic groups: Newfound- landers, French Canadians, British, Portuguese, Greek, German, and

East Indians. Criteria emphasized by respondents in defining such differences were cultural patterns and language, and the forms of social exclusion derived from these.

III.

Ethnicity and Class in Wabush

If you spent a short time in Wabush, you would probably leave with the feeling that Wabush is truly a "new town" where social relations are based on a system of social equality. Walking through the shopping center between the hours of 4–6 P.M. on any weekday, you would observe about half the adult population of Wabush passing through to shop, have coffee, or pick up mail. People would seem in high spirits; there would be constant flow of greetings, brief conversations, and joking.

This view would fit the impression the citizens of Wabush would have outsiders believe. It is common to be told when first visiting the community that "everyone gets along here." This, it would be added "goes without saying." Yet, it was said to me repeatedly when I first arrived in Wabush. A critical question was why?

After living in Wabush a while, you would discover why. In a small, relatively isolated community it is important that everyone adheres to the ideal, at least superficially, that everyone is "friendly." But this norm is belied by social reality. As one minister said: "I have never been in a town where there is as much gossip and social divisions. But people do get along everyday; sort of a hail and well met attitude. They have to; there is no one else, no nearby town to escape to."

If the normative ideal is belied by reality, what is the nature of the actual social relations, that is, how are relations structured?

If social relations are measured by the patterns of informal interaction outside of the work situation, such as friendship, then ethnicity, on the surface, would appear to be the critical factor in the structuring of relations in Wabush. Newfoundlanders, the British, French Canadians, Portuguese, Greeks, and Germans are most often singled out as the most cliquish by people in Wabush. The rest are either too few in number or not overtly recognizable as a distinct ethnic category to be mentioned.

In both open-ended interviews and the closed questionnaire, informants stated that ethnic divisions did play a role in the structuring of social relations. Respondents were asked, "Are there any social divisions in Wabush by ethnic group, that is, any ethnic groups that tend to stick together?" Forty-four percent responded "yes," 28 percent said "sometimes," and only 20 percent responded "no."

In another question respondents were asked, "Would you tell me who your friends are, that is, those people you spend most of your free time with away from work?" In the random sample, 53 Newfoundlanders listed a total of 139 friends of which only 9 were non-Newfoundlanders (see Table 3).

TABLE 3

NEWFOUNDLANDER FRIENDSHIPS BY ETHNIC STATUS

	Newfoundlander	Non-Newfoundlander
Friend	130	9
Non-friend	670	197
p < .001		

Measured as a proportion of the total number of Newfoundlanders and other ethnic-group individuals available as potential friends in Wabush, one finds that there is a significant tendency for Newfoundlanders to befriend Newfoundlanders.

In the same way, members of other ethnic groups tended significantly to befriend members of non-Newfoundlander ethnic groups (see Table 4).

TABLE 4

NON–NEWFOUNDLANDER FRIENDSHIPS BY ETHNIC STATUS

	Newfoundlander	Non-Newfoundlander
Friend	9	16
Non-friend	791	190
p < .001		

In this case all non-Newfoundlanders were lumped together owing to the small sample size in the random sample.

In the set of open-ended interviews, chosen non-randomly, informants again were asked to list their friends. Again there was a trend
toward the maintenance of social relations within one's own ethnic
group (see Table 5).

TABLE 5

FRIENDS BY ETHNIC STATUS (non-random)

	Newfoundlander	Non-Newfoundlander
Newfoundlander	65	13
Non-Newfoundlander	14	22

These findings were corroborated by observation. At various events
there were obvious ethnic biases. Certain clubs were attended primarily by Newfoundlanders, other clubs by French Canadian and
European groups, such as the Wabush Legion and the ski club respectively. For the most part, this was a result of differing interests.
Certain bands, for example, attracted a predominantly Newfoundland audience. Activities such as skiing did not appeal to most Newfoundlanders.

Portuguese, Greek, and West Indians were normally seen in distinct
groups. The Portuguese rarely mixed with other groups. For some,
this was primarily a function of language limitations. Most Portuguese did not speak English well; some spoke none at all. For the
Greeks, it stemmed from the nature of their jobs. Greeks owned and
operated three of the restaurants in the area.

On the one hand, these divisions were recognized by the informants
as a natural propensity for people of similar cultural and linguistic
backgrounds to seek each other out. As one Newfoundlander said,
"I am more comfortable with a bunch of Newfoundlanders from my
own area, as they speak my language." To the degree that these
ethnic patterns are viewed as simply a matter of personal predilection,
they were not considered by people in Wabush to present any problems. At this level there are no hostilities. People recognized the importance of similarity on a cultural plane and felt that such patterns
did not prevent mutual friendliness on the part of all groups.

On the other hand, ethnicity, in Wabush, can and does evoke hostile
feelings. Perhaps here is the analyst's first clue that ethnic divisions

do exist. One can observe signs which disparage particular ethnic groups. People complain bitterly at times about the advantages which accrue to members of particular ethnic groups. Some feel excluded from activities because of their ethnic background. A devout French Canadian Roman Catholic woman told me that she was encouraged by her priest not to join the Ladies Auxiliary because it was mainly for Newfoundland women and they would resent her becoming a member. The priest was French Canadian.

Many Newfoundlanders feel that Europeans, especially the British, have a monopoly on certain managerial positions. It is often said that being British is an advantage in gaining promotion in certain departments. Often, they add, the British are promoted by their fellows even though they are unqualified. Two Englishmen, when asked about this, replied that in some ways it was true. But they readily added that most Newfoundlanders were not capable of undertaking responsible management positions because of relative inexperience. Newfoundlanders also feel that French Canadians come to Labrador because they can obtain supervisory positions unavailable to them in Quebec.

The various ethnic groups also allude quite frequently to the supposed faults of the other groups, although this is most often done in a humorous fashion. Most common are comments about Newfoundlanders and the British. Newfoundlanders will tell you the British are overwhelmed by a sense of their own importance while the British will describe Newfoundlanders as uncivilized, rowdy, and stupid. While other groups are not talked about as frequently, they do not escape disparagement. For example, one will be told how cheap the Portuguese and Indians are; how greasy the Greeks and Portuguese are, *ad infinitum.*

While ethnic ties are important, these patterns alone will not enable the analyst to adequately describe or accurately predict, much less explain, the nature of social relations in Wabush. A deeper analysis of ethnic divisions and its implications reveals another underlying factor influencing social relations, that of class.

The most hostile ethnic division is between the British and Newfoundlanders. Other groups are disparaged but not to the extent these two are. Most of the disparagement is mutual. Partly this is a result of a traditional enmity. However, more important are the class implications of this division. Most of the British, twenty-five of thirty-one, are in the managerial class at Wabush Mines, while less than 20 percent of the Newfoundlanders hold such positions. Of the British, most are Assistant General Foremen and above. They are disliked by Newfoundlanders, not primarily because they are British, but because of their class position. The British in Wabush are seen as snobs, as self-important, and as monopolizing critical positions in the management hierarchy. That they stick together is evidence of this to Newfoundlanders. The latter feel that as a result of their position in the company the British feel themselves "too good" to associate with Newfoundlanders. However, Englishmen who are not of the supervisory class are *not* classified with the British clique. Nor are English supervisors who act pleasantly toward Newfoundlanders. During my tenure in Wabush, an English hourly employee was president of the local branch of the United Steel Workers union, which is predominantly Newfoundlander in membership.

Other groups like the Portuguese are rarely alluded to with any hostility. Yet the Portuguese are probably the most clannish ethnic group in Wabush. Greeks too are clannish, yet not recognized as snobbish. In both cases, they are not considered part of the "upper class" and so their cliquishness goes unnoticed for the most part.

Moreover, if the British are disliked and viewed as cliquish, quite often Newfoundlanders who become foreman are castigated as even more uppity. "You find that a Newfoundlander who gets ahead here feels that he is hot shit, snotty and superior" a Newfoundlander told me. His sentiments are not unique.

In Wabush, while there may be debate and discussion about status in general, there seems to be a general recognition of the class position of any given individual, and class in Wabush is defined by reference to one's relation to the productive process.

There are two major and distinct categories of class position in Wabush: "working class" and "supervisory (or middle) class." Within the latter there are additional strata. Again these are defined by an individual's place in the productive process. The class position "worker" is occupied by those individuals who do some form of manual labor, are paid by an hourly wage, and belong to a union, if one exists. Middle class individuals are those who have either a white collar or some supervisory capacity. They are salaried and do not belong to a union. Within this class, further distinctions are made in regard to vertical distance from the top of the company heirarchy. Others, who do not work for Wabush Mines are middle class if they are either in a supervisory or professional occupational role.

These distinctions are not simply categorical. They define different roles within the productive process and different opportunities and responsibilities outside it. For example, salaried employees receive compensation for long illnesses from the company while hourly employees do not. When strikes occur, the hourly employees are often laid off without pay while the staff is not affected. People in Wabush also expect different sets of behavior to some degree. Workers are expected, for example, to be responsible to the company but not loyal to it while supervisory personnel are expected to be both. These distinctions are also quite visible. Supervisory staff wear striped hard hats while those of the hourly personnel are plain yellow.

While people in Wabush recognized this positional difference, it would be difficult to obtain any unanimity on the relative status of these class groups except vis-à-vis "the company."

Informants certainly felt that class was more important than ethnicity in describing social patterns. When asked, social divisions by class were considered more pervasive than those by ethnic status (see Table 6).

TABLE 6

SOCIAL DIVISIONS BY ETHNIC AND CLASS STATUS (percentage)

	Yes	Sometimes	No	No Opinion
Ethnic Group	44.3	27.9	19.7	8.1
Class Group	66.6	21.1	8.8	3.5

As in the case of ethnicity, class divisions were a significant factor in the choice of friends. Out of 118 friends among hourly respondents in the random sample, only 9 were members of the supervisory staff (see Table 7).

TABLE 7

HOURLY FRIENDSHIPS BY CLASS STATUS—WABUSH MINES

	Hourly	Supervisory
Friend	109	9
Non-friend	576	166

$p < .001$

Given the large number of relatives that the hourly employees of Wabush Mines have who are also hourly employees, one might argue that this may influence the result. Omitting relatives, the results are still as significant (see Table 8).

TABLE 8

HOURLY FRIENDSHIPS BY CLASS—WABUSH MINES—OMITTING RELATIVES

	Hourly	Supervisory Staff
Friend	99	8
Non-friend	547	161
p < .001		

The constraining influence of class may be further strengthened if one analyzes the results more fully. Of the eight hourly-supervisory staff friendships listed, at least five are special cases. In one instance, an hourly claimed a supervisor as a friend whereas that supervisor remarked to me that "Given my position, I don't have any friends among hourly personnel." Another is between one of the few hourly men over forty-five still single with a supervisor who is one of the only single men over forty-five. One is between two Pentecostals, in Wabush a small denomination and one which demands social equality among its members. One General Foreman in the sample occupies that position in only a *pro forma* sense. Finally, one such friendship was described as problematical. The foreman, recently promoted from hourly, spoke at length about the difficulties in maintaining the friendship because of pressures he felt at work and in the community.

Staff friendships reveal a similar pattern (see Table 9).

TABLE 9

STAFF FRIENDSHIPS BY CLASS—WABUSH MINES—OMITTING RELATIVES

	Hourly	Staff
Friend	6	8
Non-friend	640	159
p < .005		

Again, as with ethnicity, the patterns in the random sample are reflected in the non-random interviews (see Table 10).

TABLE 10

FRIENDSHIPS BY CLASS—WABUSH MINES (non-random)

	Hourly	*Staff*
Hourly	29	4
Staff	3	33

Given the small random sample, it would be difficult to infer on the basis of it alone whether class or ethnicity are more important in defining the patterns of social relations in Wabush. Analysis of other evidence, however, favors class as more critical.

It was argued above that the intensity of ethnic division was underlined by the problem of class. Further, it was noted that the respondents themselves perceived class status to be of more importance in delimiting social divisions than ethnic status. In addition, when analyzing particular patterns of frienship, evidence suggests that while people tend to limit their friends to their own ethnic group, they are less constrained to befriend members of other ethnic groups than other class groups.

Out of the total number of hourly Newfoundlander friendships in the random sample, ninety-seven were other Newfoundlanders. Of these only seven were members of the supervisory class (see Table 11).

TABLE 11

FRIENDSHIPS OF NEWFOUNDLANDER HOURLY WITH NEWFOUNDLANDER
HOURLY AND STAFF—WABUSH MINES

	Hourly	*Staff*
Friend	90	7
Non-friend	511	126
p < .005		

Again, three of the hourly-staff friendships were the special cases described above.

Not only does class tend to divide ethnic groups, it also tends to divide kinsmen. Newfoundlander hourly respondents tended to maintain close contact and regular social interaction with relatives of the same class (see Table 12)—this among a group for whom relatives have been traditionally very important.

TABLE 12

NEWFOUNDLANDER HOURLY FRIENDSHIPS WITH
RELATIVES BY CLASS POSITION

	Hourly	*Staff*
Friend	33	2
Non-friend	6	4
p < .025		

Among the supervisory staff there was a greater tendency to befriend people of different ethnic groups than themselves. Newfoundland supervisors, among Newfoundlanders, showed a greater tendency to befriend non-Newfoundlanders who are also supervisors. Again the tendency is to befriend within a class group first and an ethnic group second. Staff, being fewer in number than hourly workers, have fewer potential friends among their own class and ethnic group. So they tend to cross ethnic lines rather than class lines.

Furthermore, while respondents viewed ethnic groups as natural but not necessarily constraining, class groups were a matter of some debate. There was much disagreement over the possibility and viability of cross-class friendships. While 67 percent of the respondents felt that supervisory staff should be friendly toward "hourly," only 2 percent said this was an ideal quality for a supervisor. Supervisors should be pleasant but not "buddy-buddy" with "hourly," to use a Newfoundland expression.

"Hourly" felt that when an "hourly" became a foreman, social pressure was such that they could no longer remain friends. Opinion was divided as to whether this was necessary or the result of "uppity" attitudes on the part of the new foreman. Of forty-two hourly respondents, thirty said they would not accept a promotion to foreman while only four said they would. Reasons given were too much responsibility, no meaningful increase in income, less security, and the *new constraints on social interaction* with former friends among the hourly.

Thus, in Wabush, people befriend within an ethnic group because they want to; they befriend within a class group because they have to.

IV.

Conclusion

While this is only a sample of my data, I have attempted to demonstrate the relative importance of ethnicity and class. Both play a role in defining and delimiting everyday social patterns in Wabush. However, they do not play the same role nor are they equally important.

Ethnicity does divide people in Wabush primarily as a function of personal predilection and cultural tradition. Ethnicity was recognized as a positive personal preference. Where it became hostile and divisive, it was a function of deeper rooted divisions, such as class.

Class also divides Wabush. However, it does so structurally, and is not simply a question of choice or tradition. Rather, it functions as a part of the productive relations of society; it is a structural constraint whether recognized or not. Moreover, it is a constraint whether desired or not. It is not simply a problem of cognition or ideology.

While Wabush is only one case, it does illustrate the problems of ethnic analysis. Ethnicity is important in many societies. As fundamentally a form of cognition or ideology, its role may be crucial. Nevertheless, it is not a structural relation and as a result cannot define its *raison d'etre*. Said another way, ethnicity can provide reasons for social patterns and divisions. As a social cognition, though, it needs to be explained. *Why* do people perceive and act on the social categories that they do?

In the case of Wabush, ethnicity defined important social divisions among people but class explained why these divisions were important. Class was more critical in defining social patterns than ethnicity. Emphasis on ethnicity alone would reify cognition, but would not root it in the concrete structural relations which shape and define that cognition. Class analysis, by engaging the problem of production as the basic agent of social formation, roots that analysis in the concrete without ignoring the role of cognition. Thus, it would serve anthropologists well to undertake class analysis if they are to broaden and deepen their understanding of society.

LITERATURE CITED

Barth, Fredrik, Ed.
1969 Ethnic Groups and Boundaries. Boston: Little, Brown and Co.

Cohen, Abner
1969 Custom and Politics in Africa. Los Angeles: University of California Press.

Dominion Bureau of Statistics (D.B.S.)
1970 Income Distributions by Size in Canada. Ottawa: Queen's Printer.
1972 Population Survey—Preliminary—for Labrador. Ottawa: Queen's Printer.

Goldmann, Lucien
1969 The Human Sciences and Philosophy. H. V. White and R. Anchor, Trans. London: Jonathan Cape Ltd.

Gordon, Milton
1958 Social Class in America. Durham: Duke University Press.

Lockwood, David
1958 The Blackcoated Worker. London: Allen and Unwin.

Marx, Karl
1967 Capital: A Critique of Political Economy, Vol. 2. New York: International Publishers.

Mills, C. W. and Gerth, M.
1946 From Max Weber: Essays in Sociology. New York: Oxford University Press.

Naroll, Raoul
1964 On Ethnic Unit Classification. Current Anthropology 15:283–312.

Ossowski, S.
1963 Class Structure in the Social Conciousness. Glencoe: The Free Press.

Warner, Lloyd
1957 The Study of Social Stratification. *In* Review of Sociology. Joseph Gittler, Ed. New York: John Wiley and Sons.

ETHNICITY
AND ETHNOLOGY

*

18

Franz Boas and the Study of Black Folklore*

WILLIAM S. WILLIS, JR.

Columbia University

Few know of these problems,
few who know notice them;
and yet there they are,
awaiting student, artist,
and seer,—a field for
somebody sometime to discover.

W. E. B. Du Bois

The new black militancy of the 1960s confronted white anthropologists with the problem of defining adequately the ethnic identity

* A preliminary version of this paper was read at the 1973 Joint Meeting of the Southern Anthropological Society and the American Ethnological Society, Wrightsville Beach, North Carolina, March 7–10, 1973. For essential help and valuable suggestions incorporated into this published version, I thank Morton H. Fried, Dell Hymes, Sidney W. Mintz, and John F. Szwed. I thank Regina Darnell for permission to read her unpublished paper. I thank Murphy D. Smith and the staff of the American Philosophical Society Library for their kind assistance during many months of research, and the Society for permission to quote from the Franz Boas Professional Correspondence. The responsibility for any infelicities of style and errors in content is mine.

of black people in the United States. This problem has plagued black
intellectuals for decades. For instance, it preoccupied W. E. B. Du
Bois throughout his long career (Meier 1963:190–206). I do not attempt to solve this difficult problem; but I do assume that, whatever
else may be entailed, ethnic identity involves emotion and ideology.
This being the case, folklore is probably one of the surest paths toward
understanding the ethnic identity of a people. I shall describe the persistent attempts by Franz Boas to organize anthropological studies of
the folklore of black people in the United States. That Boas did so
may surprise many anthropologists, especially since Melville Jacobs
(1959) and Gladys Reichard (1943) ignored black folklore in their
summaries of Boas's career as a folklorist.

Boas was the dominant influence in the American Folk-Lore Society
and its journal, *The Journal of American Folk-Lore,* throughout most
of his life. One of the four founders of the A.F.L.S. in 1888, he was
always a member of its Council, president in 1900, and then again in
1932 and 1934.[1] He was an associate editor of the *J.A.F.L.* until
1908, then editor until his resignation in 1924, when he again became
an associate editor. But even this list does not encompass the extent
of his influence. For instance, former students and colleagues sus-
ceptible to his wishes were frequent presidents of the A.F.L.S. He
had exerted considerable influence on William Wells Newell and
Alexander F. Chamberlain (Darnell 1972; see below), his two predeces-
sors as editors. Moreover, Ruth Benedict, his "good left hand," succeeded him as editor for the fifteen years following his term. Boas's
influence, then, did not wane until the mid-1930s. The election of
Archer Taylor as editor in 1941 was followed by the adoption of a
new editorial policy stressing shorter theoretical articles and calling
for the phasing out of single-topic issues (A.F.L.S.1941:78). By
then, Boas had less than two years to live.

Throughout most of his long period of dominance, Boas pushed for
the study of black folklore. The waning of Boas's influence partly
explains why this effort has been largely forgotten. The *J.A.F.L.*
thereupon would devote less space to black folklore; instead, more
coverage was given to other peoples in America and around the world.
The decision to end single-topic issues applied only to black folklore,
since other single-topic issues continued to appear. Since the early
1930s, black folklore has been studied by very few anthropologists.

The Great Depression jolted the United States, but anthropologists then concentrated more than ever on North American Indians isolated on out-of-the-way reservations. Later, during World War II and its aftermath, many anthropologists shifted their attention to Latin America, then Asia, and finally to Africa. As these shifts were made, anthropologists stressed economic problems and personality-in-culture and then political problems and social structure. In other words, most anthropologists ignored folklore, and very few published in the *J.A.F.L.* On the other hand, folklorists emerged as a self-conscious group, and they were oriented toward the humanities rather than the sciences. Hence, the A.F.L.S. gravitated toward the Modern Language Association and away from the American Anthropological Association (A.F.L.S.1941:76–77). Most anthropologists and folklorists began operating in different worlds, even when they studied the same peoples. This separation of anthropology and folklore, constituting a major problem in the history of anthropology, helps explain why Boas's earlier work in black folklore was forgotten. The aging Boas was not able to counteract this trend away from black folklore, especially since he faced so much hostility in the A.A.A. (Stocking 1960; 1968:270–307; Darnell 1972).

BOAS: FOLKLORE, LINGUISTICS, AND POLITICS

To a considerable extent, Boas's persistent interest in black folklore arose from political commitments that shaped his vision of anthropology. These commitments were more fundamental than the professionalization of anthropology, although professionalism was sometimes strong enough to clash successfully with Boas's politics. Professionalism also acted as a brake on Boas's political activism, at least until his later years. On the other hand, professionalism was often an apolitical mask for deeper political convictions. The intensity of Boas's politics and its influence on his scholarship are shown by his admission (to F. von Luschan 12/20/1919 BP) that the "only relief" was to "explode periodically in print" and then he felt a "little better for a while!" I suggest that the clash between politics and professionalism is the main key to Boas as a person and as a scientist.[2]

Boas's political commitments can be traced to his German Jewish background and his family's response to the Revolution of 1848. Life in the United States intensified Boas's commitments, making them more explicit as he moved into the Socialist Party and finally toward the communist movement. The red flag became a "symbol of the equality of the rights of man, symbolizing the red blood that flows in the veins of all human beings" (Boas to A. Lee 11/21/1918 BP). The basic commitment was to the extension of individual freedom, unrestricted by the "shackles" of social tradition and the merging of individuals into artificial social categories (Boas 1938a). Boas (1928:228–229, 245) explained explicitly the causal relationship of freedom with tradition and categories. Progress became defined as a matter of more freedom and equality, involving a "wider concept of humanity." This progress depended on better and more rationalism, attained when individuals discarded "traditional fetters" and minimized ascribed status. This being the case, ethnology became the study of the mental life of man (Benedict 1943) and dealt primarily with the "masses, and with the characteristic forms of their thought" (Boas [1902] 1940:314). Folklore and linguistics then became major preoccupations, and these preoccupations reenforced each other. I will now show the different ways in which politics was connected with folklore and linguistics.

Folklore and language were mental phenomena. Since folklore was also a linguistic phenomenon, it provided considerable linguistic information—hence, the collection of extensive texts. Boas saw folklore and language as important parts of mass culture. Folklore became a manifestation of the "popular life" and language had "intimate ties" with group psychology. Moreover, each people placed a distinctive stamp on its folklore, regardless of the origin of the material, and each language expressed the "individuality" of its speakers (Boas 1904:-518–519; [1914a] 1940:476; [1925] 1940:498). Since specialized thought and speech were produced by elite classes from the thought and speech of the common people, these specializations were considered derivative and thereby of secondary importance in anthropological research (Boas [1902] 1940).

Boas's politics led him to attack the extreme racist interpretations of human behavior that were so prevalent at the turn of the century. Boas subscribed to a version of the psychic unity of mankind that was closer to the eighteenth century than to the more racist version of the nineteenth century (Harris 1968:137; Willis 1972:133–134). Hence, Boas could endorse a view of the sociocultural environment as the root cause of human behavior. This stress on sociocultural causation rested upon the concept of culture, and this helped explain the centrality of this concept in Boasian anthropology. Specifically, it became the main thrust in the anti-racist attack, with both folklore and languages providing impressive ammunition. The study of folklore revealed the worldwide occurrence of psychological capacities and social conditions that explained similarities in simple plots—as opposed to specific incidents—in the world's folklore (Boas [1916] 1940:399; 1938b:611). Similarly, comparative linguistics revealed the complexity of all languages and the existence of identical processes of abstraction (Boas 1901:454; 1908:22).

The phenomenon of the diffusion of culture established that each race had contributed to, and participated in, the development of world culture. Boas (1908:21) saw folklore as "perhaps the best proof" of this diffusion; he ([1920a] 1940:215–216) also stressed linguistic diffusion across linguistic boundaries, including the possible spread of fundamental grammatical features. The uneven distribution of traits in the world's folklore—particularly the presence of proverbs and riddles in the Old World and their absence in the New World—"proved the independence of literary development from racial descent" (Boas [1925] 1940:496).

Boas had two conceptions of folklore. One conception equated folklore with the "mass of traditional material" of a people, whereas the other identified it more narrowly with literature. Hence, folklore became an aspect of traditional authority, especially when conceived broadly, and had an "immense" importance in determining thinking and actions. This function was more powerful in contemporary colored societies—seen as primitive societies—than in white societies. These colored peoples were "more easily satisfied" with tradition, since they lacked a scientific tradition. Hence, folklore as tradition constituted an obstacle to rationalism, thereby posing a challenge to Boas's politics. This is one explanation why he studied folklore. On the other hand, folklore as tradition provided an alternative to racist explanations for many real and alleged deficiencies of contemporary colored peoples. This is another reason why Boas studied folklore and why he was explicit about this function of folklore (Boas 1901:452, 456–458).

Language was similarly an obstacle to rationalism and a challenge to Boas' politics. Different grammars provided different semantic information, with each grammar arranging the world into "definite conceptual groups." Since grammatical processes were unconscious (particularly in the so-called primitive societies), these categories were "taken as objective categories" in the real world and "impose themselves" upon thought (Boas [1920b] 1940:288-289). Boas was not usually so explicit about the relationship of grammar to perception. Instead, he made this point more by implication (Hoijer 1954:92-93). That he did so is partly explained by a reluctance to give any credence to the prevailing racist notion that languages differed in their degree of primitivity. Hence, linguistic deficiencies were explained by the potentiality of every language to adapt to new needs as they arose. Since new needs arose mainly in the clash of colored societies with white societies, Boas (1911:64-67) minimized the issue of linguistic development prior to—and separate from—white expansion around the world.

Boas rejected language as an independent variable in sociocultural development. Instead, he saw language as a medium that reflected sociocultural conditions. This position is not consistent with the view that grammar affects the nature of perception. This inconsistency on the part of Boas is partly explained by his opposition to prevailing racist notions about languages. It is also explained by the difficulty of inducing linguistic change because of the unconscious character of linguistic phenomena. It was easier to make changes in other parts of culture, and Boas was committed to sociocultural change. Finally, Boas was unequivocal about lexical impediments to clearer thinking, emotional and imprecise words being stumbling blocks to accurate conclusions (Boas 1911:71-72; 1938c:142; Willis 1972:135-137).

Boas's politics led him to stress repeatedly that anthropology must become more useful to society. It must serve contemporary colored peoples, but it must serve even more in the improvement of white societies (Willis 1972:134-139). However, this assistance must not occur at the expense of scientific accuracy and advancement—hence, large museums should appeal both to the masses and to the scientists (Boas 1907). It may be surprising to some contemporary anthropologists that Boas opposed the almost total specialization of United States anthropologists in the study of North American Indians. This specialization, in his view, reduced the appeal of anthropology to men of power and wealth who could subsidize anthropological research. This specialization also contributed to the intellectual narrowness of North American anthropologists and to the marginality of anthropology to science and society. Hence Boas stressed the usefulness of anthropology to the United States and its government (Boas to L. D. Gill 12/5/1905 BP). He always wanted to shift some anthropological research to other continents and to other races (Stocking 1968:282). Boas included black people in the United States among those who should be studied, trying to get the United States Congress to extend the scope of the Bureau of American Ethnology so that attention could be given to these people (Boas to C. Schurz 8/12/1903; Boas to A. G. Bell 12/3/1903; Boas to C. P. Bowditch 12/17/1903 BP).

Boas's ideology led him to oppose class, religious, and racial discrimination and prejudice. This was especially important since Boas was a Jew and a foreigner. But Boas was genuinely alarmed at the oppression and violence of Jim Crow. Hence, he declared (to G. A. Plimpton 5/10/1907 BP): "I desire very much to contribute my share to the solution of this difficult political [black-white] problem." The study of black people and their folklore might help undermine the doctrine of white supremacy. The folklore of southern blacks might reveal the "sound feeling and judgment" found in African folklore (Boas 1905:86). This folklore might help black people overcome their shame in the African heritage and the slave background, thereby helping to instill the pride necessary for advancement. In discussing research in black folklore, Boas (to G. F. Peabody 6/13/1918 BP) explained that he wished to "devise some means of bringing home to the negroes the great achievements of their race." Moreover, the spread of public education was increasing feelings of shame, while threatening to eradicate such folklore. Finally, black folklore seemed to provide the easiest access to black studies. Most white people saw this folklore as a confirmation of comforting black stereotypes: witness the popularity of Joel Chandler Harris and Uncle Remus. Boas confidently expected money from the men of power and wealth for research in black folklore, believing it "impossible that an appeal could be made to the generosity of the American people without obtaining an adequate response" (A.F.L.S.1901:53).

BOAS AND NEWELL

Boas and William Wells Newell, another founder of the A.F.L.S. and the first editor of he *J.A.F.L.*, worked well together. The essential preconditions existed: Newell deferred to Boas's superior ability and training, giving him "virtually a free hand" in matters of publication, and Boas respected Newell for his "devotion to ideals." Moreover, Boas considered Newell "one of the most lovable men whom it was my good fortune to know." They also shared similar views about the significance of folklore and the necessity for fieldwork as well as their suspicion of theory (Newell 1890; Boas to A. Tozzer 1/31/1907 BP; Darnell 1972). Representing the abolitionist tradition in Boston, Newell had racial views that were congenial to Boas. Newell also believed that the study of black folklore was important to science and would help advance black people in this country (Newell 1894). Hence, he (to Boas 11/29/1898 BP) was "persistently preaching the collection of negro folk-song."

At the outset, a Department of Negro Folk-Lore was established as an integral part of the A.F.L.S. The editorial policy of the *J.A.F.L.* was set to devote one-fourth of its space to black folklore (Newell 1888:5; Darnell 1972). Boas and Newell succeeded surprisingly well. During Newell's editorship, more than forty articles dealt with blacks in the southern United States, the Antilles, and Africa. In addition, incidental information often appeared in "Folk-Lore Scrap Book" and "Notes and Queries" sections of the *J.A.F.L.* Finally, the first three Memoirs of the A.F.L.S. dealt with blacks: Heli Chatelain's *Folk-Tales of Angola* (1894), Alcée Fortier's *Louisiana Folk-Tales* (1895), and Charles L. Edwards' *Bahama Songs and Stories* (1895).

These publications—especially those dealing with southern black folklore—were of uneven quality and none would satisfy modern methodological standards. Yet they represented a solid achievement, especially in view of the serious obstacles that faced Boas and Newell, who soon discovered that the *J.A.F.L.* as an outlet for publication did not bring sufficient contributions in black folklore. Trained collectors did not exist, nor did money for training and research (A.F.L.S.1892:5; 1895:2–3). Since Boas and Newell depended on dues from the few hundred members of the A.F.L.S., they were forced to use these members as amateur collectors. Moreover, the members lived mainly in the North, whereas blacks lived mainly in the South. To overcome this handicap, Boas and Newell pushed for more southern chapters, thereby hoping to get on-the-spot collectors (A.F.L.S.1891:4). However, the racism of Southern white collectors constituted another obstacle to competent research. The incompetence—and the racism—offended Boas; indeed, amateurs in science offended his commitment to professionalism (Stocking 1960). However, Newell's dedication, tact, and prestige helped Boas to be realistic about his methodological standards. Newell subscribed to these standards as a goal, but urged Boas to accept amateur collectors as a temporary measure (Newell to Boas 5/9/1890 BP). That Newell won Boas's cooperation indicates the importance that Boas gave to the study of this folklore.

As a partial solution, Boas and Newell sought Southern blacks as amateur collectors. They turned to Alice M. Bacon, a white teacher at Hampton Institute. In 1893, Bacon founded the interracial Hampton Folk-Lore Society and the Department of Folk-Lore and Ethnology as part of the *Southern Workman,* the journal published by Hampton Institute. Bacon (1893; 1898) agreed with Boas and Newell on the immediate need to collect black folklore and the usefulness of black collectors. Boas and Newell aided and encouraged Bacon, expecting the H.F.S. to become of the "utmost usefulness." Newell (1894) gave the principal address at the first formal meeting of this society. They arranged for Bacon's election in 1897 to a three-year term as a councillor of the A.F.L.S. and then gave her a gramophone for collecting folklore (A.F.L.S.1898:4; Newell to Boas 3/8/1899 BP). Finally, they opened the *J.A.F.L.* to Bacon (1896:1898) and her black colleagues (Banks 1894). The story of the Hampton Society needs telling; its collections need to be studied again.

BOAS AND CHAMBERLAIN

Alexander F. Chamberlain was the editor of the *J.A.F.L.* from 1900 to 1908. He was Boas's first student to receive a Ph.D. in anthropology, having been awarded the degree at Clark University in 1892. It is not surprising that Chamberlain shared Boas's views on folklore, politics, and race. Nevertheless, attention to black folklore declined. The *J.A.F.L.* published only seven articles on this folklore during the period that Chamberlain was editor; other than these there were only short digests from other publications in the "Record of Negro Folk-Lore," a new section that appeared irregularly. The relationship with Hampton ended; black collectors were no longer sought. In these years, the *J.A.F.L.* gave more space to North American Indians.

Chamberlain was partly responsible for these changes. He did not have Newell's preoccupation with black folklore, being more interested in Indians. Despite his specialized training in ethnology, Chamberlain appears to have spread his modest talents too widely. Boas (to Tozzer 1/31/1907 BP) criticized Chamberlain for "always looking for the curious, not the ordinary material." In addition to Indians, Chamberlain studied European and North American whites as well as Southeast Asians. His interests shifted easily from ethnology to archeology to anthropometry, from architecture to criminality, from child psychology to the so-called higher religions. He was also a sometime-politician in the Progressive Movement and an occasional poet (Boas 1914b; Gilbertson 1914).

Despite the training from Boas, Chamberlain was not committed to fieldwork. Indeed, Boas (to C. D. Walcott 12/7/1903 BP) dismissed him as "entirely a literary man . . . a good bibliographer." Boas also explained (to Tozzer 1/31/1907 BP) that Chamberlain's "great mistake" was being "not sufficiently energetic in correspondence with contributors." Boas (to Tozzer 10/1/1908 BP) believed that pressure was necessary to secure contributions from non-professionals. Hence, another reason emerges for the decline in black folklore during Chamberlain's editorship. It is not surprising that Boas, with the assistance of Roland Dixon and especially Alfred Tozzer, eased Chamberlain out as editor and placed him in charge of a new section on bibliography (Boas to Tozzer 1/31/1907; Tozzer to Chamberlain 1/7/1908; Tozzer to Boas 1/12/1908 BP).

That Boas did not respect Chamberlain as he had Newell is clear. This difference, and the timidity of a former student toward a formidable teacher, may suggest an additional reason for the decline of interest in black folklore. Chamberlain did not, like Newell, obtain a relaxation of Boas's high methodological standards. At this time, Boas's commitment to professionalism was probably stronger than at any point in his career: witness the acrimonious controversy over the membership policy of the A.A.A. (Stocking 1960).

BOAS ALONE

In the first nine years that Boas edited the *J.A.F.L.*, the space devoted to black folklore did increase, perhaps by as much as four times as many pages as during Chamberlain's editorship. Nevertheless, the increase from about 50 pages to slightly more than 200 pages did not mean that Boas had stimulated a research program in black anthropology. Indeed, the increase is deceptive, for it ignores the extent of the previous decline. Under Boas, more issues of the *J.A.F.L.* were published each year, and the issues were usually larger than before. Almost half of the increase was embodied in contributions by Howard W. Odum (1911) and Anna Kranz Odum (1914), whose research was independent of Boas. Boas did not revive the relationship with Hampton nor did he initiate contacts with any other black schools. He did not seek black collectors. Boas actually accorded more space to North American Indians than had Chamberlain, and Boas himself admitted that black folklore received "only slight attention" (A.F.L.S.1916:296). Nevertheless, he regarded the study of this folklore as "very important and urgent" (A.F.L.S.1912:89); indeed, Boas proposed (to Tozzer 1/31/1907 BP) at the beginning of his editorship that it would be "quite appropriate to develop the study of negro folk-lore." I will now explain this contradiction.

The *J.A.F.L.* became crucial as an outlet providing prompt publication for Boas, his students, and their allies in anthropology. To a considerable extent, the *American Anthropologist* was controlled by anthropologists hostile to Boas (Darnell 1972). At this time, the publication of dissertations was a final requirement for the Ph.D. degree at Columbia Univerity. Since the *A.A.* was reorganized as a national journal in 1898 and Boas was soon thereafter producing Ph.D.'s, the importance of the *J.A.F.L.* obtained even during Chamblerlain's editorship. To accommodate his students, Boas expanded his definition of American folklore. Soon after becoming editor, Boas proposed (to Tozzer 3/18/1908 BP) that the *J.A.F.L.* should be renamed as the "'American Journal of Folk-Lore,'" arguing that this would justify publishing non-American material. The Council rejected the proposal, but Boas pursued his policy anyway. For instance, he published Alexander Goldenweiser's study of totemism as a single-topic issue (1911). But because he could get modest grants to train students in North American Indian ethnology but no money for black research, these publications dealt with Indians and not with blacks. That Boas undertook to accommodate his students by publishing their work in the *J.A.F.L.* probably eventuated in reducing the space available for black folklore.

The attention given to black folklore was probably lessened also because of Boas's effort at this time to develop anthropological research in Latin America. He spent the academic year 1911–12 in Mexico, during which time he established the International School of American Archaeology and Ethnology; in 1914, he made a field trip to Puerto Rico. As part of this effort, Boas opened the *J.A.F.L.* to Latin American material. For instance, a single-topic issue on Mexican folklore appeared in 1914.

There is yet another, final reason for the declining anthropological investment in black folklore at this time. Without Newell's restraining influence, Boas's high methodological standards dominated his editorial policy. Boas declared (to A. L. Kroeber 10/6/1908 BP) that the "readiness with which we invite the cooperation of amateurs, seem to me to convey the idea that nothing is as easy to become a contributor to the progress of science. This tendency is naturally particularly strong in those branches of investigation where it is so easy to pick up stray information that may be of some interest." Hence, Boas favored "longer and weightier" articles (A.F.L.S. 1911:23). This policy also rationalized the publication of long dissertations. Willy-nilly, it discriminated against black folklore, since shorter contributions were often submitted by nonprofessionals.

THE IMPACT OF WAR

World War I was a turning point for Boas and for the study of black folklore. The war brought a greater urbanization of southern blacks, both in the North and the South. This urbanization signaled the rapid disappearance of much of their folklore. It also made them more accessible for research. Moreover, it meant the emergence of a black intelligentsia that was less ashamed of Africa and of the slavery past. The northern urbanization and the new black protest— the integrationist protest of the National Association for the Advancement of Colored People and the nationalist protest of Marcus Garvey —alarmed men of power and wealth. The black problem was becoming a national problem, rather than merely a southern problem. Accordingly, the scientific world in the United States reacted to this new situation; for instance, the National Research Council and the Social Science Research Council both established committees on black research.

The war stimulated political nationalism and isolationalism which in turn fostered cultural nationalism. This induced men of power and wealth to finance more studies of sociocultural phenomena in the United States, and folklore appealed especially to the new nationalism. Hence folklore achieved a new popularity among social scientists in the 1920s (Dorson 1963:100–101). This, combined with new anxieties concerning black people, resulted in a greater interest in black folklore. Some scholars—such as the Chapel Hill folklorists, Guy B. Johnson and Howard Odum—now got funds for its study.

The war intensified national, religious, and racial hatreds. It also increased restrictions on freedom of thought and violations of academic freedom. The war also compromised the professional integrity of some scientists; specifically, four anthropologists whom Boas denounced for espionage in Mexico and for which denunciation he was censured by the A.A.A. (Stocking 1968:273–277). These were traumatic experiences for Boas and important steps in the radicalization of his politics. In view of these developments, Boas decided that the study of black folklore was needed more than ever. Indeed, he began to curb his stress on professionalism. Boas also believed that he could now get sufficient money for this research, despite his unpopularity in the scientific world of the United States. Boas announced that he would "devise means of accomplishing" the study of black folklore (A.F.L.S.1916:296).

BOAS AND PARSONS

The means came in the person of Elsie Clews Parsons, a wealthy sociologist who became Boas's good friend while she was developing a career in anthropology. They worked well together. The essential preconditions existed: deference to the superior ability and training of Boas on her part, and his respect for Parsons's character and scholarship. They shared many views on anthropology, folklore, race, and politics. Boas considered Parsons as the unofficial member of his department and arranged for her election as an associate editor of the *J.A.F.L.* (Parsons to Boas 3/15/1934 BP; A.F.L.S.1916:297). Parsons consulted Boas regularly and almost always complied with his wishes. Hence, Parsons's work was done largely under Boas's guidance and with his approval.

Parsons was especially interested in black folklore. She financed her own extensive field work and publications in black folklore of the United States and the Antilles (Whitten and Szwed 1970:32). In addition to paying the salary of Boas's private secretary so that he could devote more time to folklore (Parsons to Boas 10/8/1928 BP), Parsons financed almost all of his projects in black folklore. She subsidized the field work and publications of several of his white students, including Manuel J. Andrade (1930), Martha W. Beckwith (1924; 1928), and Melville J. Herskovits (1936). At Boas's request, she (to Boas 8/18/1926 BP) paid for the publication of Clement M. Doke's *Lamba Folk-Lore* (1927), even though Doke was not Boas's student. Parsons became special editor of the new single-topic issues on black folklore: the so-called Negro Numbers (A.F.L.S.1917:270). Fourteen "Negro

Numbers" appeared between 1917 and 1937, and Parsons paid for most of them (A.F.L.S.1929:200). When she did not, she found support among her rich friends, particularly George Foster Peabody, the Georgia-born philanthropist (Boas to Parsons 9/23/1920; Parsons to Boas 10/24/1920; Boas to Parsons 11/1/1920 BP).

Boas and Parsons revived the use of black collectors, and hoped to train blacks as professionals. In view of the emergence of a black intelligentsia, this was now more feasible, but it was still a realistic problem to find suitable blacks. In addition to alerting some white anthropologists, Boas and Parsons cultivated Carter G. Woodson, the black historian who founded the Association for the Study of Negro Life and History and was editor of its journal, *The Journal of Negro History*. Boas's contact with Woodson began with the promise of an article to the J.N.H. during its first year (Woodson to Boas 10/17/1916 BP). Later Boas helped the A.S.N.L.H. obtain a grant from the Laura Spelman Memorial (Boas to B. Ruml 3/12/1926 BP; Woodson 1925:602–603). Boas also served on the Executive Council of the A.S.N.L.H. from 1922 to 1934 (Woodson 1923a:121; 1927:4; 1931:- 6). Parsons helped Woodson finance a modest program to provide a fellowship for a black collector. Woodson agreed to find candidates, whose applications would be submitted to a Committee on Awards, consisting of Boas, Parsons, and Woodson. The successful candidate would then be trained by Boas and Parsons (Woodson 1924a:585– 586).

Without Woodson's help, Boas and Parsons found two blacks with some anthropological training: Arthur Huff Fauset and Zora Neale Hurston. Frank Speck introduced Boas and Parsons to Fauset, then a part-time graduate student in anthropology at the University of Pennsylvania. Parsons financed Fauset's field trips to study black folklore in Nova Scotia, the Deep South, and the Antilles. Three articles by Fauset (1925; 1927; 1928) were published in the "Negro Numbers." Fauset's larger report (1931) on Nova Scotia—after some revision by Boas (to Parsons 11/5/1926)—was published as a Memoir by the A.F.L.S. with Parsons paying for its publication (A.F. L.S.1932:264). This permitted Fauset to receive his M.A. degree from Pennsylvania. In 1942, Fauset was awarded the Ph.D. degree from Pennsylvania, thereby becoming one of the few black anthropologists in the United States (Fauset [1944] 1971).

In 1925, Gladys Reichard introduced Boas and Parsons to Hurston, then a Barnard undergraduate majoring in anthropology. Even before Hurston's graduation, Boas sent her to Harlem to make anthropometric measurements as Herskovits' assistant and to collect folklore (Boas to Parsons 8/6/1926 BP). After her graduation in 1926, Boas obtained a fellowship for her from Woodson and sent her to collect folklore in the Deep South. Hurston was then employed for three years by Mrs. R. Osgood Mason, a white patron of black artists, to collect folklore in the Deep South and in the Antilles. After Hurston's contract with Mrs. Mason ended, Boas helped her get a modest Rosenwald grant for a short period of graduate training at Columbia (Hemenway 1972; Boas to E. R. Embree 12/27/1934 BP). Despite the brevity of Hurston's graduate training, Boas had helped her to become a competent folklorist. Two articles by Hurston (1930; 1931) were published in the "Negro Numbers." In addition, Hurston published two books on black folklore: *Mules and Men* (1935), for which Boas wrote the introduction; and *Tell My Horse* (1938).

Boas and Parsons revived and even extended the use of amateur black collectors. At least in regard to black folklore, Boas curbed his insistence on professionalism. Like Newell, Parsons encouraged the relaxation. Parsons had the time and means to find these amateur collectors, a task made easier now that a black intelligentsia was emerging. She could give them direct supervision, something that had not been done previously and which made their use more acceptable to Boas. Moreover, Boas and Parsons had to use amateurs if they wanted black collectors and wanted to publish the "Negro Numbers." Anthropology did not appeal to many young blacks seeking a profession. In addition, Woodson's extreme caution toward black aspirants proved a stumbling block in recruiting blacks for graduate training. Even Boas complained (to W. C. Putnam 10/8/1923 BP) that blacks discovered by him and Parsons "did not appear [to Woodson] to be qualified."

Since it was mainly Parsons's job to find and work with amateur black collectors, she prepared a lecture stressing the importance of black folklore and the need to preserve this folklore. The lecture was revised and approved by Boas (Parsons to Boas 3/9/1917; Boas to Parsons 3/10/1917 BP). Parsons went to Harlem and addressed black groups, particularly new migrants from the Antilles. She encountered considerable resistance stemming from the fear of ridicule. Nevertheless, she found John H. Johnson, a black from Antigua, who agreed to collect folklore from other West Indians. Johnson was introduced to Boas, who began supervising Johnson in his work (Boas to Parsons 9/23/1920 BP). Johnson's report (1921) was published in a "Negro Number."

After Harlem, Parsons concentrated more on the South. She secured the good offices of Peabody and his friend, Natalie Curtis, both of whom had extensive connections with southern black schools (Boas to Parsons 10/22/1920 BP). Parsons sent "Negro Numbers" to these schools (Parsons to Boas 10/?/1920 BP) and paid for a subscription to Hampton Institute (Parsons to Boas 11/15/1920 BP). Parsons made visits to Hampton, Penn Normal and Agricultural Institute in South Carolina, and to several other black schools (Bacon and Parsons 1922:252; Parsons 1923). Parsons found a surprising number of black educators willing to collect folklore, especially from their students. She found Caddie S. Isham (1921), A. S. Perkins (1922a; 1922b), Clement Richardson (1919), Portia Smiley (1919), Susan D. Spinney (1921), Sadie E. Stewart (1919), Clemmie S. Terrell (1930), and Monroe W. Work (1919). Their reports were published in the "Negro Numbers." Most of these educators were graduates of Hampton, probably a testimony to the lingering tradition of the Hampton Society.

Boas and Parsons made another effort to identify amateur collectors. They arranged with Woodson to establish a contest for the best collection of folklore submitted by students attending black colleges. The prize of $200 was provided by Parsons. The contest was conducted under the joint sponsorship of the A.F.L.S. and the A.S.N.L.H., with Boas, Parsons, and Woodson constituting the Committee on Awards. In addition to seeking amateur collectors, the contest was designed as an easy and inexpensive means of collecting folklore from the black masses, since the students were required to collect only folklore "heard at home" and most students came from poor families (Woodson 1923b:470; 1924b). The contest also had the larger goal of stimulating interest among black people in their folklore "as it exists in this country" (Boas to F. Warburg 12/9/1924 BP). But after one award was made, the contest was discontinued. Many black schools did not cooperate, and Woodson was too severe in judging the contributions submitted by students (Woodson 1924:585; Boas to F. Warburg 12/9/1924 BP).

The publications of black collectors—amateurs as well as those with training—did not differ significantly from the average publications of Boas' white students. The supervision and editing afforded by Boas and Parsons, and Boas's emphasis on accurate reporting, set a minimal standard within the reach of a diligent and educated person. Boas and Parsons did not encourage theoretical innovations. They saw black collectors simply as technicians who could obtain data that was denied to even the best white field workers. Hence, the "great merit" of Hurston's work was her ability to "penetrate through that affected demeanor by which the Negro excludes the white observer effectively from participating in his true inner life" (Hurston 1935: Boas's forward). Parsons believed that only black collectors could record accurately the normal speech of lower class blacks, since the presence of a single white person induced them to try to speak "School English" instead of their "dialect" (Parsons 1923: preface).

That Boas and Parsons conceived of blacks as technicians is not evidence even of latent racial arrogance. In fact, Boas also viewed most of his white students as technicians. Moreover, the protective defenses of many black people did create a serious obstacle to research. That black collectors acquiesced in being technicians, and did not push toward making theoretical innovations, is obvious and is important for black studies today. It means that the mere existence of black anthropologists does not necessarily lead to new insights into the black experience. New insights are not likely to come from insecure black anthropologists isolated and marginal in white academia; new insights are not likely to come from frustrated black anthropologists isolated in the world of the black middle class. New insights will depend on a new kind of black anthropologist, one who is more secure with both his black and white colleagues, and nourished by solid sociopolitical relations with the black masses.

BOAS: SUCCESS AND FAILURE

The partnerships of Boas with Newell and with Parsons resulted in a considerable amount of published black folklore. This folklore was collected with augmented skill. There was an increasing technical proficiency in analyzing its structure in regard to plots, incidents, and characters. The origins of this folklore were traced with considerable success. Moreover, this occurred in a crucial period in black history, when many former slaves were still living and when the Jim Crow system was first expanded and then entrenched. Boas was articulating anthropology with one of the most serious problems in the United States, and doing so in the face of indifference and even hostility. No other anthropologist has made a similar effort. Boas introduced black intellectuals to anthropology, a step toward overcoming the embarrassment of anthropology as a lily-white science that specialized in studying colored peoples (Willis 1970:33–40). These were solid achievements. In attempting to organize black studies and in pushing for the sociopolitical relevance of anthropology, Boas was not transitional between the late nineteenth century and the early twentieth century, but decades ahead of his times.[3]

Nevertheless, the work of Boas in black folklore is disappointing to some students of black people in the United States. It is especially disappointing to students adhering to the radical perspectives that emerged in the 1960s. Boas produced very few important insights into the black experience and his work in black folklore was largely harmless to the doctrine of white supremacy. In view of Boas's politics and expectations, this failure may seem paradoxical, and demands explanation.

Lack of money was probably the main reason, however. Even Parsons's money was insufficient to sustain a program of systematic study. Boas never got a large government grant or the foundation grants he had hoped for. The men of power and wealth were afraid of the black people of the United States as a potentially dangerous people—and Boas was a foreigner, a Jew, a New Yorker, and a radical. The lack of money helps explain why he needed Newell and Parsons. It helps explain why Boas's students, except for Herskovits, did not pursue black studies in the United States. Even Herskovits shifted principally to the study of foreign blacks. This failure by Boas's students abuts on the wider problem of a "Boas School" in anthropology. Indeed, the financial history of anthropology—an aspect not yet well documented—would be essential to any complete intellectual history of the profession.

Another explanation starts with Boas's personality. He was very ambitious and energetic—and he was surprisingly unselfish. He shifted easily back and forth among the four fields of anthropology, from one problem to another, and from one culture to another. In addition to his research and teaching, Boas gave freely of himself in helping other anthropologists with their work. Boas was always involved with arduous editorial assignments, and with the exhausting politics of anthropology.

He also participated in national and international politics, especially in his later years. Personal advancement was not the sole motivation for this intense activity: witness the help he gave other anthropologists. The advancement of anthropology, according to his own conception of its tasks, was at least equally important to him. Boas saw an underlying design in many of his activities: the exposition of sociocultural causation in human behavior. Despite this design, the multiple activities help explain why Boas's work in black folklore is disappointing. Put simply, Boas was too busy and spread his considerable talents too widely to finish any major research. Indeed, he never found time to write a single article on black folklore in the United States. But one reason Boas was so busy is that he never received support sufficiently generous to allow him sustained work on one problem. Thus the explanation that starts with Boas's personality ends in economics and politics.

Another explanation is revealed in Boas's theories. Since folklore as tradition and as literature was seen as a part of culture, it reflected the "essential features" of the rest of culture. These essentials were equated with the general characteristics of a culture. Folklore was then a guide to history and sociology, especially in the urgent ethnographical study of North American Indians, who were thought to be disappearing rapidly. Indeed, this urgency frequently induced Boas to equate Indian folklore with Indian tradition. This was a pragmatic compromise with necessity. Otherwise, Boas had a deep distrust of folklore as a guide to history and sociology. Instead of reflecting actual human experience, folklore was often the product of the "play of imagination with everyday experience," and the "imagination of man knows no limits." Hence, folklore was often "fantastic," filled with "exaggerations of experiences" (Boas [1914a] 1940:457, 475; 1938b:610–611). This distrust was more operative in the case of black folklore than of Indian folklore: the same necessity for pragmatic compromise did not exist.

Blacks were long-time residents of the United States and shared in its general culture. Folklore was unnecessary as a guide to the broad outlines of black culture. Folklore was not needed to salvage black culture seen as African culture, since so much of this kind of culture seemed already to have disappeared. Hence, black folklore was defined narrowly as literature more frequently than Indian folklore. In general, black folklore was seen as a prime example of the few survivals from Africa and not as a product of experience in the South. Hence, black folklore did not obviously reflect the southern experience. Under these circumstances, the study of black culture required deep penetration, and this kind of penetration via folklore required symbolic interpretations. At this point, Boas was stymied by his literalism. For instance, he saw animals as animals and not as persons in animal fables —and such fables constituted a goodly part of black folklore. Put simply, Boas strongly resisted symbolic interpretations. To attack the search for hidden meanings, Boas ([1933] 1940) cited the "exaggerations" in folklore as well as secondary rationalizations of diffused elements. Boas's distrust of folklore severely restricted his insights into the black experience in slavery and under Jim Crow.

This distrust limited Boas's historical interest to problems of diffusion. Indeed, these problems became his main preoccupation. Many parallels were revealed in the folklore of blacks in the United States, the Antilles, and Africa. These parallels were used to establish diffusion and provenience. This was made easier by recourse to the slave trade as an explanation, since the trade eliminated the difficulty of discontinuous distribution. Boas's stress on the diffusion of black folklore from Africa provided a starting-point from which Herskovits developed Afro-American studies and the postulation of substantial African survivals in the South. At present, this constitutes Boas's most significant contribution to the problem of black ethnic identity. I suggest that Boas suspected long before Herskovits that African survivals were more numerous than generally believed. In studying North American Indians, Boas ([1891] 1940:443) stressed that folklore and other customs frequently diffused together. The impact of Boas on Herskovits bears further investigation.

There is another side to this question. Preoccupation with diffusion and provenience coincided with the needs of white rule and its doctrine of black inferiority. It tended to shift blame for black sociocultural differences and inferiorities from white oppression to the African heritage. Moreover, Boas ([1914a] 1940:464) and his students (Parsons 1919:234; Espinosa 1930:130–132) found the ultimate origin of important parts of black folklore in Europe and Asia. This ultimate provenience presented a potential and unresolved conflict with Boas's contention ([1906] 1945) that African peoples had contributed importantly to the early inventions of mankind. It was also congenial to the racist notion that black people lack inventive potential.

Boas contended that folklore must be placed in its sociocultural environment. This contention is valid. Too often, however, this environ-

ment was ignored. When not ignored, the trouble was then in its definition. Boas defined the sociocultural environment too narrowly, this
narrowness being made easier by the frequent equation of black folk-
lore with black literature. What was most important to Boas was the
"intimate setting in the social life" of black people. This "homely life"
would provide the "true inner life" (Hurston 1935: Boas's foreword).
This usually meant only sketchy biographies of informants and brief
descriptions of the immediate scene of storytelling. The definition of
the sociocultural environment seldom included the whole segregated black
community (Whitten and Szwed 1970:34). When the black community
was included, its isolation resembled the presumed isolation of Indian
communities, and then the broader conception of folklore as tradition
became more operative, as in Parsons's study of Sea Islands blacks
(1923). The surrounding world of the dominant white people was
excluded. Hence, white oppression was ignored. Whenever this oppression is ignored or even minimized, then African survivals become
congenial to the detractors of black people.

Since white oppression was ignored, the black struggle for survival,
for freedom, and for equality was likewise ignored. This struggle,
however, permeates the black experience. In different ways, the plea
for survival and the tricks to attain survival abound in this folklore.
Hence, Boas overlooked and even distorted important dimensions. That
Boas did so is surprising, since he saw folklore as filled with "ardent
desire" (1938b:610). Boas's literalism is only part of the answer to this
neglect, since the demand for survival, for freedom, and for equality is
frequently explicit. Boas was strongly opposed to all forms of nationalism. Perhaps Boas sensed the nationalistic strivings in black folklore,
and he (to D. S. Andron 10/26/1933) was "absolutely opposed to all
kinds of attempts to foster racial solidarity." Hence, Boas did not direct research toward the Garvey Movement, centered in nearby Harlem.
Boas also ignored the old tradition among black intellectuals, from
Frederick Douglass to Du Bois, that interpreted black folklore in terms
of the struggle for survival and the struggle for freedom and equality
(Stuckey 1971).

There is need today to place the black folklore collected at Boas's
instigation into its wider context. This is one important task for contemporary students of black people in the United States, and a special
task for the young black anthropologists who are now appearing. They
must not study only black people in foreign countries; they must not

study only blacks in northern ghettos. The southern experience of black people was a crushing experience, and its effects are still operative even in the North. Since Boas's folklore was collected at a crucial period in black history, its reexamination can provide important insights into the development of the intricate ethnic identities of black people in the United States.

NOTES

[1] The other founders were T. Frederick Crane, J. Owen Dorsey, and William Wells Newell.

[2] George W. Stocking, Jr. (1960) believed that the professionalization of anthropology was the basic commitment of Boas.

[3] In regard to the development of the culture concept, Stocking (1968:230–231) has interpreted Boas as transitional between the late nineteenth century and the early twentieth century.

LITERATURE CITED

American Folk-Lore Society

    1891   2nd Annual Meeting of the American Folk-Lore Society. Journal of American Folk-Lore 4:1–12.

    1892   3rd Annual Meeting of the American Folk-Lore Society. Journal of American Folk-Lore 5:1–8.

    1895   6th Annual Meeting of the American Folk-Lore Society. Journal of American Folk-Lore 8:1–6.

    1898   9th Annual Meeting of the American Folk-Lore Society. Journal of American Folk-Lore 11:1–6.

    1901   12th Annual Meeting of the American Folk-Lore Society. Journal of American Folk-Lore 14:52–55.

    1911   22nd Annual Meeting of the American Folk-Lore Society. Journal of American Folk-Lore 24:21–25.

    1912   23rd Annual Meeting of the American Folk-Lore Society. Journal of American Folk-Lore 25:87–92.

    1916   27th Annual Meeting of the American Folk-Lore Society. Journal of American Folk-Lore 29:295–298.

1917 28th Annual Meeting of the American Folk-Lore Society. Journal of American Folk-Lore 30:269–271.

1929 40th Annual Meeting of the American Folk-Lore Society. Journal of American Folk-Lore 42:197–200.

1932 43rd Annual Meeting of the American Folk-Lore Society. Journal of American Folk-Lore 45:261–264.

1941 52nd Annual Meeting of the American Folk-Lore Society. Journal of American Folk-Lore 54:76–78.

American Philosophical Society Library
n.d. Franz Boas Professional Papers.

Andrade, Manuel J.
1930 Folk-Lore from the Dominican Republic. Memoir 23, American Folk-Lore Society.

Bacon, Alice M.
1893 Proposals for Folk-Lore Research at Hampton, VA. Journal of American Folk-Lore 6:305–309.

1896 Conjuring and Conjure Doctors in the Southern United States. Journal of American Folk-Lore 9:143–147, 224–226.

1898 Work and Methods of the Hampton Folk-Lore Society. Journal of American Folk-Lore 11:17–21.

Bacon, Alice M., and Elsie Clews Parsons
1922 Folk-Lore from Elizabeth City County, VA. Journal of American Folk-Lore 35:250–327.

Banks, Frank D.
1894 Plantation Courtship. Journal of American Folk-Lore 7:147–149.

Beckwith, Martha W.
1924 Jamaica Anansi Stories. Memoir 17, American Folk-Lore Society.

1928 Jamaica Folk-Lore. Memoir 21, American Folk-Lore Society.

Benedict, Ruth F.
1943 Franz Boas as an Ethnologist. *In* Franz Boas: 1858–1942. Memoir 61, American Anthropological Association.

Boas, Franz
[1891] 1940 Dissemination of Tales among the Natives of North America. *In* Race, Language, and Culture. Franz Boas, Ed. New York: Macmillan. pp. 437–445.

1901 The Mind of Primitive Man. Journal of American Folk-Lore 14:451–460.

[1902] 1940   The Ethnological Significance of Esoteric Doctrines. *In* Race, Language, and Culture. Franz Boas, Ed. New York: Macmillan. pp. 312–315.

1904   The History of Anthropology. Science 20:513–524.

1905   The Negro and the Demands of Modern Life. Charities 15:85–88.

[1906] 1945   Commencement Address at Atlanta University. *In* Race and Democratic Society. Ernst P. Boas, Ed. New York: J. J. Augustin. pp. 61–69.

1907   Some Principles of Museum Administration. Science 25:921–933.

1908   Anthropology: A Lecture Delivered at Columbia University in the Series on Science, Philosophy, and Art, December 18, 1907. New York: Columbia University Press. pp. 5–28.

1911   Introduction. *In* Handbook of American Indian Languages. Franz Boas, Ed. Bureau of American Ethnology, Bulletin 40, Part 1. Washington, DC: Government Printing Office. pp. 5–83.

[1914a] 1940   Mythology and Folk-Tales of the North American Indians. *In* Race, Language, and Culture. Franz Boas, Ed. New York: Macmillan. pp. 451–490.

1914b   Alexander Francis Chamberlain. Journal of American Folk-Lore 27:326–327.

[1916] 1940   The Development of Folk-Tales and Myths. *In* Race, Language, and Culture. Franz Boas, Ed. New York: Macmillan. pp. 397–406.

[1920a] 1940   Introduction, International Journal of American Linguistics. *In* Race, Language, and Culture. Franz Boas, Ed. New York: Macmillan. pp. 199–225.

[1920b] 1940   The Methods of Ethnology. *In* Race, Language, and Culture. Franz Boas, Ed. New York: Macmillan. pp. 281–289.

[1925] 1940   Stylistic Aspects of Primitive Literature. *In* Race, Language, and Culture. Franz Boas, Ed. New York: Macmillan. pp. 491–502.

1928   Anthropology and Modern Life. New York: W. W. Norton.

[1933] 1940   Review of The Serpent in Kwakiutl Religion: A Study in Primitive Culture, by G. W. Locher. *In* Race, Language, and Culture. Franz Boas, Ed. New York: Macmillan. pp. 446–450.

1938a   An Anthropologist's Credo. Nation 147:201–204.

1938b   Mythology and Folklore. *In* General Anthropology. Franz Boas, Ed. Boston: D. C. Heath. pp. 609–626.

1938c   Language. *In* General Anthropology. Franz Boas, Ed. Boston: D. C. Heath. pp. 124–145.

Chatelain, Heli
1894 Folk-Tales of Angola. Memoir 1, American Folk-Lore Society.

Darnell, Regina
1972 American Anthropology and the Development of Folklore Scholarship. Unpublished paper.

Doke, Clement M.
1927 Lambda Folk-Lore. Memoir 20, American Folk-Lore Society.

Dorson, Richard M.
1963 Current Folklore Theories. Current Anthropology 4:93–112.

Edwards, Chafles L.
1895 Bahama Songs and Stories. Memoir 3, American Folk-Lore Society.

Espinosa, Aurelio M.
1930 Notes on the Origin and History of the Tar-Baby Story. Journal of American Folk-Lore 43:129–209.

Fauset, Arthur Huff
1925 Folk-Lore from the Half-Breeds of Nova Scotia. Journal of American Folk-Lore 38:300–315.
1927 Negro Folk Tales from the South (Alabama, Mississippi, and Louisiana). Journal of American Folk-Lore 40:213–303.
1928 Tales and Riddles Collected in Philadelphia. Journal of American Folk-Lore 41:529–557.
1931 Folk-Lore from Nova Scotia. Memoir 25, American Folk-Lore Society.
[1944] 1971 Black Gods of the Metropolis: Negro Religious Cults in the Urban North. New Introduction by John F. Szwed. Philadelphia: University of Pennsylvania Press.

Fortier, Alcée
1895 Louisiana Folk-Tales. Memoir 3, American Folk-Lore Society.

Gilbertson, Albert N.
1914 In Memoriam: Alexander Francis Chamberlain. American Anthropologist 16:337–348.

Goldenweiser, Alexander
1911 Totemism, An Analytical Study. Journal of American Folk-Lore 23:179–293.

Harris, Marvin
1968 The Rise of Anthropological Theory: A History of Theories of Culture. New York: Thomas Y. Crowell.

Hemenway, Robert
1972 Zora Neale Hurston and the Eatonville Anthropology. *In* The Harlem Renaissance Remembered. Arna Bontempts, Ed. New York: Dodd, Mead. pp. 190–214.

Herskovits, Melville J., and Frances S. Herskovits
1936 Suriname Folk-Lore. New York: Columbia University Press.

Hoijer, Harry
1954 The Sapir-Whorf Hypothesis. *In* Language and Culture: Proceedings of a Conference on the Interrelations of Language and Other Aspects of Culture. Harry Hoijer, Ed. Memoir 79, American Anthropological Association. pp. 92–105.

Hurston, Zora Neale
1930 Dance Songs and Tales from the Bahamas. Journal of American Folk-Lore 43:294–312.
1931 Hoodoo in America. Journal of American Folk-Lore 44:320–417.
1935 Mules and Men. Philadelphia: J. B. Lippincott.
1938 Tell My Horse. Philadelphia: J. B. Lippincott.

Isham, Caddie S.
1921 Games of Danville, VA. Journal of American Folk-Lore 34:116–120.

Jacobs, Melville
1959 Folklore. *In* The Anthropology of Franz Boas: Essays on the Centennial of His Birth. Walter Goldschmidt, Ed. Memoir 89, American Anthropological Association. pp. 119–138.

Johnson, John H.
1921 Folk-Lore from Antigua, British West Indies. Journal of American Folk-Lore 34:40–88.

Meier, August
1963 Negro Thought in America, 1880–1915: Racial Ideologies in the Age of Booker T. Washington. Ann Arbor: University of Michigan Press.

Newell, William Wells
1888 Editorial. Journal of American Folk-Lore 1:11.
1890 Additional Collection Essential to Correct Theory in Folk-Lore and Mythology. Journal of American Folk-Lore 3:23–32.
1894 Hampton, VA. Folk-Lore Society. Journal of American Folk-Lore 7:163.

Odum, Anna Kranz
1914 Some Negro Folk-Songs from Tennessee. Journal of American Folk-Lore 27:255–265.

Odum, Howard K.
1911   Folk-Song and Folk-Poetry as found in the Secular Songs of the Southern Negroes. Journal of American Folk-Lore 24:255–294, 351–396.

Parsons, Elsie Clews
1919   The Provenience of Certain Negro Folk-Tales, III, Tar Baby. Folklore 30:227–234.
1923   Folk-Lore from the Sea Islands, South Carolina. Memoir 16, American Folk-Lore Society.

Perkins, A. S.
1922a Riddles from Negro School-Children in New Orleans, LA. Journal of American Folk-Lore 35:105–115.
1922b Negro Spirituals in the Far South. Journal of American Folk-Lore 35:223–249.

Richardson, Clement and Monroe W. Work
1919   Folk-Tales from Students at Tuskegee Institute, Alabama. Journal of American Folk-Lore 32:397–401.

Reichard, Gladys A.
1943   Franz Boas and Folklore. *In* Franz Boas, 1858–1942. Memoir 61, American Anthropological Association. pp. 52–57.

Spinney, Susan D.
1921   Riddles and Ring-Games from Raleigh, N.C. Journal of American Folk-Lore 34:110–115.

Smiley, Portia
1919   Folk-Lore from Virginia, South Carolina, Georgia, and Florida. Journal of American Folk-Lore 32:357–383.

Stewart, Sadie E.
1919   Seven Folk-Tales from the Sea Islands, South Carolina. Journal of American Folk-Lore 32:394–396.

Stocking, George W., Jr.
1960   Franz Boas and the Founding of the American Anthropological Association. American Anthropologist 62:1–17.
1968   Race, Culture, and Evolution: Essays in the History of Anthropology. London: Free Press.

Stuckey, Sterling
1971   Through the Prism of Folklore: The Black Ethos in Slavery. *In* Black and White in American Culture: An Anthropology from The Massachusetts Review. Judith Chametzky and Sidney Kaplan, Eds. New York: Viking. pp. 172–192.

Terrell, Clemmie S.
  1930   Spirituals from Alabama.   Journal of American Folk-Lore
         43:322–324.

Whitten, Norman E., Jr., and John F. Szwed
  1970   Introduction. *In* Afro-American Anthropology: Contemporary
         Perspectives. Morman E. Whitten, Jr. and John F. Szwed, Eds.
         New York: Free Press. pp. 23–60.

Willis, William S., Jr.
  1970   Anthropology and Negroes on the Southern Colonial Frontier.
         In The Black Experience in America: Selected Essays. James
         C. Curtis and Lewis L. Gould, Eds. Austin and London: Uni-
         versity of Texas Press. pp. 33–50.
  1972   Skeletons in the Anthropological Closet. *In* Reinventing An-
         thropology. Dell Hymes, Ed. New York: Pantheon. pp. 121–
         152.

Woodson, Carter G.
  1923a The Proceedings of the Annual Meeting of the Association for
         the Study of Negro Life and History held in Louisville, KY,
         Nov. 22–24, 1922. Journal of Negro History 8:116–124.
  1923b The Annual Report of the Director, 1922–1923. Journal of
         Negro History 8:466–471.
  1924a The Annual Report of the Director, 1923–1924. Journal of
         Negro History 9:579–586.
  1924b Notes. Journal of Negro History 9:239–240.
  1925   Ten Years of Collecting and Publishing the Records of the Negro.
         Journal of Negro History 10:598–606.
  1931   The Proceedings of the Association for the Study of Negro Life
         and History held in Cleveland, OH, Oct. 26–30, 1930. Journal
         of Negro History 16:1–8.

Work, Monroe D.
  1919   Folk-Tales from Students in the Georgia State College. Jour-
         nal of American Folk-Lore 32:402–405.

†